ADVANCED CONCEPTS IN DEFENSIVE TACTICS

A SURVIVAL GUIDE FOR LAW ENFORCEMENT

ADVANCED CONCEPTS IN DEFENSIVE TACTICS

A SURVIVAL GUIDE FOR LAW ENFORCEMENT

CHUCK JOYNER

CRC Press
Taylor & Francis Group
Boca Raton London New York

CRC Press is an imprint of the
Taylor & Francis Group, an **informa** business

CRC Press
Taylor & Francis Group
6000 Broken Sound Parkway NW, Suite 300
Boca Raton, FL 33487-2742

Printed in the United States of America on acid-free paper
10 9 8 7 6 5 4 3 2 1

International Standard Book Number: 978-1-4398-4500-4 (Hardback)

Library of Congress Cataloging-in-Publication Data

Joyner, Chuck.
Advanced concepts in defensive tactics : a survival guide for law enforcement / Chuck Joyner.
p. cm.
Includes bibliographical references and index.
ISBN 978-1-4398-4500-4
1. Self-defense for police. 2. Police training. 3. Law enforcement--Safety measures. I. Title.

HV8080.S34J69 2011
363.2'3--dc22 2010027608

Visit the Taylor & Francis Web site at
http://www.taylorandfrancis.com

and the CRC Press Web site at
http://www.crcpress.com

In memory of Randy Joyner—

coach, mentor, role model, and Dad.

When making decisions in life, he put his family first.

Table of Contents

Introduction

The purpose of this book is to make every officer safer, to minimize the possibility of an officer lying on the ground, looking up into the barrel of a gun, and relying on a criminal's mercy for survival. It should prove useful to officers who wish to increase their survival skills, instructors with the objective of improving a current use of force program, and law enforcement executives interested in reducing liability while enhancing officer safety and professionalism.

Presented here are advanced concepts (rather than simply techniques) with a broad application to increasing officer safety. The focus is on defensive principles and tactics that are easily taught, understood, retained, and applied by officers. The tenets presented are based on extensive research and actual street experience. Using a risk management approach, the most common and dangerous attacks on officers were identified. Actual assaults on officers were studied, the best response to attacks was developed, and the Survival Sciences Defensive Tactics (SSDT) program was devised to successfully overcome those situations in which officers get injured, sued, or killed.

The goal of any law enforcement academy's defensive tactics (DT) curriculum is to provide the necessary knowledge and skills to make officers safer on the streets. Almost all come up short in this endeavor. The emphasis of most DT programs is an overabundance of techniques. The types of techniques taught are usually based upon the particular expertise of the lead instructor. If the lead instructor is a karate practitioner, students learn kicks and strikes. If the instructor is a wrestler, students learn takedowns and pins. And if the instructor really has no expertise in DT but is in great physical condition, the students do a lot of running and calisthenics. All of these approaches have merit if we had unlimited time to train in DT, but we don't. If we don't recognize the limited time devoted to DT training and adjust accordingly, DT programs are destined to fail.

The problem is most DT programs are administered as if they are martial arts studios, wrestling teams, or boxing gyms. DT instructors, most of whom have extensive experience and training in their method of self-defense, train officers in the same manner as they were trained. It's natural to do so. This approach will work if the training environment and hours are similar, but they are not. Most DT programs are run as if they are attempting to prepare a fighter for sports competition rather than training officers to survive a street battle. There is no doubt an individual can become a proficient fighter given proper training and time. But how much time is actually devoted to law enforcement DT training? In the FBI Academy, new agent trainees receive ninety hours of DT training. Once they graduate, they receive approximately four hours a year. In conversations with instructors from departments throughout the country, I learned the majority of departments devote two to six hours a year to DT refresher training. And some have no DT training at all once an officer graduates from the academy. This is a recipe for disaster. How good would a football or baseball team be if they practiced four hours a year? How many games do you think they would win? Probably none. Yet law enforcement officers must win every encounter. One loss can mean death.

Elite athletes will tell you that spending only a few hours a year on a physical skill doesn't come close to being sufficient training time to maintain that skill. In many ways, the training becomes counterproductive. Officers are taught a variety of techniques that are somewhat complex and complicated. In the hands of an expert who trains regularly, the techniques are effective. However, these same techniques are useless to the officer who has failed to commit them to muscle memory.

I repeatedly experimented with FBI special agents during quarterly scheduled DT training to determine their level of practical DT expertise. I would have agents form two lines—designating one line to be the FBI agents and the line facing them to be the subjects. On my command, the agents were to approach the subjects and execute a random technique I called out. Although this was stressful to some agents, it certainly didn't approximate the stress of a real-life confrontation. After I was certain everyone clearly understood the exercise, I would call out a DT technique taught to the agents while at the academy and during refresher training in the field. All of the agents had to pass a proficiency exam on these identical techniques to graduate from the academy. In addition, all agents were given annual reviews of these techniques. This should have been a simple exercise to complete, but it quickly became evident it was not. The result of my experiment was approximately 10% of the agents could successfully perform the requested technique on a cooperative partner, approximately 50% struggled to perform the technique but were able to stumble through it with assistance from a DT instructor, and the remaining 40% had no clue what I was talking about. I had serious doubts any of the agents, with very few exceptions, could effectively use the techniques on a resistive, noncooperative subject. I repeated this experiment with officers from other agencies and the results were the same.

How could this happen? After the hours devoted to DT training in the academy and in the field, it was clear the vast majority of agents would be unable to adequately defend themselves in a street brawl. The time spent learning countless DT techniques was apparently not well spent. We had failed to provide necessary, life-saving training.

I'm fortunate in that I've had the privilege of training with some of the best and most highly acclaimed martial artists in the world. While I was the lead DT instructor for the Los Angeles Field Office of the FBI, I would invite internationally respected martial arts grand masters to provide training seminars for agents. The presentations were always awe inspiring, as the physical accomplishments of some of these individuals were truly remarkable. A typical seminar by a grand master included demonstrating and practicing a small number of complex and impressive-looking techniques for a two-hour period. The agents enjoyed the seminars and were excited about being exposed to new techniques, but how effective were the seminars in achieving their objective (i.e., increasing agents' safety)? Most of the agents couldn't adequately perform the majority of the techniques even while the class was in session. Even the DT instructors in attendance were unable to remember or perform the techniques a few days later. Unfortunately, none of the participants retained any of the knowledge they had gained. Other than the motivational factor, the training was a complete waste of time.

Dr. Masaaki Hatsumi is the thirty-fourth grand master of Budo Taijutsu (Ninpo) and founder of the Bujinkan Dojo in Japan. He is the most talented martial artist and instructor I have seen. He is also a big supporter of law enforcement and the military, believing they are the last warriors in our modern society. In a meeting with high-ranking black belts, Dr. Hatsumi lamented that many of the senior black belts had become "technique collectors" rather than focusing on the underlying principles. He emphasized this is incorrect thinking. Dr. Hatsumi said that without understanding the core principles, techniques are useless.

Focusing on the collection of techniques is a trap many skilled DT instructors fall into. The typical DT instructor has spent many years perfecting his or her skills and is passionate about sharing these skills with fellow officers. The instructor knows hundreds of techniques and wants to teach them all. And then the instructor tries to impart ten, twenty, or even thirty or more years of knowledge in a two-hour block of time.

As a DT instructor, I was frustrated by the inability of the majority of officers to successfully defend themselves against an attack. I was determined to find a solution and devise a more effective and realistic DT program. I knew there was a better way to reach the officers who lacked sufficient DT skills in the limited training time provided. Part of developing a viable solution was to first determine what didn't work. What didn't work was teaching an unlimited number of complex techniques in response to an infinite number of possible attacks. It's not that complex techniques are necessarily bad. It just takes a major commitment to be able to perform complex maneuvers in a life-or-death struggle. I've dedicated my life to learning, developing, and teaching martial arts. It's a way of life. For those who have chosen to walk a similar path, I thank you and appreciate your dedication. Most people (and yes, that includes most law enforcement officers) do not spend their lives improving their defensive capabilities. There are other demands and priorities in life, and they have chosen to focus their attention elsewhere. This does not make them bad officers or bad people. Actually, it makes them normal. It's the job of the DT instructor to prepare them as best as possible using the limited time and limited resources granted by our respective agencies.

The answer to our problem is a DT program must be based on broad, wide-ranging concepts that have proven effective in the street. The focus must be on understanding a few key principles. Next, the techniques that are selected to complement those principles must be instinctive, practical, easily committed to muscle memory, and reliable under stress. This means they must emphasize large muscle groups and not fine motor skills. When faced with a violent and unexpected confrontation, an officer is better off attempting a basic, but effective technique. Attempting to complete a fancy move taught in DT class without adequate training time will only get the officer hurt or killed.

The FBI DT program was and is a good program upon which many law enforcement DT programs throughout the country are based. However, it shares the same dilemma as other DT programs in that it doesn't realistically address the limited time allotted to training. Using the FBI program as a starting point, I studied recent research and conducted interviews to identify and mitigate program weaknesses. I consulted a number of experts. My instructor, Par Ford, was instrumental in providing a large number of the concepts presented here based upon the teachings of Dr. Hatsumi. Par introduced me to the simplest, yet most effective strategies I've seen in over thirty years of martial arts training. That information, combined with others' research and studies, as well as my own experiences, interviews, and analysis resulted in the SSDT program.

The SSDT program contains proven effective philosophy, principles, and techniques to successfully combat an aggressor. The tactical elements focus on general awareness and a commonsense approach to maintaining your safety. The mental attitude focuses on the warrior mindset and the psychology of survival. Finally, instinctual, street-proven techniques based on scientific principles, research, and concepts are presented. The SSDT program is effective for all officers, regardless of size, strength, or athleticism.

The book is organized in the same sequence I would recommend for DT training. Officers should first be taught the core concepts, tactics, and principles. Once the essential fundamentals are presented, comprehended, and adapted, then the actual techniques may be taught in a systematic fashion. The logical order is to first address those subjects that present the lowest level of threat and then address increasingly dangerous subjects. Therefore, compliant, or nonresistant, subjects are discussed first. After that, instruction regarding passively resistant subjects is provided, followed by aggressively resistant subjects. Next, information regarding deadly resistant subjects is presented. The book concludes with a special section on liability, which should be of particular importance to law enforcement executives and use of force instructors.

Some chapters end with drills to successfully prepare the officer for a violent encounter. Please don't ignore these. A little time invested in reviewing and practicing the drills will pay big dividends in increased safety and confidence. Also included throughout the book are links to the Survival Sciences website so videos of various applications can be viewed to supplement the writing. No matter how carefully a technique may be explained, sometimes the "ah-ha!" moment occurs only after seeing it in practice. Please take the time to visit the website to view the videos to reinforce what has been learned in the book. To access the videos, go to www.SurvivalSciences.com and click on the "Videos" page. Under user ID, type *access@SurvivalSciences.com*. The password is *dtconcepts*.

I have been privileged to meet thousands of individuals who chose a career in law enforcement. This book is intended to help protect those officers who put their lives on the line protecting their communities. If you have any questions or comments, please feel free to contact me at www.SurvivalSciences.com.

Acknowledgments

Gigi Joyner. When it comes to wives, I hit the jackpot—gorgeous, bright, athletic, and the nicest person I ever met. She has been supportive of this project, understanding of the training that takes me away from home, a great motivator, and provided her incredible business insight to keep me pointed in the right direction. Gigi portrays the female officer in the book and videos (as a female, this was a logical role for her). In addition, once I developed the idea of the Dynamic Resistance-Response Model (DRM), Gigi created the diagram to go with the concept.

Cole Joyner. Cole is my first, last, and only child, as well as my pride and joy. He is love personified. Cole "supervised" me as I wrote several chapters. For some reason, he thought it was funny to sit on my shoulders like a gargoyle as I typed away on my laptop. I wrote this book to enhance the safety of all officers so they can return home each day to those they love.

Dr. Masaaki Hatsumi. Dr. Hatsumi is the thirty-fourth grand master of the thirteen schools of Ninjutsu/Ninpo. He is a fervent advocate of the military and law enforcement. His teachings have been adopted throughout the world, making it a safer place. Many of the concepts presented in this book originated from Dr. Hatsumi.

Par Ford. With over thirty years experience in the martial arts, I thought I had pretty much seen it all and knew it all. Then I met Par. He introduced me to Bujinkan Ninpo and a whole new way of looking at things. I had never seen an art with absolutely no sport's application but with dead-on application for law enforcement and military. Par was the source of many of the techniques that appear in this book.

Hugh Coleman. Hugh and I worked on the same criminal squad for years and were on SWAT during some exciting times in Los Angeles. We have taught countless firearms, defensive tactics, tactics, and chemical agents courses together. Hugh has also been my martial arts training partner for over a decade. He is my training partner in the photographs and videos.

Tom Yi. Tom was involved in my business plan from the beginning, providing input, guidance, and his uplifting philosophical outlook on life. Tom also generously allowed us to shoot photographs and videos at his martial arts studio, MUDO Integrated Martial Arts, located in Santa Monica, California.

Genevieve Staats (CreatEve Web Design). Gen is Tom's better half. Not only is she a former model from Australia, but she is an incredibly talented website designer and artist. She created my website, designed my logo, designed the cover for this book, and has been an invaluable asset. Gen also directed, filmed, and produced the training videos.

Dr. John Pi. In addition to being an FBI agent, John is also an emergency room physician and on the teaching staff of UCLA Medical School. His passion and dedication to helping make law enforcement safer resulted in his creation of a panel to research carotid-type restraints. The result was the bilateral vascular restraint (BVR) presented in Chapter 13.

Keith Teller. Although I began my martial arts training prior to meeting Keith, I've always considered him to be my original instructor. We met in 1979 and have continued our friendship. Keith is a tenth-degree black belt in USA Goju and owns the Gainesville Goju Dojo (Urban Hall #47) in Gainesville, Florida.

Don Schmidt. Don does computer forensic exams for the FBI. He is a computer wizard and a talented artist. Don did the artwork to turn a rough sketch of the DRM into the diagram you see in this book.

Chad Basile. Chad and I have worked together for many years. If you need an attorney, he should be your first call. After I created the DRM and drafted the first article, Chad provided the legal review and editing.

Joel Nussbaum. Joel is a retired photographer from the FBI and now a beach bum. We all want to be like Joel one day. Joel did the still photography for the book.

Mike Conrad. Mike and I were classmates at the FBI Academy in 1987. He is a respected investigator and talented DT (defensive tactics) instructor currently serving in the Phoenix office. Mike reviewed the first drafts of the manuscript and gave me his suggestions. His help and guidance made the book a better product.

Dave Freihon. Dave is another FBI friend and fellow SWAT operator. When I needed someone who looked like a tough, biker type, I instantly thought of Dave. Dave good naturedly agreed to be the "bad guy" in the photos and videos.

The FBI. I have had a wonderful career with the premier law enforcement agency in the world. The FBI has given me endless training opportunities and sent me around the world meeting the finest law enforcement officers. It's been a fantastic ride.

Carolyn Spence, David Fausel, and the fine people at CRC Press. My ignorance of the book-writing and publishing process probably accounted for my optimism. Carolyn and David have professionally and patiently provided me with the guidance I needed.

Rob Roy. Rob and I have been friends since we were in middle school. During one of our many political discussions, I described my plan to help law enforcement. Rob came up with an ingenious idea on how to combine our resources and provide a necessary, valuable, and life-saving product to the law enforcement community. The result is the Law Enforcement Training and Tracking System (LETTS).

Legal Disclaimer

Please note that the publisher and the author of this instructional book are not responsible in any manner whatsoever for any injury that may result from practicing the techniques or following the instructions given within. Defensive tactics (DT) training is inherently dangerous, and the reader assumes all risk and responsibility. The reader knowingly and voluntarily accepts and assumes all risks of injury, death, or other loss or damage.

If you are in doubt about any information in the book, consult with a certified DT Instructor prior to proceeding. Since the physical activities described herein may be too strenuous for some readers, it is necessary to consult with a physician prior to beginning any physical training.

Gender-Neutral Intent

I attempted (and hopefully succeeded) to portray officers in gender-neutral terms. However, I consistently referred to subjects in masculine terms (e.g., "bad guy"). This was done for two reasons. First, photos of the resistive subject role player were always depicted by a male. Second, I recognize female offenders assault officers and are equally dangerous, but approximately 90% of the attacks on officers are by males. Therefore, for simplicity, I chose to refer to subjects in masculine terms. I hope I have not offended any female criminals by doing so.

About the Author

Chuck Joyner is a recognized expert in the field of use of force and has lectured throughout the United States and internationally on myriad law enforcement topics. He is the creator of the Dynamic Resistance-Response Model (DRM), a modern use of force model, which first appeared in the September 2007 issue of the *FBI Law Enforcement Bulletin.*

Mr. Joyner holds FBI certifications as a master police instructor, general police instructor, defensive tactics instructor, firearms instructor, chemical agents instructor, and physical fitness instructor. He holds Peace Officer Standards and Training (POST) certifications as a SWAT and sniper instructor. Mr. Joyner is also a certified TASER instructor and ASP baton instructor.

Mr. Joyner began his martial arts training in 1976, earning his first black belt in 1980. He has been awarded black belts in four martial arts and holds master rank in two styles. Mr. Joyner is a former competitive kick boxer and boxer. He was inducted into the Martial Arts Masters Hall of Fame as instructor of the year in 2006.

Mr. Joyner was employed by the CIA from 1983 to 1987, and has worked as a special agent for the FBI since 1987. He served as the principal firearms and defensive tactics instructor for the FBI Los Angeles Field Office, providing lead instruction to thousands of FBI agents, law enforcement officers, and military personnel in firearms, defensive tactics, chemical agents deployment, and arrest and raid tactics. He served as a SWAT team operator (entry team), sniper, and grenadier for seven years. He was appointed as the SWAT team commander for three years until being promoted to an FBI headquarters position.

Mr. Joyner has a BS in biology, a BA in psychology, and an MA in organizational-industrial psychology.

Use of Force

1

The International Association of Chiefs of Police (IACP) conducted an informative study entitled "Police Use of Force in America 2001."[1] The collection of information for this project began in 1996, but the results were just recently published. The IACP research and a number of other use of force studies were reviewed, and the results were determined to be consistent. All of the time, resources, and effort in conducting these research projects are wasted, however, unless we carefully examine the results and make systemic improvements to better serve law enforcement and the public. Before designing a defensive tactics (DT) program, or upgrading an existing program, it makes sense to first determine who is attacking law enforcement officers, how officers are attacked, and under what circumstances officers are injured and sued. Completed use of force research has answered these questions—now we just have to address them properly. The IACP study appears to be the most comprehensive, so it is referenced to the greatest extent in this chapter.

The IACP categorized different types of force used by officers, to include physical force (fighting), chemical force (typically pepper spray), electronic force, impact force (typically batons), and firearms force. The IACP also had these same categories of force as used by subjects. Since subjects may use whatever is available as a weapon, the IACP also includes "other" types of force used by subjects to include active aggression, edged weapons, verbal threats, and automobiles.[2]

When Do Officers Use Force?

The first topic to consider is when officers use force. This won't be a surprise to experienced officers, but officers are required to use force primarily during arrests. Yep, bad guys sometimes aren't too excited about going to jail and they put up a fight. According to the IACP study, 39% of the use of force incidents occurred during arrests.[3] What does this tell us? Although we should always be alert and aware of potential threats, we should be hyperalert while making arrests. It's also helpful to remember there is an inverse correlation between the officer's stress level and the subject's stress level. As an officer, you are probably experiencing some tension as you approach a subject to make an arrest. Your body is in the fight-or-flight mode as you prepare yourself for something bad to happen. The subject as this time has no stress, as he is not even aware you exist in his world yet. Once you make contact and the subject is aware of your presence, you both are at high levels of anxiety until you are able to gain some control (either willingly or unwillingly on the part of the subject) and begin to put on the handcuffs. You start thinking, "Whew, glad that's over," and the bad guy starts thinking, "Crap! I don't want to go to jail!" Officers tend to relax about now, and it's just too soon. Don't do it. The subject is probably getting more and more agitated as the reality of losing constitutionally guaranteed freedoms is sinking in. As the subject gets more anxious, it is a safe bet he is also getting more dangerous. Just like a caged animal, the subject may be frantically looking for any means of escape—and his escape plan may include hurting you.

The second most common situation in which officers are required to use force is for disturbance calls. Again, this is not a surprise. You are going someplace where there are angry people who want to fight. In addition, you probably have the added mixture of alcohol and drugs. I would expect every officer to have heightened awareness on this call.

The next most common is traffic stops. Traffic stops are always potentially hazardous. It is incredibly dangerous to walk up on a vehicle for some minor traffic violation, not knowing who, or how many, are in that vehicle.

Who Assaults Officers?

Who is it that assaults law enforcement officers? Your first thought is probably "someone who is not too bright," and I would tend to agree with you. It doesn't make sense to attack an officer—one who stands for freedom, justice, apple pie, and the American way. Chris Rock created a humorous video titled "How Not to Get Your Ass Beat by the Police."[4] Mr. Rock's first rule was to obey the law. Another rule was, if you ignore the first rule, stop immediately and don't run from the police. It's funny because it is sound advice and it would solve a lot of problems if people abided by these two rules. Actually, if everyone abided by rule 1, we would no longer need to have any law enforcement. Wouldn't that be utopia? I would gladly look for another line of work if it meant my son would grow up in a world without crime. But I'm not holding my breath, nor am I quitting my day job anytime soon.

Changing the topic slightly, see if you agree with the following advice provided to the public about how to best interact with the police:

"Don't get into an argument with the police."
"Think carefully about your words, movement, body language, and emotions."
"Keep your hands where the police can see them."
"Don't run. Don't touch a police officer."

"Don't bad-mouth the police officer…."
"Don't resist even if you believe you are innocent."
"If you're given a ticket, you should sign it."

I don't know about you, but I like these pearls of wisdom. Again, if everyone followed these guidelines, the world would be a much better place—particularly for those in law enforcement. But where did I find this sage advice? Probably from the IACP, you may (logically) guess. Or perhaps it's from some other law enforcement agency? No, it's not. The above statements are from the article "Know Your Rights: What to Do If You're Stopped by the Police,"[5] which appears on the American Civil Liberties Union (ACLU) website. Surprised? The ACLU has a different perspective than most in law enforcement. This is one of the extremely rare times I agree with their message. The purported purpose of the ACLU is to protect the public, just as it is the mission of law enforcement. We may certainly disagree on how best to accomplish that, but I think we can all agree the above recommendations are good ones. Now if we can just get everyone to abide by them.

Going back to the original question of who assaults officers, the answer, as documented in the IACP report, is people under the influence.[6] Per the study, 53% of the males and 35% of the females who were involved in use of force incidents were under the influence of alcohol or drugs. Females account for about 10% of the assaults on police officers.[7] Who else assaults officers? Emotionally disturbed subjects (EDSs). The report further states in arrests of female EDSs, 58% were involved in a use of force incident. Of male EDSs being arrested, 52% were involved in a use of force event. The lesson here is mentally ill people and those under the influence of alcohol or drugs are less likely to be logical and, therefore, can be dangerous.

On a related topic, those with excited delirium are a major problem for law enforcement. During a conference on use of force sponsored by the Police Officers' Association of Los Angeles County (POALAC) on October 27, 2009, retired LAPD Captain Greg Meyer stated physicians estimate it takes a minimum of six officers to successfully control an individual with excited delirium. Almost all the officers at the conference seemed to agree with this number. Due to the effects of PCP and similar drugs, these individuals have extremely high body heat. So, if you arrive on scene and find a naked, sweaty man acting in a bizarre fashion, go ahead and save yourself some time and trouble—call for backup and medical assistance.

Who else assaults officers? Juveniles assault officers.[8] Twenty-seven percent of the reported assaults on police officers during the study period (1995–2000) were committed by juveniles.[9] Seven percent of all reported firearms assaults were committed by juveniles ten years old or younger. This is scary. When you are visualizing your if-then scenarios (discussed in Chapter 3), do you ever visualize an eight-year-old trying to shoot you? Have you prepared yourself mentally to handle this type of threat—not only as it is occurring, but also the aftermath?

Finally, it is not only one-on-one conflicts you have to deal with. Many times, you will be outnumbered.[10] The ICAP report indicates approximately 94% of the use of force incidents involved one subject. Doing the math, that means 6% involved more than one subject. In the time period of 1995–2000 there were three reported incidents of one officer and twelve subjects. That's a really bad day. From a training standpoint, this means our defensive tactics can't always focus on one-on-one drills. We need to be aware of additional threats at all times and know how to deal with multiple subjects.

So who is it that assaults police officers? The answer is lots of people. Most of those people are not of right mind, which makes them even more dangerous. We are attacked by people under the influence, mentally ill people, juveniles, several at one time, and don't forget, committed bad guys who would rather fight or kill you than comply.

Types of Force Used

If we want to implement a valid DT training system, we need to know how we are being attacked and develop a strategy for combating those attacks. In the IACP study, officers were attacked with physical force in approximately 87% of the reported use of force incidents, chemical force in 10% of the incidents (yes, the public has access to Mace and pepper spray too), impact force in 1 to 2% of the incidents, and firearms in 1 to 2% of the incidents.[11] In the large "other" category, the IACP listed attacks by subjects using things such as edged weapons, automobiles, and tools (like a screwdriver) as weapons against officers.[12] In a Bureau of Justice Statistics (BJS) report,[13] it was determined that suspects use weaponless tactics in 5.5% of all arrests. Of these, wrestling moves were the most common, followed by pushing or shoving.

A report titled "Arrest and Control Unit Statistical Summary, The First Two Years in Retrospect" prepared by LAPD Sergeant Greg Dossey, discussed a study Sgt. Dossey conducted as the officer in charge of the LAPD Arrest and Control Unit.[14] Sgt. Dossey's research results were similar to those of the IACP study. Sgt. Dossey further broke down the type of physical assaults on officers. He determined approximately 23% of the suspects kicked the officer, 16% punched the officer, 15% wrestled the officer to the ground, and 11% bit the officer.

Knowing how the subject will attack dictates how training time should be allotted. The more serious the threat and the more often the threat occurs should lead to increased training time on defending against that particular method of attack. The most prevalent type of attack comes under the broad category of physical force. Specifically, per Sgt. Dossey's research, resisters attempted to kick, punch, tackle, or bite officers. This is where the bulk of DT training needs to focus. A good DT program will address these issues and provide officers with a simple and effective response.

What is interesting is the IACP report indicates that even though the size of the reporting departments and jurisdictions vary greatly, the occurrence and parameters of use of force incidents are fairly consistent.[5]

Injuries and Lawsuits

To look objectively at evaluating and developing a DT program, we need to determine when bad things happen. For law enforcement administrators (for that matter, all of us), bad things include officers getting hurt or getting sued. We'd like to avoid both situations entirely.

The goal of any good DT program is to increase the safety of officers while serving the public. Per the IACP report, injuries are most likely to occur during a physical struggle.[16] How much risk is there (for both the officer and the suspect) when force is used? Specifically, what are the comparative rates of injury when officers use empty-hand techniques (control holds and personal weapons), impact weapons, pepper spray, TASER, and carotid-type neck restraints? Sgt. Chris Butler of the Calgary (Alberta) Police Service and Dr. Christine Hall of the Canadian Police Research Center conducted a study to determine the risks associated with each of the five major force options listed.[17] Not surprisingly, the ranking, from safest to most likely to cause injury, is:

1. Pepper spray
2. Carotid type of restraint hold
3. TASER
4. Empty-hand techniques
5. Impact weapons

Pepper spray (oleoresin capsicum) produced the lowest rate of injury in that 80% of sprayed subjects had no injury, about 15% had minor injuries, and 4% had injuries resulting in outpatient medical care. Officers suffered no injury in 89% of the cases and only minor injuries for the remainder. One of the expected hazards of using pepper spray is receiving secondary or residual exposure. This is justification for exposing officers to pepper spray during training prior to its use in the field. On a number of occasions I experienced some minor coughing and constriction of my throat after a fellow agent was a little too energetic in the dispersal of pepper spray. Admittedly, I also caused a friend and fellow SWAT operator to get some exposure as he was downwind when I chose to spray a dog rather than shoot it. I don't think he's ever forgiven me.

The research further stated that TASER, which seems to get an abundance of inaccurate and unfair press, had no injuries in 45% of the cases, 42% had minor injuries, 12% needed minor outpatient medical care, and 1% required hospitalization. Many departments require that the TASER probes be removed from the subject by medical personnel. This would lead to an increased percentage of outpatient care for the use of a TASER. Of officers deploying the TASER, 83% were not injured. It should be noted that a TASER is typically used on the most violent resisters, increasing the likelihood of some injury, yet it still had excellent results for safety.

For the more injurious options, the study indicated over 61% of the subjects had injuries when a baton was used, and the injuries were of a more serious nature. Twenty-nine percent of the officers deploying a baton sustained at least some injury. Empty-hand techniques resulted in injuries to 77% of the subjects and about 22% of the officers.

What does the study by Sgt. Butler and Dr. Hall tell us? It indicates it's very dangerous for officers to go hands-on with a resistive subject. Given the choice, the safest options are those that allow the officer to gain compliance or control at the greatest distance. Those would be the TASER and pepper spray. It also demonstrated that a carotid type of restraint (the bilateral vascular restraint is discussed in Chapter 13) is a safe, viable option if an officer is required to close with a subject.

The BJS study[18] stated the most common type of use of force (77%) by officers is the use of their hands and arms in some type of DT technique, usually grabbing or holding a suspect. The BJS research indicated that officers are "significantly at risk for injury when they use force, particularly when they strike a suspect with their fists or use their hands and arms to control a suspect." This is consistent with the other cited research. Bad things happen when subjects resist arrest, and the most common injuries to officers occur when they go hands-on with a subject.

The emphasis must be on officer safety, but we can't ignore lawsuits or bad conduct. Some of the lawsuits I have researched resulted from inadequate training, poor training, or bad policy. This is not the officer's fault. This is the department's fault. One way to evaluate the effectiveness of training is to look at officer injuries and sustained lawsuits against officers as indicators. Well-trained, professional officers, with proper supervision, typically have fewer injuries and aren't sued successfully for violating civil rights.

Going back to the IACP study, in 1995–1999, the overwhelming majority (80 to 99%) of excessive force complaints against officers occurred during arrests. In 1995–1997, the use of physical force by officers comprised 68% of the complaints, chemical agents comprised 4% of the complaints, electronic devices comprised 6% of the complaints, impact weapons comprised 3% of the complaints, and firearms comprised less than 1% of the complaints.[19]

A continuing trend is the acceptance and adoption of the TASER by law enforcement agencies throughout the country. I'm a big fan of the TASER. I think it's an incredible tool that has increased the safety of law enforcement officers and the general public. There are officers alive today because of this tool. Undeniably, there are a large number of citizens who are alive today due to the advent of the TASER. The problem occurs when any good tool is misused. The highest percentage of sustained citizen complaints, per category, involves the use of electronic tools by officers.[20] It is incumbent upon departments to provide current legal updates to its officers and to have policy based on the law. It surprises me some departments have written policy permitting the use of an electronic control device (ECD) on a passively resisting subject. One department's policy was described as ask, tell, tase. This is simply bad policy, and the courts are repeatedly indicating such by awarding large settlements. I know if people would abide by the ACLU guidelines listed above, we wouldn't have this problem. As a law enforcement officer it offends my sense of justice when someone doesn't obey the law. I understand. But I also understand the courts have repeatedly ruled it is not "reasonable" force to use an ECD (or pepper spray, impact weapons, or personal weapons) on a passively resisting subject who, in the officer's own words, is not a threat.

Plaintiff's attorneys love "bad facts." The public becomes concerned when they hear about an unarmed, fragile elderly man or woman (who admittedly may be verbally abusive) getting hit with an ECD. Regardless of the circumstances, it is bad facts when an obviously pregnant woman, who is not a physical threat to an officer, has an ECD deployed against her. The good news for officers and departments is less than 1% of all excessive force complaints are sustained. Let's not spoil this and have valuable, life-saving tools taken away from us because we begin using them too indiscriminately.

I'm proud to have served for seven years on the FBI Los Angeles SWAT team as an entry team member and sniper, and three additional years as the team's commander. Our team was frequently the busiest in the FBI, averaging more than forty operations a year. Most of those involved very dangerous people, some who had publicly vowed they "would never be taken alive." I would like to say that we faced incredible danger and walked in the shadow of death every day. I would like to say that because it sounds really cool. But I can't, because it's not true. We planned, we practiced, and we controlled our operating environment. We minimized threats through careful preparation. In SWAT we have the element of surprise. In most police work, the bad guys get that tremendous advantage. The IACP report confirms what you probably already knew. Working in law enforcement is dangerous, particularly when you are arresting people, dealing with angry people, or even issuing a ticket for a minor traffic violation. Now that we know this, what are we doing about it? Are we planning, practicing, and preparing ourselves now for those occasions in which we will need to use force to gain control? Are we training and strategizing for those inevitable confrontations? We will discuss the survivor mindset in Chapter 3, but the fact you're reading this indicates you have grasped the concept that law enforcement is dangerous and you are taking steps to make it less so by proper planning and training. Please ensure your DT training is also taking into account the lessons learned from completed use of force research.

Endnotes

1. International Association of Chiefs of Police (IACP), "Police Use of Force in America 2001," www.cops.usdoj.gov/html/cr-rom/resources_law_enf/pubs/PoliceUseofForceAmerica2001.pdf (accessed August 27, 2009).
2. Ibid., pp. 33–34.
3. Ibid., p. iii.
4. Rock, Chris, "How Not to Get Your Ass Beat by the Police," Chris Rock Show, April 17, 2005, TV lesson, www.tvlesson.com/video/11888_how-not-to-get-your-ass-kicked-by-the-police-by-Chris-Rock.html (accessed August 22, 2009).
5. American Civil Liberties Union (ACLU), ACLU website, July 30, 2005, www.aclu-wa.org/library_files/You%20and%20the%20Police.pdf (accessed August 27, 2009.
6. IACP, "Police Use of Force in America 2001," p. 40.
7. Ibid., p. 32.
8. Ibid., p. 28.
9. Ibid., p. 31.
10. Ibid., p. 47.
11. Ibid., pp. 29–30.
12. Ibid., p. 34.
13. Adams, K., Alpert, G. P., Dunlam, R. G., Garner, J. H., Greenfeld, L. A., Henriquez, M. A., Langan, P. A., Maxwell, C. D., and Smith, S. K., "Use of Force by Police: Overview of National and Local Data," Bureau of Justice Statistics, November 1, 1999, p. 32.
14. Dossey, G., "Arrest and Control Unit Statistical Summary, The First Two Years in Retrospect," Los Angeles Police Department (LAPD, February 24, 1998).
15. IACP, "Police Use of Force in America 2001," p. 7.
16. Ibid., p. 24.
17. Butler, C., and Hall, C., "New Study Ranks Risks of Injury from 5 Major Force Options,"www.forcescience.org/fsinews/2008/07/new-study-ranks-risks-of-injury-for-5-major-force-options. Force Science News #102 (accessed July 19, 2008).
18. Adams, K., et al., "Use of Force by Police," p. 13.
19. IACP, "Police Use of Force in America 2001," p. 60.
20. Ibid., p. 14.

Dynamic Resistance-Response Model

2

When you go to arrest someone, who determines how much force you will use? Do you make that decision? Or is it the person you are arresting? I hosted many VIP groups at the FBI, and I would always include a demonstration of the firearms "shoot–don't shoot" simulator. It was my objective to ensure every person who attended left with an accurate perception of a use of force incident. Some people got the answer to the above question right immediately and some had to be convinced. The correct answer is the bad guy always determines how much force an officer uses. It is the bad guy's level of resistance that directly determines the necessary force required. If the subject follows commands and complies completely, then great. We slap on the handcuffs and off we go to jail. We're all safe for another day. But if the subject wants to run away, fight, or shoot, then we don't necessarily have the fairy tale happy ending.

Let's face reality. The use of force is never pretty. Actually, it can be downright ugly. Anytime a physical confrontation occurs, it should be expected injuries will happen. If an officer uses force, it is because a subject is resisting. Obviously, the law and the officer's departmental policies are also vital in determining the appropriate response.

Knowing we have several viable options to deal with a resistive subject, we need to understand what we can use and when. Following is a compilation of several actual events:

> A pregnant, 4-foot-10-inch, 90-pound, 92-year-old woman with diabetes is on her way to church. After speeding through a stop sign, she is pulled over by Officer Dogood. Officer Dogood writes her a ticket and politely requests the driver to sign the ticket to acknowledge she is receiving the ticket and agrees to appear in court. The driver calls Officer Dogood lots of really bad names. She then insults his mother, his dog, and tells him his kids are ugly. She finishes her tirade by telling Officer Dogood that if he thinks she is going to sign the ticket, he can just kiss her wrinkly, ninety-two-year-old butt. Feeling somewhat nauseous upon visualizing that suggestion, Officer Dogood asks the driver to step out of the car. The driver refuses. Officer Dogood then commands the driver to get out of the car as she is now under arrest. The driver again refuses. Officer Dogood attempts to forcefully remove the driver from the car, but she thwarts his efforts by firmly holding onto the steering wheel. Failing all attempts to remove the driver and place her under arrest, Officer Dogood tells the driver he will use his TASER on her if she doesn't get out of the car. The driver ridicules Officer Dogood and questions his manhood. Zap! Officer Dogood tases the driver and she falls out of her car fracturing her hip. The driver then lets out a stream of obscenities to include suggesting Officer Dogood commit a physically impossible act. Zap, zap goes the TASER.

Some of you may be thinking this is a wonderful bedtime story you're going to read to your kids tonight. I get it. If people abided by the guidance provided by Chris Rock and the ACLU, this wouldn't be a problem. Unfortunately, today's society is becoming more belligerent and distrustful of law enforcement. Even though it shouldn't happen, more people in society are resisting lawful commands by officers. The result, of course, is bad things happen—bad things for the resisters and, sometimes, bad things for the officers. Do you think Officer Dogood and the department will get sued? Uh, yep! Do you think the ninety-two-year-old woman will be awarded at least some monetary damages? Uh, yep! Do you think the department will then come out with some policy not to use a TASER on pregnant ninety-two-year-old ladies with diabetes? Possibly, but they shouldn't. Whether or not an officer should use a TASER should come down to one thing: Can the officer reasonably articulate why the person was a threat. If the answer is yes, then tase away. If the answer is no, then keep the TASER in its holster.

The problem is most law enforcement agencies will rely on a traditional use of force model for guidance in establishing policies. Traditional models place the emphasis on the officer's actions first, and then belatedly view the actions of the resister. This misleads citizens and jurors into erroneously analyzing why all possible lesser force options were not used. In *Graham v. Connor*,[1] the Supreme Court determined the "reasonable officer" standard for guiding officer conduct. But what do most departments do? They implement a more restrictive policy than required by the court in an attempt to reduce liability, but this strategy usually backfires. After facing a civil suit for alleged excessive force, departments tend to prohibit or greatly restrict the use of nonlethal equipment. This results in officers becoming increasingly reluctant to use valuable tools that were created specifically to increase the safety of both officers and the public. The misuse of a credible tool by one officer should not lead to an automatic policy change affecting an entire agency. Before adopting a more restrictive policy, departments should first consider the ramifications of such changes and the impact on safety.

There are several types of traditional use of force models being used today, but they primarily fall into one of two categories: the ladder (or continuum) model and the wheel model.

First, looking at the ladder diagram (Figure 2.1), we see use of force options presented in an escalating pattern. Right away, you should notice a problem with this model. What are you looking at? To use this traditional model, you first look at the level of force used by the officer. This puts the officer in a defensive position at the outset and does not accurately depict what actually happened. Did the officer just randomly walk up to someone and whack him with a baton? (If this is the case, you have big problems.) Or, more realistically, did the subject first resist and behave aggressively? Another problem is that those unfamiliar with law enforcement look at the ladder and

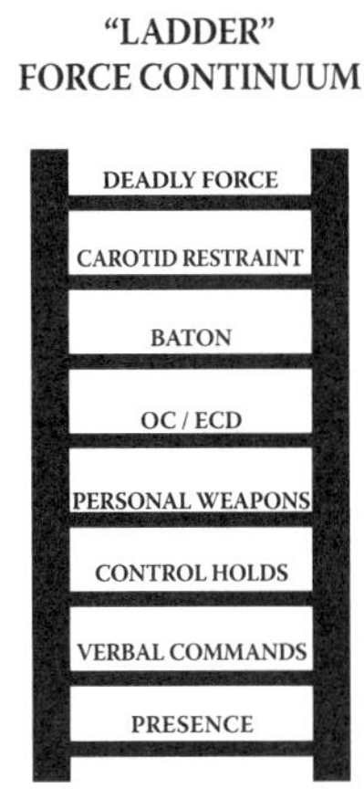

Figure 2.1 The ladder force continuum.

believe an officer should climb the ladder one rung at a time until the suspect complies. The ladder portrays a confrontational relationship in which the officer is always trying to use ever-increasing levels of force. It is not unusual for non–law enforcement people to think an officer should attempt to use every tool on the ladder prior to deploying deadly force.

As an example of this, I was a member of a panel composed primarily of medical doctors to research the use of carotid-type restraints (discussed in Chapter 13). The doctors on the panel were all incredibly pro-law enforcement. Many volunteered their time to train and work with law enforcement tactical teams. In a conversation with one of these doctors, he said officers should never shoot an unarmed assailant. I was surprised and asked why he thought this. His response was the gap between the officer and subject on the continuum ladder was too great—the subject was at the very bottom of the ladder and the officer had used force at the top of the ladder. This is coming from a highly educated person who loves and respects law enforcement. Using the ladder as a use of force model reinforces this flawed thinking.

In an attempt to correct this problem, some departments reverted to the wheel model (Figure 2.2). The wheel typically depicts the officer in the middle of a circle or wagon wheel configuration. The various force options available to officers are listed among several spokes radiating from the center of the wheel. The idea was to represent the officer's ability to reach out and choose whatever tool was appropriate for the situation, permitting greater flexibility. It was a good concept, but it failed to provide officers with guidance as to what tool to use when. The result was officers would mentally revert back to a continuum type of model when determining the appropriate force option. It also would lead the public to ask, and second-guess, why one particular weapon was chosen over all of the other available options.

Figure 2.2 The wheel model.

These traditional uses of force models fail to represent the dynamic encounter between an officer and a resistive subject. Worse, they represent an ever-increasing escalation of force that misleads the public and makes decision making for the officer more difficult.

Recognizing the limitations of traditional use of force models, I had begun teaching a modern approach during defensive tactics (DT) training in the late 1990s. It was suggested I publicize the model as officers found the new approach more accurate and easier to understand. I asked Chad Basile, an FBI agent and attorney, to research current case law and provide a legal opinion of my model. My wife created a diagram depicting the dynamic resistance-response model (DRM).[2] The resulting article appeared in the September 2007 issue of the *FBI Law Enforcement Bulletin*.

The DRM addresses the shortcomings of traditional models. When officers clearly understand their use of force options and receive adequate training, they are better prepared to make appropriate decisions in critical incidents. Officers in life-threatening situations must have unambiguous and consistent guidelines.

The origin of the name of the DRM requires some explanation. The word *dynamic* as used to emphasize encounters with subjects can be fluid and, therefore, so is the model. Subjects can move rapidly from one category of resistance to the next. Officers must never assume a compliant subject will continue to remain compliant. As will be discussed in Chapter 3, officers should be prepared for an attack regardless of how compliant an individual initially appears.

As was mentioned at the beginning of this chapter, *resistance* indicates it is the subject who controls the interaction with the officer. A major failing of traditional models is the initial focus is on the officer's actions and the force used prior to examining the resister's actions. This is misleading and places the officer in an untenable position if an accusation of excessive force is made. The DRM emphasizes it is the suspect's level of resistance that determines the officer's response. In other words, the resister's actions establish the appropriate reaction (i.e., the level of force or tools used) by the officer. To use the DRM, the reviewer is required to first determine the category of resistance by the subject.

The DRM combines force options with four broad categories of subjects. The four categories are not resistant (compliant), passively resistant, aggressively resistant, and deadly resistant. The number of possible subject categories and descriptions is unlimited, but it serves no purpose to create additional categories if the force options available to the officer can be limited, and simplified, to four categories. These categories were selected because court decisions typically place subjects in one of the four following broad groups:

Not resistant: Under the mindset of "hope for the best and prepare for the worst," a suspect who is not resistant is the best possible situation on every encounter. If presence and verbal commands are all that is required, then hallelujah! This is what we want. No coercive physical contact is required and no one gets hurt.

Passively resistant: A passively resistant suspect fails to follow commands and may be verbally abusive. Presence and verbal commands aren't working on this person. The suspect may attempt to curl into a fetal position or pull away from the officer. The officer deems the subject's actions as neutral or defensive. The key to this classification is the officer doesn't feel threatened. Since the officer doesn't feel threatened, and using the reasonable officer standard, the officer may not use items such as pepper spray, baton, or a TASER. The officer may use pressure points or control holds to obtain compliance.

Aggressively resistant: An officer feels threatened by an aggressively resistant suspect. This resister takes offensive action by attempting to push, throw, strike, tackle, or physically harm the officer or another person. Or the resister gives preattack indicators that cause the officer to feel reasonably threatened. It is necessary for officers to recognize and articulate verbal and nonverbal preattack behavior. The subject's verbal preattack indicators are usually relatively simple (e.g., "I'm going to kick your ass!"). The nonverbal is more difficult, but the more likely to occur. It also requires significant, careful report writing later. The importance of accurate, comprehensive report writing will be discussed in Chapter 18.

Nonverbal preattack indicators could include the subject shifting balance to a more balanced stance, the "target" glance in which the subject unintentionally looks at the area of the officer he intends to attack, clenching of the fists, the 1,000-yard stare, failure to obey lawful commands, and dramatic and excessive gestures. One of the best indicators is the subject attempts to close the distance in a subtle or not so subtle way. The best response to someone trying to "step on your toes" or close the distance will be covered in Chapter 6.

Justified responses to an aggressively resistant suspect include the use of personal weapons, TASER, chemical agents, and impact weapons.

Deadly resistant: If deadly resistant, the officer believes the suspect will seriously injure or kill the officer or another person if action is not taken to stop the threat. The officer is justified in using deadly force to overcome the offender and gain control.

For each of the four suspect categories, officers have all of the tools in preceding categories available. In each situation, the officer should give commands if doing so doesn't jeopardize the officer's safety (Figure 2.3).

In the DRM diagram, no resistance, or compliance, is placed in the center of the triangle. This emphasizes the officer's objective in every encounter is to have the suspect comply. If a suspect's resistance places him on one of the three corners of the triangle, the officer's proper response is intended to move the suspect's behavior to the center of the triangle and compliance. The

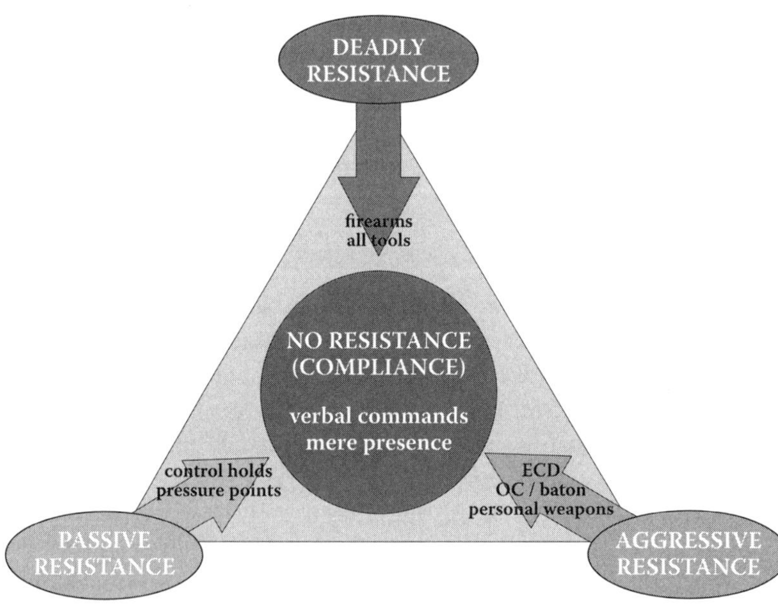

Figure 2.3 The DRM.

purpose of any use of force by an officer is never to punish, but to gain control or compliance of the resister. Even when using deadly force, the officer's intention is to gain control—either by the resister becoming killed or incapacitated, or preferably by the resister ceasing the resistance and complying with the officer's commands.

Unlike traditional models, which represent a continuous escalation of force, the DRM clearly depicts every confrontation moving toward compliance—the true goal of the officer. This is more easily understood and accurately applied by officers and the public (potential jurors). The DRM places the initial analysis on the actions of the resister and then reviews the appropriate response of the officer. The DRM also simplifies training, as suspects can easily be classified into one of four groups. Officers are then trained as to the appropriate tools to use for each of the four subject categories. Officers have a better understanding of their force options, enhancing their safety and the effectiveness of the department.

Concluding with our ninety-two-year-old pregnant diabetic—what is the appropriate response if you were the officer on scene? We've already determined the use of a TASER will probably lead to taxpayers' dollars going into her bank account. Also, other bad things for you and your department are likely to occur, to include appearing on YouTube and being embarrassed. First, determine in which of the four resister categories the woman belongs. She certainly isn't compliant, as much as you'd like for her to be to avoid this whole ugly mess. She also is not aggressively resistant, as she is not trying to punch, kick, or hurt you. What is her resistive action? She gripped the steering wheel tightly so she couldn't be removed from the car. She didn't display any weapons, nor did she do anything to indicate she would use the car as a weapon. It would be difficult for you to articulate how you felt threatened by this driver, unless of course you were a 110-year-old crippled police officer. I'll assume you're not. Therefore, she is clearly passively resistant. Based on the DRM, what are your force options? They include a firm grip, control holds, and pressure points.

As was mentioned at the beginning of the chapter, any use of force is likely to be ugly and result in injuries. Even using these mildly coercive methods, due to the woman's age, it is likely she will suffer bruising and possibly tearing of the skin simply by you grabbing her wrist or arm. You are justified in using these options. You may want to ensure your dash cam is working properly. Depending on your department's policy, you may have the option of writing "refused to sign" on the ticket and walk away. If she fails to appear in court, then a warrant could be issued. Many departments require a supervisor to appear on scene for these situations. It's amazing how many people refuse to sign a ticket for an officer, but once a sergeant arrives and says, "Yep, the officer is correct. You will go to jail if you don't sign the ticket," the light bulb clicks on and they become compliant. At worse, you have another witness to the resistance. The bottom line is, it's a tough job, isn't it? But we can make it a little simpler by having a use of force model that officers, the public, and the courts understand, and which accurately reflects the confrontations on the street.

Endnotes

1. *Graham v. Connor*, 490 U.S. 386 (1989).
2. Joyner, C., and Basile, C., "The Dynamic Resistance Response Model, A Modern Approach to the Use of Force," *FBI Law Enforcement Bulletin*, September 2007, pp. 15–20. The acronym was changed from DRRM in the original article to DRM in this book simply because it is easier to say.

Choosing to Survive
The Warrior Mindset
3

The objectives of this chapter are to increase your awareness, increase your survival instincts, increase your safety, and motivate you to make positive changes. Along these lines, we will discuss what a warrior is. Finally, after doing a self-assessment, you should determine your status as a warrior.

First, what is the meaning of life? No, this isn't a misprint, and no, I didn't go off the deep end (at least I don't think I did). Even though this may sound esoteric, I'm still on topic. I'm sure you have thought about it at some point, and some may have even come up with an answer. I'm confident most would recognize the meaning of life if they heard it. Then there are those of you who immediately thought of the 1982 Arnold Schwarzenegger film *Conan the Barbarian*, in which Conan defines the meaning of life as "to crush your enemies, to see them driven before you, and to hear the lamentations of their women." Uh no, that's not it.

So what is the meaning of life? There is no need to climb to the top of a mountain and seek out an old man with a long beard. You probably see the answer every day. I was walking along one afternoon when it appeared out of nowhere, like a sign from the heavens. Actually, it was written on the side of a patrol car, but it had the same effect. What I read, and the meaning of life, is simply this: to protect and to serve. That is why you are here. That is why you exist. That is why you have chosen a career in law enforcement. It's because, on some level, you recognize a life well lived is one in which you protect and serve your fellow citizens.

While attending martial arts training in Japan in 2007, I noticed a group of people wearing shirts that had the following printed on them:

> Wherever I go, everyone is a little bit safer because I am there.
> Wherever I am, anyone in need has a friend.
> Whenever I return home, everyone is happy I am there.[1]

This was quite a bit different than the typical macho "kill or be killed" type of slogan you see in most martial arts studios. It really impressed me. I particularly liked the last sentence. Sometimes we become so focused on saving the world, we forget the most important people to protect and serve—our own families. I later learned the t-shirts were worn by students of Jack Hoban, a former U.S. Marine, master martial artist, gifted musician, and a remarkable man in his own right. The quote was from Robert Humphrey, a professor of Jack Hoban's when Jack was a young Marine attending college.

Robert Humphrey was a semiprofessional boxer during the Great Depression, a Marine platoon commander on Iwo Jima, held a law degree from Harvard, and taught economics at MIT. He developed the life values theory, which was used successfully throughout the world to quell violence and was the precursor to the present-day strategy of "winning the hearts and minds" of a local population. I think Dr. Humphrey succinctly defined a warrior.

Dr. Masaaki Hatsumi (mentioned in the introduction) defines a warrior as someone who is a person of justice, one who has a sincere heart, and one who helps everyone. Conan the Barbarian was wrong. People like Dr. Hatsumi, Jack Hoban, and Robert Humphrey, those who are true warriors, recognize being a warrior is about self-sacrifice, serving others, and having the strength to protect others.

Are you in a warrior profession? Absolutely! Does that automatically make you a warrior? Unfortunately no, but it's a good start. Job satisfaction is typically high in warrior professions. What a tremendous responsibility it is to protect and to serve. What a tremendous blessing it is to have a career that allows you to protect and serve your fellow man and woman in such a meaningful way.

Most people I know in law enforcement or the military saw the movie *300* about King Leonidas and the 300 Spartans at the battle of Thermopylae. This battle occurred in approximately 400 B.C., yet we still remember it today. Why? Why does it still have such an emotional impact? For those of you who haven't seen it (shame on you), 300 Spartans and other soldiers under the leadership of King Leonidas set up defensive positions at Thermopylae to slow the advancing Persian army of King Xerxes. Estimates of the size of Xerxes' forces ranged from 250,000 to over a million. An indicator of the fierce reputation of the Spartans is exemplified in Xerxes' proposal to King Leonidas. Xerxes offered Leonidas the kingship of all Greece if he joined him. Leonidas' reply was, "If you had any knowledge of the noble things in life, you would refrain from coveting other's possessions; but for me to die for Greece is better than to be the sole ruler over the people of my race!"[2] The reason this story still affects us today is it's a story about the Spartans' service and sacrifice for their people, their nation, and their ideals. It's a story about warriors. To protect and to serve.

Why should you worry about practicing defensive tactics (DT)? Why should you worry about being a warrior? If you are serving in a law enforcement profession, there are people out there who want to hurt you and kill you because of who you are and what you represent. If this is your chosen career and you're out on the job, the potential to be seriously injured or killed exists every second of every day. Tragically, I was training in Japan in early December 2009 when I first learned of four officers brutally murdered while sitting in a coffee shop outside of Tacoma, Washington, prior to their shift. The cowardice of the shooter and the senseless ultimate sacrifice of these four heroes are shocking. Odds are about 12% of all officers will be feloniously assaulted this year, and approximately seventy will be murdered.[3] If you are a law enforcement officer, you will be assaulted during your career, possibly on multiple occasions. You will have to draw your weapon in defense of your life. The good old days are gone (if they ever existed). Criminals are becoming increasingly violent. What are you doing, right now, to prepare for this deadly encounter? Are you preparing yourself tactically, mentally, and physically for this inevitable life-or-death struggle?

The first step in preparing ourselves for this pending violent confrontation is the realization we are training to be the warriors and the protectors of society. If we can't protect ourselves, we are incapable of protecting others. Unless we first develop a warrior mindset, we are doomed to fail in a crisis situation. And that's what we are all really training for, isn't it? We're training for a worst-case scenario, the critical incident. No matter how good our tactics and techniques may be, they are useless unless we are fully prepared to deal with the stress of a life-threatening crisis and use our tactics and techniques effectively. We are doomed unless we are prepared to be warriors.

In a video created by the FBI, several inmates were interviewed. All of the inmates were serving life sentences, with no possibility of parole, for murdering police officers. They were asked to describe the confrontation that led to the murder and the actions of the police officer. Their responses were insightful. One inmate was in the process of robbing a liquor store when an off-duty police officer, who was armed, chose to attempt to tackle the robber instead of shooting him or waiting for a tactical advantage. The inmate said, "I don't think he really wanted to shoot me. Otherwise, he probably would have from the beginning." Another inmate said, "Most police officers aren't conditioned. They're overweight, they drink a lot of booze, they don't sleep very well." One inmate provided this assessment: "If the police officer had been better prepared, if he had known what to do, he wouldn't have been killed." Listen carefully to what these cop killers are saying. They are our enemies and they are providing us with some incredible insight. What they are saying is, "I kill you because I can."

A noteworthy story involved another cop killer who believed he received a message from God to kill a police officer because the police were ruining his drug business.[4] After arriving at a location in his neighborhood, he observed a police officer to determine if he would kill the officer. After watching the police officer, however, the killer decided the officer would be too difficult to overcome. After that officer left the area, the killer remained for two hours until a traffic accident occurred. After watching a second officer for only a short while, the killer concluded this officer would be his victim. The killer calmly walked over to the officer, struck him, knocked the officer to the ground, took the officer's weapon, and shot him six times. The killer didn't know it, but the second officer had recently received a poor performance evaluation and refused to wear his department-issued body armor. This officer also had his weapon taken away from him by a subject a year earlier, but the officer's partner had killed the subject. What was this officer doing that communicated to the killer he was an easy target? What was the first officer doing that indicated he was not? It appears as if the first officer was fit, alert, professional, and followed departmental policies. The drug dealer didn't try to kill the first officer because he didn't think he could. The second officer, however, was not tactically prepared. The subject killed the second officer simply because he could.

As a side note, it is not my intention to bad-mouth any officer, particularly one who has given his life in the line of duty. However, I think we are many times too hesitant to look at the circumstances surrounding the murder of an officer in an attempt to determine what went wrong, what could have been done better, and what can be done to prevent the tragedy from reoccurring. If I should die in a confrontation, I would hope the sacrifice could have some meaning by allowing others to learn from my mistakes. I would hope the training that would result would save other officers' lives. What better way to honor officers killed in the line of duty than to use their stories to provide life-saving training to other officers?

In approximately my ninth year as an FBI special agent, I was assigned to a gang squad and multiagency task force that was working a major Mexican Mafia (La Eme) case. It was an incredibly successful investigation that led to the arrest and prosecution of the top echelon of the Mexican Mafia in the Los Angeles area. The investigation involved countless hours of wiretaps, and we became infinitely familiar with all of the gangsters. One thing that has always stayed with me after listening to their conversations was how they were constantly training. A typical conversation was something like this:

"Hey Chupo! Whatcha doing?"
"Ah, I just got back from the desert. I was shooting my pistolas, man."
"Whatcha doing tomorrow?"
"I'm goin' run at the high school track."

These hard-core gangsters were frequently training with weapons, almost always had a weapon on their person, and were serious about maintaining their physical fitness. They also didn't hesitate to use deadly force.

In the FBI publication "In the Line of Fire," offenders who assaulted police officers were profiled.[5] Interestingly, there was no singular profile developed. This means offenders who are willing to assault officers don't behave in a particular way, nor do they have a particular look. Officers who think they can "read" people and tell if someone is dangerous by looking at them are only fooling themselves.

The study did determine offenders who assaulted officers tended to have criminal records and use drugs. This is not a surprise. As was mentioned in Chapter 1, most offenders who attack officers are under the influence of narcotics or alcohol. Several of the offenders grew up in environments where violence was a routine occurrence. The majority of the offenders practiced with a handgun at least once a year, and one-third practiced shooting at least once a month. Many of the offenders assessed the officer prior to the assault and believed the officer would be unwilling to use deadly force. The people who assault police officers are generally in good condition, practice with firearms, grew up being exposed regularly to violence, and have no hesitation to use deadly force. These are our enemies and they are preparing for battle. Are you?

Sun Tzu wrote *The Art of War* in approximately 500 B.C. What's amazing is the book is still very much valid today. In fact, *The Art of War* is mandatory reading in all of the U.S. military academies and many military academies throughout the world. Sun Tzu wrote, "If you know the enemy and know yourself, you need not fear the result of a hundred battles."[6] Our enemies are studying us. In our prisons, the inmates practice techniques to disarm and kill us. They are studying our policies, procedures, and techniques. We must study them as well. We must know them by constantly studying how they attack us. We need to fully comprehend how officers have been injured and killed and determine how to prevent the tragedy from reoccurring. We must know our enemies as completely as possible so we can best prepare ourselves for the inevitable confrontation we will face. As stated by Sun Tzu, "The art of war teaches us to rely not on the likelihood of the enemy's not coming, but on our readiness to receive him; not on the chance of his not attacking, but rather on the fact that we have made our position unassailable."[7] We must not only know our enemy, but also ourselves. What are our strengths and weaknesses? What are we doing to maximize our strengths and minimize, or eliminate, our weaknesses?

Medical Survival

If you are injured during a confrontation, you must have the will to survive. If you have been wounded, you must first realize the greatest threat to your survival is the person who wounded you. If you don't quickly neutralize that person, that threat, you will die. You must have the determination, the persistence, and the will to fight on no matter what the injury. If you don't, the bad guy will stop you—permanently.

Here's the good news in surviving an injury: if you've been wounded in a fight and you're thinking about how much pain you're in and how much it sucks, there's over a 98% chance you'll survive. I think that's better than the general survival rate on any Los Angeles freeway! And if you're unconscious (greatly increasing the chances of death), you won't even know it. So there's nothing to worry about. It's all good! Either you're thinking, "Man this sucks, but I'm alive and I'm going to keep fighting to stay alive," or you're in blissful sleep. Just remember, if you're conscious, fight on, find your attacker, and neutralize the threat. Since I first began giving lectures on the survivor mindset in 1995, the survival rate has steadily improved from an original percentage of 95%.

Just as an injury to you is not likely to be fatal, don't assume an injury to a bad guy is either, no matter how horrendous it looks. The human body is amazing in its resiliency and its ability to survive wounds. In the video *Ultimate Survivors*, police officers who survived being shot talked about their experiences and what kept them focused on survival.[8] One undercover drug agent told of shooting a drug dealer during a drug deal that went bad with his .45 caliber handgun. The agent was shocked the subject kept coming toward him after being shot several times. Later, during another drug buy, the agent was shot. He thought back to his earlier experience. This agent rationalized that he was bigger than the previous subject. He also figured if that guy could get up, he certainly could. And so he did. The agent was able to fight back and save his life. Remember, if you're conscious, you are still in the fight—so fight!

Causes of Death

There are four general causes of officer deaths in the line of duty. They are lack of training, lack of planning, carelessness, and overconfidence.

Lack of Training

Most departments throughout the United States are doing a good job in the majority of their training. If you did not receive adequate training, then it's your responsibility to get it. This is not the time to whine about the cost or having to take leave to attend outside training. After all, it's your life. If you want to be a warrior, the first step in ensuring your survival is knowing what to do. Unlike the Spartans, we weren't trained in draconian, barbaric methods in the ways of war (and that's a good thing since some of us would have been thrown off of a cliff for being "imperfect" infants). However, since you've chosen a warrior profession, you have an obligation to learn the warrior ways, to learn the safest and most effective methods of dealing with bad people. I've been impressed by the attitude of most officers I've met in this regard. Most officers understand the need to continuously update their training, and they spare no expense in ensuring they are prepared. Completing this book will go a long way toward providing you with the necessary DT skills to survive a violent encounter.

Lack of Planning

Lack of planning is only excusable if you are responding to an emergency that doesn't permit the proper time to plan. I could argue, however, that you could have seen the potential of this particular incident occurring, or something similar, and visualized (planned) how you would respond to it. Many times, lack of planning is due to nothing more than pure laziness. When I was a young agent in 1988, I was assigned to a multiagency task force. On my first arrest with this task force, we were all gathered around the hood of a sergeant's car. He laid out a map book and a photograph. The sergeant looked at all of us and said, "We are going to this address and we're going to arrest this guy." I was pumped and excited. I asked what the plan was. The sergeant looked at me and repeated, "We're going to this address and arrest this guy." I was still pumped and excited and I said, "Yeah, yeah, but what's the plan?" The sergeant looked at me like I was an idiot and he spoke very slowly, "We ... are ... going ... to ... this ... address. We ... will ... arrest ... this ... guy." It finally dawned on me. I decided at that moment it may be best if I stayed near the back on this run to see how these guys did things. We hopped in our cars and sped to the designated address. Tires squealed as the task force members braked to a stop. Agents and officers ran screaming to the front of the house. "AAAAAAIIIIIIIIEEEEEEE!" they yelled. It was really quite exciting. It seemed as if the fastest guys got the front door, the next fastest got the sides of the house, and the slowest got the back of the house. It was truly chaos. No one remembered to bring a ram, so one of the officers went running back to the cars, grabbed a ram, and ran back up to the front door. "AAAAAIIIIIIIEEEEEEE!" he screamed again as he approached the front door holding the ram in a menacing fashion.

Is that good planning? Is that planning at all? Would you feel comfortable going on an arrest with those guys? My bet is you have. You haven't gone on an arrest with the same guys obviously, but you probably have with folks just like them. What's worse is you may still be going on arrests like this, even though your gut feeling tells you it's unsafe. Well stop it! Stop doing stupid things that will get you killed! We allow this behavior to become our norm. We begin to think we don't need to plan. We begin to think we don't need to be that careful. And we don't. At least not until things go badly; then we wish we would have taken the time to plan to prevent the death of a friend and of a fellow officer.

I have a good friend who is an FBI agent, firearms instructor, and former SWAT operator. He also provides me with a lot of great stories of what not to do. He told me about an arrest he made with a fugitive task force he was assigned to. The fugitive was considered armed and dangerous. The task force found out where the fugitive was staying and hurried to the residence to make the arrest. They all huddled together at the front door, knocked and announced, and waited for a response. They continued to wait even after hearing movement inside. They broke in the door and ran like banshees through the house, passing open doorways and passing obvious danger areas. They finally found the subject and made the arrest without incident. At first glance, you could say it was a successful mission and they are all superstars. That's what they would tell each other over a beer later as they slapped each other on the back. But was it really done well? My friend said they later learned the subject had a loaded M-16 and had been watching all of the task force members as they gathered by the front door. The fugitive could have easily killed all of them, but chose not to. They also learned that a friend of the fugitive was in a bedroom and the team had blown by the open bedroom door where the fugitive's friend was located. The fugitive's friend, too, could have killed several of the task force members by casually shooting them in the back as they ran down the hall. I later asked my friend if this came up during the debriefing. He said he tried, but the tactical leader was an old-timer and wasn't receptive to any criticism. I only hope the team leader's fragile ego and unwillingness to explore better, safer options doesn't get someone killed.

Carelessness

I don't know how many times I've heard, "But I've always done it this way!" or "I've been doing it like this for over fifteen years!" To which I think, "Yeah, and you still royally suck." I wouldn't say that out loud because it's not very nice, but I can think it. We have become the victims of our own success. Because you may have made hundreds of arrests, conducted countless searches, and cleared houses on multiple occasions without incident, you begin to think that you are you pretty good at this law enforcement stuff. And you may be right. But are you good, or just lucky? I would say that any officer who has worked any significant amount of time on the job and has never been injured is just plain lucky. Why? Because we've all made mistakes. We've all been careless and have taken tactical shortcuts. We've just been lucky in those times of being careless that there was not a committed bad guy who wanted to hurt us.

In a disastrous incident that occurred in Santa Clarita, California, in December 2001, a county sheriff's deputy was killed. A federal law enforcement agency was serving a warrant and had requested the sheriff's department's assistance. It became tragic when the subject decided to shoot it out with the officers. I was deeply saddened by this senseless tragedy, but I was outraged by what I read in the local newspaper after the shooting. The December 16, 2001, *Los Angeles Times* newspaper quoted two executives from the federal agency. An assistant special in charge (ASAC) stated: "Obviously, we had no expectations of this reaction. Had we had any indication there was going to be this type of reaction or emotional instability, this operation would have (had) an entirely different flavor."

Is the ASAC an embarrassment to law enforcement? Perhaps he should have just said, "I'm an idiot, so don't ask me any questions." It would have been a lot better response than this one. It would have been a whole lot smarter if he *had* expected "this type of reaction" and planned accordingly. How rude of this murderer not to call the law enforcement agency ahead of time and advise the officers of his "emotional instability" and let them know he would violently resist arrest. We can't see into the future and we don't know who will be compliant and who will not. Doesn't it make sense then to always plan and prepare for the worst? If the subject does go quietly, then you've lost nothing but a little time. I don't even think it's a waste of time because you've now effectively prepared for the next incident where something does go wrong. You are practicing to do it the safe, correct way each and every time. If this happens to be the time you do get deadly resistance, it's not a surprise and you're prepared. You planned for this contingency and you're ready to deal with it effectively without loss of life. It's called being a professional.

To make it worse, a regional director from the same agency was then quoted in the same *Los Angeles Times* article as saying, "You are there with a lawful warrant under the color of law.... You don't think some moron is going to start shooting at you. You try to be prepared, but you think people will abide by the law."

If everyone abided by the law, there would be no need for law enforcement officers. As warriors, we expect people will *not* abide by the law. We expect people to resist arrest. We do not suffer from the delusion that we are invincible and bad guys will throw their hands in the air and fall to their knees at the sight of us. On every arrest, search, or contact with an unknown individual, I always think, "This person wants to kill me, and if I give him half a chance, he will." You can be professional, you can be courteous, but just make sure you're alert and prepared to react.

After teaching movement and footwork drills to agents or officers, I'll run a drill in which one plays the bad person and the other the officer. The officer stands in an interview stance at an appropriate distance from the bad person to conduct a field interview (FI). The bad person will rush forward at any given moment and attempt to stab the officer in the stomach with a rubber knife, take the officer's training weapon, or tackle the officer to the ground. Each and every time, the officer easily sidesteps the attack and draws a "red gun" (a rubber or plastic training gun). I always ask why this is so simple to do successfully. Why is it none of the bad people come close to successfully disarming the officers? The answer is always, "Because we knew the attack was going to come." My response is, "But we should always be expecting an attack when dealing with a subject!" In every credible law enforcement academy, we are taught to be prepared, to always expect to be attacked, to have our guard up. So why do so many of us (possibly all of us at times) fail to do this? The only possible answer is complacency.

Overconfidence

Closely related to carelessness is overconfidence. Each time we arrest someone or conduct a field interview without any problems, we think we've done it correctly. We get in the habit of preparing for these events with the assumption of success and with the assumption of compliance. This is fine until you run into the subject who doesn't play by these rules. Frank Harrill, a fellow FBI agent, once said to me, "You know, for 99% of our arrests, we could go in stark naked with a feather duster stuck up our butt and still be okay." I like this analogy because it is such an ugly visual. I've since taken to calling this the feather duster syndrome. The feather duster syndrome is what leads to complacency and overconfidence. If we realized how ridiculously easy it is to make an arrest when the subject complies, and how incredibly dangerous it can be when the subject doesn't, perhaps we'd be more cautious in these situations. So the next time fellow officers tell you how great they are at tactics, apply the feather duster rule: Could they have had the same results with a feather duster? (I'll leave it up to you if you also want to visualize them with a feather duster stuck in one of their orifices.)

Officers need mental preparation and physical fitness to survive a critical incident. We will address mental preparation first, then the physical preparation.

Mental Preparation

The first topic in mental preparation is fear. We must prepare for crisis situations. We must be prepared to deal with fear. We must inoculate ourselves against fear and its potentially disastrous effects. Is it unusual to feel fear in a critical incident? Absolutely not. Anyone who tells you he or she felt no fear in a life-threatening battle is either lying or a sociopath. Early in his career as the youngest heavyweight boxing champion of the world, Mike Tyson was asked if he was ever afraid when he stepped into the ring. Mr. Tyson answered he was always terrified in every fight and that's why he fought so ferociously. Wild animals are afraid. That fear causes them to be more alert, their nerves on edge, and their adrenalin pumping. All of this is to allow them to react with more quickness and power. We all feel fear, and it's a wonderful, necessary survival tool.

What are the physiological effects of fear? First, your heart rate increases, blood pressure increases, and you have increased blood flow to the muscles and organs. This is the body preparing to fight or flee. Also, the body releases large quantities of glucose (sugar) into your system, which provides you with an abundance of quick energy. Isn't that also a good thing to have in battle? The depletion of glucose after the battle is what leads to the incredible fatigue after a fight. Another physiological reaction is that blood-clotting enzymes are activated and the capillaries begin to close down. This is a normal, healthy, beneficial response to stress. All of this represents our bodies preparing to fight vigorously, preparing to be wounded, preparing for battle, preparing to be warriors. What a beautiful and incredible response to a life-threatening event.

A key to our survival is our response to the fear, and this can be controlled by adequate training. If we are faced with a crisis situation that we've never prepared for, never trained for, and never visualized, the response may be indecision and panic. And this will lead to some very ugly results. As law enforcement officers, we know (or at least we should know) most of the threats that face us. Our training should be reality based, to include scenarios, force-on-force exercises, and role playing. We should also frequently employ visualization techniques in which we vividly imagine all conceivable situations we face and then visualize responding calmly, effectively, and successfully. We should think out the solution to critical incidents prior to their occurrence so we can immediately respond. If you are prepared, you won't be caught flat-footed. You may experience the rush of adrenalin, but you will then take appropriate action and respond to the threat.

How do we mentally prepare to survive? What is a recurring trait in officers killed in the line of duty? It's the reluctance to use deadly force, even when the need to use deadly force is clearly evident. In his excellent audiotape *The Bulletproof Mind*, Lt. Colonel Dave Grossman tells of an interview question for police officer candidates.[9] The interview question is: If you are separated from your partner by a high fence with barb wire on the top that you can't climb over, dig under, or go around, and your partner, is on the other side of the fence, is on the ground, getting repeatedly kicked in the head by a bad guy, what do you do? The answer seems pretty simple, right? You perhaps give the bad guy a quick command to freeze and, if he fails to do so immediately, you shoot him. What's amazing is that 20% of the candidates would refuse to shoot no matter what. Now remember, this isn't a random sample of the population. This is a group of people who have decided they want to be law enforcement officers. I'd also be willing to bet that, if the situation were real, some of the 80% who said they would shoot wouldn't.

A similar example was when I was going through the FBI Academy in 1987. In the first week of the academy, an instructor showed us a re-creation of the Miami shootout that occurred in April 1986 in which two FBI special agents were killed and five others were wounded. The instructor regaled us with additional gruesome stories of agents who had been killed or seriously wounded in the line of duty. He then went on to explain how we would eventually be carrying firearms and the possibility of being in a firefight was a very real threat. As he continued to go on about the dangers of the job, I was thinking, "Duh, like we hadn't thought about all of this long before we ever made the commitment to join the FBI?" But you know what? I was wrong. Some in the class had never seriously considered the possibility of having to use deadly force or having it used against them. The next day a chair was vacant. One new agent trainee had thought about it and decided this wasn't for him. I applaud him for coming to his senses, but I also wondered why he hadn't thought about these issues sometime in the year and a half it took to get processed for hire. I later learned that almost every class lost at least one person after this deadly force presentation.

If someone has any doubts whether they are capable of using deadly force (or more bluntly, killing another human being), then they have no business being a law enforcement officer. That reluctance makes the job much too dangerous, and worse, too dangerous for any partners they may have. There are people in your department who have not made this decision. This means if they are in a violent confrontation in which it becomes necessary to use deadly force, they will hesitate and probably die. What's worse, there are people in your department who have decided they can *not* ever use deadly force, yet they continue to work alongside of you every day, hoping the time will never come when they are placed in the situation in which their decision will cost them life—possibly your life and the lives of innocent bystanders.

Some of you may have religious concerns about the use of deadly force. Some refer to the Tenth Commandment of "Thou shall not kill." Biblical scholars tell us that this is not an accurate translation. The actual commandment was "Thou shall not murder." David was one of God's favorites, and David was responsible for the deaths of thousands of men. Only when David arranged for a man to be killed in battle to get his wife, Bathsheba, did David fall out of God's graces. Bob Vernon, former assistant chief of LAPD, gave me a book that states, "The proper use of force is not a necessary evil. It's a necessary good!"[10] Romans 13:4 reads, "But if you do what is wrong, you should be afraid. The government has the right to carry out the death sentence. It is God's servant, an avenger to execute God's anger on anyone who does what is wrong." As a law enforcement officer, you are the avenger and the sword of God. You have the responsibility and the right to use deadly force to protect society. In the Book of Romans, God lays the foundation for the good and necessary role of police officers in society. Romans 13:1–4 states that a peace officer's authority comes from God, and Romans 13:4 says law enforcement officers have a God-given duty to use lawful and necessary force. Any hesitancy you have to use lawful deadly force should not be based on religious misinterpretations.

A key component of mental preparation is understanding your ability to use deadly force and visualizing situations in which you would use deadly force. Generally speaking, there are three deadly force policies you should be concerned with. They are the lawful use of deadly force as defined by the U.S. Constitution, your department's deadly force policy, and your deadly force policy. In *Tennessee v. Garner*, the court has defined the legal use of deadly force by a peace officer fairly broadly.[11] In layman's terms, you can use deadly force any time you believe you or another individual faces the threat of death or serious bodily injury. The courts have permitted the use of deadly force to shoot someone who is running from you, if their escape would logically result in death or serious bodily injury to someone at a later time.

Your department's deadly force policy may be more restrictive than the court's. If your personal deadly force policy is broader than your department's and the Supreme Court's, get out of law enforcement now before you break the law and end up in prison. For some people, their personal deadly force policy is even more restrictive than their department's. This is dangerous too. The ideal is to have a personal deadly force policy exactly synchronized to that of your department and the Supreme Court. Your personal deadly force policy is the one you have established for yourself as to when you would be willing to kill another person. For some people, they have no compunction in killing another person. We call them sociopaths. If this describes you, I pray you are not wearing a badge, but that you're rotting away in prison. But for the rest of us decent folks, there is a great hesitancy to kill a member of our own species. We must come to grips with that long before we must face a real life-or-death situation.

Most officers are unwilling to shoot even when the justification to do so is clearly evident. I can think of one instance when two fellow FBI SWAT operators were involved in a surveillance of a bank robbery suspect. The suspect "made" the surveillance and the two agents decided to arrest him in a parking lot. Both agents ended up getting in a fight with the subject and were having difficulty subduing him. At one point, the subject said he had a gun and made a movement to his waistline as if he were drawing a gun. Could you shoot him at this point? By most department's policies, absolutely. By FBI policy, absolutely. But because both of these agents were good, decent people, they hesitated and wanted to be certain he was armed before firing. We've all been trained in our academies that action beats reaction, so if the subject did have a gun, both agents could have been killed. The subject was shot and killed moments later when he made it to his car and attempted to run over one of the agents.

I had a watershed moment shortly after the Los Angeles riots (described by some local newspapers as a "civil disturbance"). During the riots, our SWAT team was working long days. We would typically work a twelve-hour shift, drive home, get a few hours sleep, and get up and start the process all over again. Our duty was to ride with the Long Beach Fire Department on their calls and to prevent them from being shot at, as happened in the first days of the riots. I developed an incredible respect for all of the firefighters. I never could understand how anyone could even think of shooting at them.

After the riots ended, the FBI and local law enforcement agencies joined forces to identify and indict gang members who were instrumental in much of the violence that occurred during those dark days in Los Angeles. During Operation Sunrise, our SWAT team served multiple warrants in gang-infested neighborhoods. Due to the vast number of warrants that were to be served, our SWAT team was broken down into smaller units and perimeter responsibilities were handled by regular FBI street agents. At one particular location, we were able to call out from the residence the subject's father and grandmother. Strangely enough, the father was a retired police officer. The father and grandmother were not completely cooperative, and they certainly weren't very friendly to us, but they did follow our commands and came out of the house, where they were detained by agents on the perimeter team. The son, a hard-core gang banger about twenty years old, was back in his bedroom and did not initially respond to our commands. Another operator and I made entry into the house and into the first room, a living room. At this point, the gang banger called out from his bedroom that he was coming out. My partner and I moved to the front doorway of the house where we thought we had sufficient cover and still had a view of his bedroom door. We ordered the subject to come out with his hands up. He appeared in his doorway wearing baggy pants and no shirt. We ordered him to turn around, face away from us, put his hands straight up in the air, and walk back toward our voices. Instead of complying, the gang banger was belligerent and mouthy. He raised his hands only halfway, keeping his elbows bent at a 90° angle, and refused to face away from us. Immediately our warning alarms were going off, because this kid just wasn't grasping the seriousness of the situation. As he continued to walk toward us he suddenly stopped, and then quickly brought both hands to the waistband of his pants.

At this point it's important to explain a technique that was being practiced by several gang members at that time. They would wear baggy pants and drop a gun into the crotch area. To draw the weapon, they would slap the gun up from the crotch area, grab the gun with the other hand, and then bring the gun up into a firing position. When I saw the gang banger quickly and smoothly drop his hands to his pants, I was certain he was going for a gun. Based upon my experience, training, and knowledge of this technique, would I have been within policy to use deadly force? Definitely. But should I have? Let's explore that question further.

At the time this happened, my partner and I were in relatively good position of cover. We were also wearing ballistic helmets and vests. The vests contained ceramic plates that would stop almost all rifle rounds, and the entire vest was rated to stop all handgun rounds. We were armed with H&K 10 mm MP-5s, fully automatic submachine guns, and our weapons' selector switches were set to fully automatic. At the time the gangster dropped his hands to his waistband, my partner and I both shouted orders at the subject. I had dropped my finger onto the trigger and taken up all of the slack. I was beginning to press through the hard portion of the trigger squeeze and must have been only millimeters away from firing a quick burst. After talking to my partner, he had done the same, but neither of us had fired a shot. The gang member had come within a hair's width of being riddled with 10 mm Hydra-Shok bullets.

It turned out he didn't have a weapon. He immediately put his hands back in the air and began following our commands, perhaps finally understanding how dangerous the situation was for all of us—particularly him. I asked him what he was doing. His reply was, "My pants were falling down." It would have been funny if it weren't for how close we came to killing him. Many people, upon hearing this story, tell me it was a good thing my partner and I didn't shoot. In one sense, they're right. I would not have relished going through the administrative inquiries, civil court proceedings, and all of the related hell of a shooting incident, especially one in which the subject was unarmed. However, after a few days of reflection, I think my partner and I made a tactical error. We had felt relatively safe since we were behind good cover, had our weapons trained on the subject, and were fully prepared to shoot. In hindsight, I recall seeing his father and grandmother out in the front yard, secured, and in the subject's line of fire if he had a weapon and chose to fight it out. If my partner and I had allowed the subject to fire off a round and that round struck the father or grandmother, wouldn't we, to some extent, be responsible? Also, what if a stray round had struck an agent who was on the perimeter or watching the father and grandmother? If I were in the same situation today, I would be more willing to use deadly force, realizing we may have jeopardized the safety of our fellow agents and innocent people by waiting that split second longer to see a gun. As we all know (or should know), if you wait to see the gun, then it's already too late to keep that gun from firing.

I had the pleasure of listening to LAPD Sergeant Andy Markel speak at a recent Police Officers Association of Los Angeles County (POALAC) meeting. Andy developed what I believe to one of the clearest explanations of a use of force timeline. In summary, Andy defined the time that exists between when an officer is legally justified in using deadly force and when the officer actually uses deadly force as opportunity time. This is the opportunity you have given the bad guy to kill you or someone else. So, once you have legal justification to shoot, every second that ticks away as you are trying to make up your mind whether to use deadly force, the bad guy is gaining tactical advantage and possibly taking advantage of the time you have so generously provided to murder you and others.

Andy followed this up with a clear example of what may happen if you delay making that deadly force decision. Assume you are in a store as a regular customer, off-duty, and armed (of course). Suddenly a robber rushes through the front door, points a gun at the terrified clerk, and demands money from the cash register. You look around the store, determine the robber is acting alone, and decide the best and safest course of action at this point is to be a good witness. Suddenly the clerk falls to the floor and you see the robber jumping and reaching over the counter in an apparent attempt to shoot the clerk. You decide not to use deadly force at this time. The robber fires a fatal shot into the head of the clerk and then looks in your direction. You fire your service weapon killing the robber. What is the aftermath? Your peers will slap you on the back and tell you what a great job you did. Your supervisor will be thrilled it's such a "clean" shoot and will probably write you up for an award for your bravery. The district attorney's office will congratulate you and will be relieved it's obviously a righteous shoot, since someone was murdered in your presence. Everyone will congratulate you and call you a hero. But every morning, for the rest of your life, you'll wake up, look in the mirror, and see the face of the clerk you could have saved. You'll know the truth.

In Lt. Col. Dave Grossman's book *On Killing,* he describes the reluctance of man to kill his fellow man, even in combat.[12] The same is true for law enforcement officers. The way we prepare ourselves to use deadly force is by a number of methods. The first is visualization. We must practice if-then thinking. What will I do if, as I'm driving home tonight, someone attempts to carjack me? What will I do if I wake up in the middle of the night to the sound of a window being broken? The more if-then thinking you practice and the more realistic you make it, the better you'll perform when that critical situation actually occurs.

Another method used by most modern departments is the use of a Firearms Training Simulator (FATS) or a similar device. FATS is a high-tech video in which officers are placed in shoot–no shoot situations. They are required to make split-second decisions and then, when warranted, deliver effective rounds against an adversary. This is a highly effective tool in desensitizing officers to using deadly force. Still another method that I incorporated when I was the principal firearms instructor for the Los Angeles FBI was the addition of life-like paper targets for firearms qualifications. Using targets that are photographs of real people enhances the training and again prepares the agents to use deadly force. I would also design combat courses based on actual police shootings in an attempt to provide as much realism as possible.

Do a self-assessment right now. Ask yourself, "Have I ever seriously considered the need to use deadly force? Am I prepared to use deadly force? Have I imagined multiple situations in which I'm required to use deadly force and I do so with success?" If the answers to these questions aren't an overwhelming yes, then you need to begin working on your warrior mindset. You need to prepare yourself *now* to use deadly force, because tomorrow may be too late. Tomorrow you may hesitate when you are justified and tactically required to use deadly force, and that hesitation may get you, your partner, and others killed.

I first heard the analogy of police officers as sheepdogs when I read Lt. Col. Grossman's outstanding book *On Combat.*[13] Lt. Col. Grossman wrote that he first heard the analogy in a letter from a Vietnam veteran. I'll summarize the concept below.

You can divide the population into three general groups. First there are the sheep—peaceful, wonderful creatures who would never intentionally hurt anyone. They eat, sleep, and play at peace with the universe. Everything would be wonderful except for one thing. There are wolves, and the wolves kill sheep. Wolves are predators. They seek out the weak and eat them. The sheep are completely defenseless against the wolves. Even if they had the tools available to them, such as sharp teeth and claws, the sheep would not use them because it's against their nature. The sheep just don't have the disposition for fighting and abhor all violence, even to save themselves. The sheep live in constant denial. They think, "My life is good. My pasture is not like other pastures. My pasture is safe. No wolves would ever come here." When the wolves do come and one of the sheep is eaten, they are just grateful it didn't happen to them. They may even blame the eaten sheep, believing the victim sheep should have been more careful, or thinking perhaps the victim sheep did something to provoke the wolves.

Fortunately, there are also sheepdogs. The sheepdogs are valiant creatures who protect the sheep. They would never intentionally hurt a sheep, but they have no reluctance to do great harm to the wolves if necessary. The sheepdogs are vigilantly at watch protecting those who are unable or unwilling to protect themselves.

Sometimes the sheep are happy to see the sheepdogs running around, recognizing that when the sheepdog is there, it's less likely the sheep will get eaten. Other times, however, the sheep are distrustful of the sheepdog. They recognize that the sheepdog, in many ways, is much like the wolves. The sheepdog, unlike the sheep, is at times capable of carrying out violent acts. Even when the sheep recognize that this violence is done purely to protect the sheep, it still makes them nervous because it is so un-sheep-like. The sheep also get angry when the wolves are able to evade the sheepdogs and eat a sheep. "How could the sheepdog fail us when that is what he exists for?" wail the sheep. And the wolves, of course, will always despise the sheepdogs.

The sheepdogs do not live in denial. They know the wolves are out there and it's their duty to protect the sheep. They also know, as Clint Smith, owner of Thunder Ranch, once said, "If you don't want to get eaten, don't look like food." The sheepdogs, like the wolves, are capable of violence. There is a major difference in their capacity for violence, however. The wolves use violence for their own gain or are violent just for the sake of doing harm. The sheepdogs are only capable of violence to protect themselves or the sheep. If you are a sheepdog, you are blessed. You have been blessed with an innate aggression and a deep love for others. Take pride in this gift and use it responsibly.

When I was going to graduate school, I was required to take a few counseling courses for my MA in organizational-industrial psychology. I readily determined that I didn't really fit in with this group in terms of my beliefs. In a child psychology class, it seemed as if everyone in the class, except me, was strongly opposed to any type of corporal punishment regardless of the behavior. The overriding theme was that spanking is bad because it teaches children to be violent. My response was if I had a child, I'd want him to be capable of tremendous violence. Although I wouldn't have used the same words back then, what I was saying was I would want my child to be a warrior. I would want my child to have the ability to protect himself and those he cared about. I would want my child to be a sheepdog and not a sheep. Otherwise, I reasoned, my child would be a victim. Now that I am a father, I feel even more strongly that I am right (and no, I don't beat my child—but he has earned a swift swat on the rear on rare occasions). I never want my child to be a victim, a sheep. I never want my child to have to rely on someone else for his own protection or for the protection of those he loves.

I agree with my former classmates in principle. It would be a wonderful world if everyone were a pacifist, if everyone were a sheep. However, as long as one wolf exists, the world is not safe for us to be sheep. My wife and I have taught our child that it is not acceptable to hurt others. It is not acceptable to be a wolf. I want my child to be a polite, loving, well-mannered gentleman, but capable of incredible violence when justified. My son loves superheroes. He also loves people in the military, law enforcement, and firefighters (and aren't they all superheroes?). The reason for his love and respect is he realizes, even at four years old, that these people protect and serve—that they are sheepdogs. He wants to be a superhero when he grows up, and I couldn't be more proud.

We must have warriors who are willing to go forth, spilling their own blood, in the protection of society. Otherwise, the wolves will win and the sheep will die. When you study and practice DT, you are learning violence. You are learning to be better sheepdogs, to be better warriors. You are learning controlled, disciplined violence that has been driven by the actions of the bad guy. Remember, it's the bad guy who determines the amount of force used in making the arrest. If he complies with your commands, then there is no need for coercive contact. If he fails to comply, you are then required to use the reasonable force necessary to gain control.

Physical Fitness

Every year you get a year older, but the bad guys are twenty years old forever. You may be getting a little slower, a little weaker, a little fatter, but the bad guys never do. You can't help getting older, but you can do something about your fitness level. Even though the bad guys may always be younger than you, you can still defeat them through superior tactics, experience, and conditioning. You know you are going to be in some confrontations, right? And you know that if you lose even one fight, you're at the mercy of the bad guy. Personally, I never want to have some bad guy standing over me with my life in his hands. Decide right now to be a warrior and start acting like one. Warriors prepare for battle. Your battle is waiting for you every day on every street corner and in every alley. Prepare for that battle now by committing to fitness. Even if the battle never comes, you will still enjoy the victory of a better quality of life.

When I was in high school, a friend's father was involved in a terrible car accident. This man was in his forties at the time of the accident and was sitting in the front passenger seat (also known as the "suicide seat") when the car he was riding in collided with a big rig. He should have been killed. This was in the mid-seventies during a time period when almost no one seriously worked out after high school or college. This man, however, was the exception. He religiously ran almost every day and regularly lifted weights. The treating physician said his aerobic conditioning and the muscle mass he developed by weight training had saved his life.

Think about the athletes you see playing professional football on Sunday. You repeatedly see a running back colliding at full speed with a 300-pound monster. And then what happens? He gets up and does it again and again and again. These are hits that would seriously injure or even kill the average person, but because of incredible conditioning, the running back is capable of absorbing the blows with no damage to the body. Your conditioning plays a vital role to how well you will survive being injured. Your conditioning will determine how effectively you can defend yourself.

We all want to be respected. If you are overweight and out of shape, you do not have the respect of other officers. Even worse, you do not have the respect of the bad guy who is instantly sizing you up. Part of being a law enforcement officer, part of being a warrior, is looking like a warrior. Genetically, you may never be Arnold Schwarzenegger. I certainly never will be. You can, however (as the U.S. Army likes to say), be all that you can be. As I get older, I realize I can't work out to the same level I once did. I can't run on hard pavement for 40+ miles a week. My knees just won't stand for it. I also can't lift as heavy as I once did because my joints and ligaments will give out. But I can work out and maintain a high level of fitness. I just have to be smarter about it. Instead of running on the streets, I now run on a rubberized track that provides adequate cushioning. I also substitute time on a treadmill and elliptical machine. I may have to lift lighter weights, but I still lift. What I've discovered is, fortunately, as I've gotten older, I've also gotten smarter. I can punch a bag longer and harder than I used to simply because my body mechanics are better and I learned to throw punches from a more relaxed posture. George Foreman was an awesome fighter as a young man. When he made a comeback in his forties, he was a joy to watch, winning the heavyweight championship at forty-five with a knockout victory over Michael Moorer. No longer the physical specimen he once was, he instead fought with the relaxed confidence of a wise fighter. He said during an interview he wished he knew as a young man what he now knew, and that was how to fight without tension.

Warrior Checklist

Are you preparing to be a warrior? Are you training for the day when you will be in a critical incident? Here are some questions to ask yourself right now:

- Am I staying physically fit?
- Am I training to improve/maintain my cardiovascular fitness level?
- Am I training to improve/maintain my muscular strength and endurance?
- Am I participating in any type of DT training in addition to that offered by my department?
- Am I honing my firearms skills?
- Am I improving my tactics by constantly seeking out new training and ideas?
- Am I visualizing myself in a variety of critical incidents and planning *now* how to succeed in these situations?
- Have I determined my personal deadly force policy and incorporated it into my visualizations?
- Do I always assume the subject will attack and act accordingly as opposed to assuming compliance?
- On every search and arrest, am I constantly prepared for a worst-case scenario?
- If I'm injured, have I developed the mindset that I will not, cannot, must not quit, and I will fight, fight, fight until the threat is eliminated?

How did you answer these questions? You know how a warrior would answer them.

While I was going through the FBI Academy in 1987, my favorite instructor was Bob Rogers. "Coach" Rogers was a former captain in the U.S. Marine Corps and a decorated Vietnam War veteran. He was close to fifty years old at the time, but he was incredibly fit for a man of any age. On the first day of physical training (PT), all of the members of my new agents class were required to take a physical fitness exam consisting of pull-ups, sit-ups, push-ups, a shuttle run, and a 2-mile run. As we finished the first four events, we were led outdoors to the track and into a hot, humid July day in Virginia. It was classified as a "black flag" day, or a day in which strenuous outdoor activity was prohibited due to the heat index. Our instructors ignored the black flag classification as our class was on a schedule and the schedule for the day was to complete the fitness test. As everyone was finishing the timed 2-mile event, I saw one of my classmates struggling to stand after he had just crossed the finish line. Immediately, two other classmates rushed to his side, each took one of his arms, and assisted him in walking toward a water fountain. My first thought was it was a good show of camaraderie and teamwork. Coach Rogers thought differently. I saw the anger in his face and heard his booming voice as he yelled, "What are you doing? Leave him alone, let him go! **Let … the … weak … die!"** It certainly made an impression on us. Coach Rogers believed that arriving at the academy out of shape showed great disrespect for the FBI. The clear message was this was not a job for the weak. This was not a job for sheep. This was a calling for warriors.

Coach Rogers later told us a story about how one of his close friends died in the line of duty while wearing the FBI badge. He told us of how his friend was an outstanding and respected agent, and how he died honorably in the service of his country. He then looked each of us in the eye and said, "How dare you think you are worthy of wearing the same badge! How dare you show up in my gym fat, slow, and weak."

Coach Rogers would regale us with stories of Vietnam and his Bureau career, and gleefully tell us which one of us he would kill first if he were a sniper (whoever was last in the daily run). He motivated us with praise and he motivated us with criticism ("You people disgust me! You're not human beings! I don't even know if you're animal life, at best you may be plant life!"), but you never doubted that he cared deeply about each and every one of us. You never doubted he wanted every one of us to survive. And you never doubted he loved the FBI and his country.

Even while fighting cancer, Coach Rogers would provide motivational speeches. In the middle of a presentation, he would drop down to the floor while wearing a suit and start cranking out one-handed push-ups. I heard he died of cancer, but I don't believe it. Warriors like Coach Rogers never die. I'm sure your academy had a Bob Rogers. I hope so. I hope you had an instructor who inspired you to be better than you are now, who motivated you to be the best law enforcement officer you could be. Don't let that person down. Live up to his or her expectations. Take the job seriously. Recognize the risks. Prepare yourself for the battle you will ultimately face.

Drills for Warriors

1. Exercise aerobically at least three times a week.
2. Do strength training at least twice a week.
3. Practice the DT drills listed elsewhere in this book.
4. Seek out tactical training from credible sources.
5. Get to the firearms range whenever possible.
6. Practice visualization and always see yourself winning.
7. Determine your personal deadly force policy right now!
8. Most importantly, spend time with your family and don't forget they are the most important people to protect and serve.

Endnotes

1. Humphrey, R. L., Dr. Humphrey's life values homepage, www.LifeValues.com, www.winjutsu.com/warrior-creed.html (accessed October 2, 2009).
2. Wikipedia, 300 Spartans, Plutarch, "Sayings of Spartans," 208B-236E. En.wikipedia.org/wiki/Battle_of_Thermopylae (accessed October 5, 2009).
3. U.S. Department of Justice, Federal Bureau of Investigation, *Law Enforcement Officers Killed and Assaulted, 2002*, pp. 5, 73.
4. Pinizzotto, A. J., and Davis, E. F., "Offenders' Perceptual Shorthand, What Messages Are Law Enforcement Officers Sending to Offenders?" *FBI Law Enforcement Bulletin*, June 1999, pp. 1–4.
5. Pinizzotto, A. J., Davis, E. F., and Miller III, C. E., "In the Line of Fire: Violence against Law Enforcement, A Study of Selected Assaults on Law Enforcement Officers," FBI Publication 0163, October 1997, pp. 23–31.
6. Tzu, S., *The Art of War,* edited by James Clavell, New York, Delacorte Press, 2003, p. 2.
7. Ibid., p. 39.
8. *Ultimate Survivors*, Calibre Press, 1992.
9. Grossman, D., *The Bulletproof Mind: Prevailing in Violent Encounters … and After*, Calibre Press, 1999.
10. Lee, S., *God's Word for Peace Officers*, World Publishing, Grand Rapids, MI, 1995, p. XIII.
11. *Tennessee v. Garner*, 471 U.S. 1 (1985).
12. Grossman, D., *On Killing, The Psychological Cost of Learning to Kill in War and Society*, Little, Brown and Company, Boston, 1996.
13. Grossman, D., with Christensen, L. W., *On Combat, The Psychology and Physiology of Deadly Conflict in War and Peace*, PPCT Research Publications, 2004, pp. 176–82.

4 Staying Safe

In discussions with defensive tactics (DT) instructors from various agencies, I was told an average of four students per academy class are injured during DT training and the injuries are serious enough to warrant surgery. This is unacceptable and is an indicator program revisions are needed. The training activities leading to these injuries need to be identified and evaluated. Prior to any DT session, the instructor should discuss the absolute need for strict adherence to all safety rules. Not only is it just being nice to ensure you are not injuring your training partner, but it is also common sense. As a DT instructor with the FBI, I was constantly imploring agents to start slowly at first and increase speed gradually. The older agents had no problem with this concept. In fact, some of the older agents started so slowly it almost looked as if they weren't participating at all. And I must say, even if some of the old dogs were horrible at DT, they never had any injuries. The young bucks, however, were another story. Nothing makes a DT instructor's heart beat more proudly or bring a tear to the eye than to see folks paying attention, completing the exercises as described, having fun, and actually working hard to get better. The challenge was always to thoroughly brief safety rules prior to the start of each session, continuously remind students of the safety rules during the training, and closely monitor all students to ensure those rules were being followed. As I told the agents, "We only give you one partner. If you break that one, you don't get another one."

As a new FBI instructor in 1991 and a long-time martial arts instructor, I was gung ho about several drills that served as "gut checks." These drills would pit one student against another or sometimes one student against two or more opponents. Most of the drills were more about mental and physical toughness rather than the development of defensive skills. But they were fun, a good workout, and seemed to be motivational for the students.

One of the drills developed by the FBI Academy was called the fugitive crawl. The fugitive crawl would have a student (the fugitive) start at one end of the mat on hands and knees. Lying on the other side of the mat approximately 25 feet away was a red gun (a nonoperating, rubber gun). The student's objective was to crawl on hands and knees and grab the rubber gun. Another student (in the role of an FBI agent) would be positioned to the side and slightly behind the fugitive. The agent's objective was to keep the fugitive from reaching the gun. The rules of the game were that neither of the students was allowed to rise to their feet. More than anything, it was a test of the individual's fighting spirit, the will to win. I and another instructor, Dennis, were running the drills as part of an advanced DT class for agents. The drills were humming along and we were rotating all the agents into the different positions so they had the opportunity to work against people of different sizes and strengths. I selected an agent named Joe to take the FBI agent's role for the exercise and an agent named Chris to take the role of the fugitive. Joe, a former attorney and the son of a retired Boston police officer, was average height and weight. Chris, a former linebacker for the New England Patriots, was considerably bigger, heavier, and much stronger than average—not to mention he was previously a professional athlete who was still in incredible shape. Chris started on his hands and knees, with Joe kneeling beside him. On the whistle, Chris took off on his knees like lightning and Joe was immediately on top of him. For being the much smaller guy, Joe was scrappy and was putting forth a tremendous effort. That is, at least, until he blew out his knee trying to hold Chris down. The class came to a screeching halt as Joe writhed in agony. Dennis, a much senior instructor and a mentor to me in many ways, took me aside and explained that this is why it's so necessary to take every reasonable precaution to avoid injuries during DT training. In Dennis' words, when someone gets hurt in class, everything the students learned up to that point gets flushed, and all of them are then afraid to continue to participate. My first thought was, "It sure would have been nice if you had imparted this sage wisdom *before* someone got hurt." But it made a lasting impression on me, and everything Dennis said about that instance was absolutely true. Our only concern was to get Joe to the hospital as soon as possible and everyone lost any desire to continue training for the day. Joe, a truly classy guy, handled it as if it wasn't a big deal and had no ill will toward anyone. Chris, a gentle giant, felt bad because he had unintentionally hurt Joe. I was miserable because I was in charge of the exercise and knew I was to blame.

The learning point, and how it relates to safety, is this: for every exercise or drill you do in DT training, and I do mean absolutely each and every one, do a cost-benefit analysis. Determine the benefit of the exercise in terms of skill building or other desirable outcome (the benefit). Weigh that against the potential risk of injury (the cost). I'm certainly not saying to avoid all training that has potential for injury. DT training, by its nature, is somewhat hazardous. And some of the best training exercises carry some risk. Nothing approximates a real situation better than actually fighting in a controlled environment. But if an exercise carries significant risk, be darn sure it is critical for the development of necessary survival skills. And even then, give it a hard look to see if there is a safer way of accomplishing the same thing.

I believe the more realistic the training, the more valuable. One of the best training tools is having an instructor gear up in a protective suit and attack students in a variety of realistic scenarios. Is there potential for injury?

Yes. Would you expect to see an accurate representation of how the student would perform in a real crisis? Definitely. Would you be able to teach core survival skills based upon the exercise? You bet.

A task force targeting child predators and consisting of a squad of FBI agents and police officers underwent training by a private company. One of the scenarios involved two of the task force members having to arrest a role player in a protective suit. So far, so good, right? The scenario was realistic, the instructor was wearing a quality protective suit, and there was an element of the unknown to keep the students guessing. The problem was the drill was done in a locker room with a concrete floor, metal lockers with sharp edges, and metal benches secured to the floor by bolts. Anyone see a problem with this? I hope so. Not surprisingly, there were several (fortunately minor) injuries during the day. A little extra effort could have made the training environment safer and avoided the real potential of serious injuries.

Before you start the actual training, it's necessary to adhere to the following rules:

1. No firearms are ever allowed in the classroom or training area. A basic firearms safety rule is there is no such thing as an empty weapon. No matter how many times you've checked to ensure a weapon is safe and clear, you still treat it as a live weapon. Therefore, it makes absolutely no sense to ever use a real weapon during DT training. Always use a red gun or a rubber, nonoperating weapon. Too many officers have been killed during training by ignoring this rule.

   In 2005, the National Tactical Officers Association (NTOA) compiled and distributed a report on law enforcement training deaths. All of the incidents documented by the NTOA are tragic. A recurring theme in those disastrous situations is the presence of live weapons in the training area. No matter how many times you have checked the weapon, you should still follow the basic weapon safety rules: treat all weapons as loaded, never point the weapon at anything you don't intend to destroy, and keep your finger off the trigger until you are ready to fire. Any time you use a real weapon in DT training, you are violating basic safety rules. Don't do it. Pay the extra $50 and buy a rubber gun. It's worth it to prevent the death of a fellow officer.
2. Related to the first rule, no weapons of any type or any potentially dangerous items are to be allowed in the training area. This includes knives, pencils, pens, or anything that can cause injury during DT training. However, this doesn't preclude conducting DT training in full uniform with all gear at times. Just recognize the elevated potential for injury and adjust accordingly.

3. How do you ensure rules 1 and 2 are followed? It's up to every instructor to check all students prior to training, prior to conducting drills, and after any breaks. Most training-related injuries and deaths occur after a meal break. Officers arm themselves prior to going to eat and forget to secure their weapons prior to returning to class. I've done it myself. It's the responsibility of every instructor and every student to make certain this never happens. Check and then check again.
4. Have a predetermined signal to immediately cease all activities. We always use "code red" because it clearly indicates a dangerous situation has been observed and it is imperative for all students to immediately freeze. Some agencies simplify it by yelling "stop" or blowing a whistle. Those work as well as any other previously agreed upon signal. I personally like code red because it isn't a phrase that typically appears in day-to-day conversation and people tend to respond more quickly. Everyone must be briefed, understand, and comply with the expectation that everyone instantly freezes in place once the code red announcement has been made. No milling around, completing the technique, or chatting with your partner is permitted. All activity stops—period.
5. Everyone, both instructors and students, is a safety officer. Every individual present is responsible for safety. Everyone has the authority to call a code red. Once a code red has been called and all movement has instantly ceased, the person calling the code red can then explain the issue and the instructors will address it.
6. No jewelry should be worn by any participants. Necklaces, rings, and earrings can lead to injuries, so have them removed prior to training.
7. Ensure you have adequate space to avoid unintentional collisions. Even if you watch all of the students closely, if there is not enough space, sooner or later someone will trip over or step on someone on the ground and a serious injury could result.
8. Prior to beginning any drills, warm up thoroughly. Any surprises here? I hope not. Exercise experts have been saying this for decades. Don't start doing complicated wrist twists, joint locks, and throws without first loosening up the body.

   I don't like wasting precious DT time doing mindless calisthenics. I prefer to warm up a class doing the same motions you would do in a self-defense situation. Instead of doing jumping jacks, mountain climbers, or whatnot, I suggest starting a class doing fast footwork drills to get the heart rate up. Then proceed to some stretching, followed immediately by a review of techniques in a shadowboxing format.

9. For every technique practiced, do it slowly at first and then gradually increase speed after an instructor has checked that the technique is done correctly. On a related note, when you first demonstrate a technique, do it at full speed. This allows the students to see the technique and assess its effectiveness. Then show the same technique in slow motion. Lastly, break down the technique into separate, key elements, and explain the importance of each to the overall effectiveness of the technique. If you watch legitimate martial arts grand masters in a demonstration, you'll notice they'll typically alter their speed in different phases of the technique. They may perform the initial deflection with effortless speed, switch to slow motion to show the intricacies of a particular grab or joint lock, and then finish the technique in a blinding fury. The variations in speed make the demonstration more interesting and also have a teaching purpose.
10. Tell the students on the receiving end of the technique (the "uke" in Judo terms or the "bad guys" in law enforcement terms) to offer only passive resistance. Then tell them again. Then tell them again. Then constantly remind them throughout the day. This is where most injuries occur during DT training. You get a bunch of type A personalities and strong egos thinking, "I bet ya I can fight this!" And they try. And their partner tries harder to make the technique work. And then you have people yanking on each other's joints, and before long, a full-fledged fight breaks out. It's the instructor's job to keep the egos in check and ensure the focus is on teamwork, playing well with others, and creating a cooperative environment. It is useful to slowly increase the resistance to challenge the student performing the technique, but it must be done safely and in a partnership mindset. Save the true testosterone tests for scenarios with a protective suit. If a technique works performing it slowly, you know it will work performing it at "street" speed.
11. Explain and demonstrate "slapping out" or "tapping out." When you slap out, it's like crying uncle. It means the technique is working, you acknowledge the technique is working, and now is a good time for your partner to stop applying pressure to your elbow (or wrist, knee, etc.) before it breaks. You slap out by slapping the mat, tapping against your body, or tapping repeatedly against your opponent's body. Saying "that's enough," "stop," or "ouch" should work also.

All students must be made to realize that DT training is always done, must be done, in the spirit of partnership and friendship. We are all the good folks preparing ourselves as a team to defend ourselves from the bad folks. We are the righteous warriors, a band of brothers and sisters brought together to fight for a common good and to protect society. The last thing we want to do is to hurt each other before we have a chance to prepare for battle on the streets.

Unfortunately, occasionally you have a student who seems to like to hurt other people. Whether this is because of a weak ego, the need to show off, or just because he's mean, I don't know. Whatever the reason for this behavior, it can't be tolerated. See above for what happens when someone gets injured. It's your job, Mr. or Ms. Instructor, to ensure this doesn't happen on your watch. Try to reason with the individual, discipline him if it's within your power to do so, or get rid of him. If you can't get rid of him, at least separate him from the rest of the class so he can't cause any harm.

Another problem is that you'll have the "tough guys" or "tough gals" who think it's a personal weakness to tap out. This is usually seen in the younger pups, and rarely seen in the older, and much wiser, personnel. As you get older, you realize there really is no benefit to your partner or to you to wait until your elbow is within a fraction of an inch of shattering before tapping out. As an instructor, you should stress the purpose of the training is to improve, not to show your superhuman resistance to pain.

12. No horseplay! Okay, I'm one of the worst violators of this rule. DT training is fun. Martial arts are fun. And it's particularly fun to sneak up on your buddy and get him in a headlock or bear hug, which usually leads to a full-fledged war. Most folks involved in DT training love to train (at least all of the good ones I know do). This means they have fun during DT training, they laugh a lot, and it's a positive experience for everyone. Yes, we're learning to become better warriors. Yes, we're training to save our lives, the lives of a friend, or the life of an unknown citizen. But it doesn't have to be deadly serious all of the time. Nor should it be. As the instructor, however, it's your job to make sure that every activity has a purpose and you are in complete control of that activity to ensure maximum benefit and minimal risk of injury. Nothing is done during class that the instructor doesn't control and supervise.
13. Use appropriate protective gear and ensure it's in good condition. Appropriate gear runs the gamut from protective cups for men, comfortable workout clothing (although I encourage some training be conducted in street clothes and in uniforms—for FBI agents that means a suit), high-quality striking pads, mouthpieces, and rubber guns (never use a real gun in DT training, no matter how many times you checked to see it's unloaded—see rule 1), to a first-rate protective suit for the instructor. Having worn high-quality protective suits on countless occasions, I can assure you students are quite adept at

finding the weak link in any protective gear. If there's a 1-inch gap, they'll find it with the tip of a baton.

14. Be aware of the fitness level and fatigue level of your students. A good instructor is constantly monitoring the students, not only for the proper application of DT skills and safety, but also to see when it's necessary to take a break. I believe in pushing people past their comfort zone. Way past. Most people have no idea what they are truly capable of achieving. It's our job to show them, instill the will to survive, and develop the warrior spirit. But it's also our job to ensure they have a safe environment in which to learn these skills. Insist that students drink water throughout the day and closely monitor students for signs of fatigue. Teach skill drills when they are fresh. Teach stamina and relaxation techniques when they are tired. Having students practice personal weapons or skill drills when they're dead tired leads to poor technique. That improper technique then becomes ingrained via muscle memory. This is bad. Teach proper muscle memory and have students continuously repeat the proper technique to develop the muscle memory. Continue to do this until the students become so fatigued the techniques are starting to suffer. Then stop! Any technical training beyond this point is counterproductive.

In conclusion, train hard, have fun, and stay safe.

Essential Fundamentals 5

Without strong fundamentals, no athlete will be successful. Similarly, without strong fundamentals, no officer will be able to consistently survive a physical confrontation. The greatest baseball players in the world start off every spring training season working on fundamentals. NFL players during preseason workouts concentrate on fundamentals. And the vast majority of the time boxers spend in the gym prior to a fight is practicing (you guessed it) fundamentals. Without a strong foundation, nothing else is of use. The best athletes in the world are successful because they have mastered the fundamentals of their physical endeavor. To master any physical skill, you must master the fundamentals.

It is paramount that fundamentals are taught to all officers initially, stressed during continued training, and become muscle memory. In order for this to happen, the defensive tactics (DT) program must be based on body movements that occur naturally in day-to-day life and employ large muscle groups (such as running and jumping) rather than fine motor skills (such as putting a key into a key lock). Even with the limited DT training time allotted to officers, a program based on core concepts and instinctual, natural movements can be highly successful.

There are four generally accepted DT fundamental principles. These are balance, redirection of force, position of survival (sometimes referred to as position of advantage), and body mechanics.

Balance

Balance is the most important principle in the execution of almost any physical skill. Without balance, you will struggle to generate power, you will not be consistent in the application of techniques, and you will be susceptible to attacks from your opponent. Bruce Lee wrote that without balance at all times, a fighter can never be effective.[1] As a law enforcement officer involved in a physical confrontation, your primary objective is to survive. You accomplish this by (1) maintaining your balance and (2) taking the resister's balance. Wrestlers and jiu-jitsu practitioners frequently discuss balance in terms of a table. A table with four legs is stable. A table with three legs is not, and a table with two legs is even less so.

The first thing to look at when evaluating your own balance is your stance—both the interview stance and what is commonly referred to as a fighting stance. Instead of using the term *fighting stance*, I refer to this as a *response stance* or *survival stance*. This is not done to be politically correct, but to more accurately describe the resistance-response event. As was previously discussed in Chapter 2 on the Dynamic Resistance-Response Model (DRM), officers do not have a first-strike option. We are always responding to a resister's actions. In addition, our objective is not to fight; our objective is to obtain compliance or control as quickly and safely as possible. So when we are attacked or threatened by a resister, we assume a response/survival stance. Our purpose when taking the response/survival stance is to ensure our survival and safely avoid the attack. We can then obtain control and compliance so we can complete the arrest.

The interview stance is used every time you are dealing with the public. Actually, the interview stance should become second nature. It just becomes the way you stand no matter where you are or what you're doing. Rather than standing off-balance or in an awkward configuration, you will always strive to be balanced. The interview stance should be stable with the feet about shoulder width apart and the weapon-side foot (right foot for right-handed people) dropped back slightly so the toe of your weapon-side foot is on the same line as the heel of your forward foot (Figure 5.1). This will cause your body to be slightly bladed. Your hands should be about waist level.

Figure 5.1 Proper interview stance.

The response, or survival, stance should also come naturally. Think of it this way: You're walking down the street and suddenly you hear a loud bang that sounds like a gunshot. What do you do instinctively? If your answer is to stand on your tiptoes and crane your neck to see where the sound came from, then go sell insurance or find some other honorable profession. Law enforcement may not be a good career choice for you. Hopefully you answered that you would automatically go into a crouched position as a natural startle (i.e., survival) reflex as well as heading toward cover. Without thinking, you lowered your center of gravity, thereby increasing your stability. We don't have to think about it; it should just happen as an instinctive survival reaction. That's your response stance. Your hands should come up to protect your head and your elbows should be tucked in against your sides (Figure 5.2).

If you are dealing with a subject, it is best if you don't give him advance warning you intend to arrest him. Rather than taking a fighting stance in which your fists are tightly clenched and you stare at the subject aggressively, it is usually best to assume a nonapparent survival stance. This is the sneaky/smart way to approach a bad guy. You don't want to look like you are going to move forward or do anything belligerent. Instead, you initially look as if you

Figure 5.2 Balanced response/survival stance.

are in a peacekeeper role. Now comes the sneaky part. Your hands are open, palms facing your subject, and up by your head. Your body language is saying, "Calm down. I'm not a threat to you," yet your body is bladed, ready to move, and your hands are up and ready to protect yourself or strike out.

To break down the response/survival stance further, you should be balanced, with your weight equally distributed over each foot. Your feet should be a little wider than shoulder's width apart and your weapon-side foot should be a little more than shoulder's width to the rear. The response/survival stance is a slightly wider, deeper stance than the interview stance, and your center of gravity is lower. If you look down, your feet should appear to be at the corners of a box or, using the earlier analogy, a square table. The more rectangular, or thinner, a table becomes, the easier it is to knock over. Eventually, a table (or your stance) could become so narrow that it is essentially a line. This offers no stability whatsoever.

Here is a simple drill to test your stance: Get in your response/survival stance and then have a buddy gently push you from the four primary directions (front, back, and each side) (Figure 5.2). You should be solid and resistant to the push. If you are strong when pushed from the front or rear, but fall over easily when pushed from the sides, then your stance is too narrow (a common mistake). You need to spread your feet wider so they are a little more than shoulder's width apart. Conversely, if you are stable when pushed from the sides, but tend to topple over when pushed from the front or back, then your stance is too shallow. To correct this, step farther back with your rear foot. If you are off-balance regardless of where the push is directed, then you are just one messed up dude/dudette! Actually, your stance is too narrow and too shallow. You're like a one-legged table. Fix it!

The interview stance is simply a less extreme version of the response stance. It should look more comfortable and natural. The center of gravity is at a more natural height (you are standing erect), your knees are slightly bent (don't lock them out), and your base is not as wide or as deep. In both stances, your weapon side is bladed away. There is no reason to have your sternum, groin area, and other vital organs directly facing the resister screaming, "Hit me! Hit me!" Get them off-line of a potential attack by angling your body slightly to the other person.

Common weaknesses include leaning against something or locking out your joints for comfort. We all do this at times because we're all lazy at times. Just pick those times wisely and don't stand off-balance when dealing with anyone who has the potential to harm you. And by the way, that's about everybody. I'm not asking you to be paranoid. I'm just suggesting that if you do this regularly, it becomes habit. Good habits save lives, including yours. Another common bad habit is to lean into your opponent, making it easier for him to control you. Maintain balance at all times.

Figure 5.3 The o-soto-gari during the "reaping" (or sweeping) portion of the trip.

The corollary to maintaining your balance is your goal to upset the balance of the resister. Several methods of accomplishing this will be covered in Chapter 8 on subject control. Any technique is much easier to accomplish successfully if you first take the resister's balance. An example of this is a basic judo throw/trip, called o-soto-gari, or major outer reaping throw (Figure 5.3).

Many people watch this throw being executed and focus on the big movement of the sweeping leg. They erroneously think that the throw is all about kicking the opponent's leg out from under him. It's not. The first, and most important, aspect of the throw is to take the balance of the resister by effectively using proper body mechanics, your weight, and momentum. This is accomplished by driving your arm nearest to the resister into his opposite shoulder while simultaneously drawing the resister's near arm into your chest. Your body weight and momentum drive past the resister, forcing him back at a 45° angle (Figure 5.4).

Once you have successfully broken the resister's balance in a rearward 45° angle, the sweeping motion of the leg is almost an unnecessary afterthought (Figure 5.5). The sweep primarily prevents the resister from stepping

Figure 5.4 The initial setup of the o-soto-gari.

Figure 5.5 The sweeping motion once the resister's balance has been taken.

Video 5.1 at www.SurvivalSciences.com demonstrates the o-soto-gari using correct technique to first take the opponent's balance. As was mentioned near the end of the introduction, go to the "videos" page at www.SurvivalSciences.com, and type in *access@SurvivalSciences.com* as the user and *dtconcepts* as the password to gain access to the video section.

back to regain balance. In addition, one of the key components is to maintain your balance throughout the technique. In simpler terms, always maintain your balance and always strive to take the resister's balance.

Redirection of Force

Redirection of force is a fundamental principle of all "soft" martial arts. I know, law enforcement is a macho profession and there is nothing soft about it. Bear with me, though. There is nothing wrong with being big and strong. I think most of us would like to be bigger and stronger. Strength works great for an officer in a force-on-force encounter when the officer is much bigger and stronger than the resister. In a force vs. force encounter, with force applied in a linear fashion, the stronger force will win. It would be wonderful if you were the biggest and strongest person in the world. But here's a wild guess—you're not. And here's another wild guess: If someone chooses to attack you, that person probably is not smaller, weaker, slower, and older than you. I always train with the mindset the person who will attack me will be bigger, stronger, faster, and younger. And as I continue to get older (which is a good thing considering the alternative), this becomes even more likely. The answer must work for all officers and in all circumstances. The answer is not that you will power through the bad guy. It's just not realistic, particularly considering the resister almost always gets the first move. The answer is to redirect the resister's attack. The answer is to get out of the way (you'll see this phrase a lot later).

Purportedly, the concept of redirection of force is credited to Akiyama, one of several individuals credited with founding jiu-jitsu. As the story goes, Akiyama was walking along on a winter day in Japan. He observed several strong tree branches had broken under the weight of the fallen snow. He then noted how the supple branches of the willow tree would bend, yielding to the weight of the snow. The willow tree branches would softly deposit the accumulating snow on the ground and then gracefully return to their original position. From this, Akiyama determined how a smaller person could defeat a much bigger, stronger person, and that was by redirecting the force of the more powerful opponent.

Imagine this: Let's say your level of strength is three strength units (with strength units being a fictitious measure of strength). Your resister has nine strength units, or is three times stronger than you. If the two of you stood toe-to-toe and pushed each other, who would win? Stupid question, right? Let's do the math: 9 (pushing in one direction) – 3 (pushing in the opposite direction) = 6 (favoring the bad guy). Since the resister has six more strength units than you, the resister will easily push you backwards (Figures 5.6 and 5.7).

Now, in the next situation, you initially push back with your three strength units and then suddenly pull the resister instead of pushing (Figure 5.8). What happens? Most likely he'll go flying. The resister was pushing against you with all of his nine strength units and only meeting weak resistance from your puny three strength units. However, when you unexpectedly pulled the resister, there are now twelve strength units taking him in one direction. That is redirection of force. That is how a smaller, weaker officer can defeat a bigger, stronger resister. That is being smart (and devious).

Figure 5.6 A smaller, weaker officer pushing directly against a bigger, stronger resister. Obviously, force against force will not work well for the officer in this situation.

Figure 5.7 The result of the above force-against-force confrontation. The smaller, weaker person is easily pushed backwards.

Figure 5.8 The result of the smaller person pulling as the larger, stronger opponent pushes (redirection of force).

Position of Survival

This is usually referred to as position of advantage. As a law enforcement officer, it is often difficult, if not impossible, to get into a position of advantage. Many times, we are fortunate if we can just get in a position to survive. Sometimes it is taught for the officer to always be at the subject's 45° angle, and preferably to the rear. This is great in theory and true, but all the bad guy has to do is rotate his body and the officer is facing the bad guy straight on. However, there are positions that are better to be in than others.

Here is one axiom that should be easy to remember: **"behind is better."** Given the choice, you strive to be behind the resister. The worst place to be is directly in front of the attacker, where he can easily bring to bear all of his weapons against you (Figure 5.9). Slightly better is being just outside of the attacker's arms, as demonstrated in Figure 5.10. The best (i.e., safest) place to be is behind the attacker (Figure 5.11).

As will be discussed in more detail in Chapter 6, you always want to avoid moving straight in on a resister. If you are directly in front of your opponent, all of his personal weapons are available to hurt you. Moving in at a slight angle at least puts you outside of your opponent's strength zone. At a minimum, you force him to turn to strike you effectively. Never move straight in on an attacker; always move in at an angle to provide you with more protection and reaction time.

Here's another adage: **"always face your butt kicking."** It's amazing to me how many people curl up in a fetal position when attacked. Animals do this as a sign of submission. It's not a good idea to place your survival in the

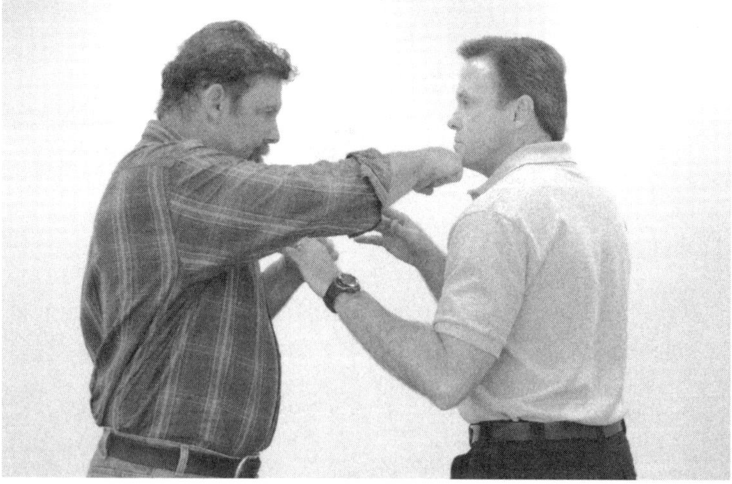

Figure 5.9 Being directly in front of the attacker—not where I want to be. You never want to be directly in front of the attacker.

Figure 5.10 I'm slightly off-center to the attacker. This is not the ideal position, but it is much better than being directly in front of the subject.

Figure 5.11 I'm in a much better tactical position. Behind is better!

hands of someone who has already clearly indicated he wants to hurt you. For those of you who are ardent mixed martial arts (MMA) fans, think of the fights where one competitor turned his back on the other. Almost always, this is the beginning of the end. The one in the turtle position is now defenseless and the other fighter is now free to reign down blows with impunity. When teaching defensive tactics to agents, law enforcement personnel, and military personnel, I could always tell during the grappling exercises the former high school wrestlers. They were the ones who instinctively went to their stomachs when they got in trouble. It's great in wrestling to avoid getting pinned, but it will sure get you in a heap of trouble in a street fight.

Body Mechanics

Body mechanics are critical to any physical activity. Body mechanics are what separates the nonathlete from the world-class athlete. When Tiger Woods was just beginning his professional career, he wasn't the buffed athlete we see today. He was, to put it politely, skinny. In spite of this, he averaged over 300 yards a drive in competition. For the nongolfers, that is a really, really, really long way to hit a golf ball. How is this possible when other people, some of whom are tremendous athletes and much bigger and stronger than was Tiger, couldn't hit a golf ball nearly as far? The two-word answer is body mechanics. Tiger Woods had, and still has, incredible body mechanics. The way he deployed his muscles to drive a golf ball was almost perfectly synchronized, resulting in incredible power. In Chapter 11, I will discuss the proper body mechanics involved in striking.

Generally, proper body mechanics can be defined as the timely deployment of specific muscle groups directed toward completing a physical task. The weight of the entire body is used in the execution of a DT technique. In striking, the trunk (or core) muscles are the source of power, resulting in an "explosion" of the technique. This is enhanced with proper breathing. When striking, you must exhale forcefully as the technique travels and lands. Think of boxers, martial artists, and even tennis players, who exhale in grunts when they strike. It is also a psychological edge to grunt, kiai, or yell to intimidate your attacker. Exhaling causes the core muscles to contract, creating more power. It also offers some protection to the body if the resister strikes you. Inhalation relaxes the core muscles. The worst time to get hit is when you are taking a deep breath and will lead to what is commonly referred to as "having the wind knocked out."

Since it is a concept we will repeat throughout the book, let's look at the proper use of your body weight. The techniques that will be presented later involve the use of your full body weight for maximum effectiveness. Try this drill: Stand on an old-fashioned mechanical scale and determine your weight. Wouldn't it be nice, if someone tried to pick you up and throw you off a cliff, if you could dramatically increase your weight? You can! Look at the dial on the scale and suddenly relax your body. Don't tense up, jump, or try to force your weight down; just relax and let your muscles go limp. What happens? The dial on your mechanical scale probably spun around rapidly, making it appear as if you doubled or tripled your weight. Remember this feeling of relaxing and dropping your weight, as you will use it a number of times as you complete the drills listed in this book.

All four of the essential fundamentals are of paramount importance in the execution of all DT techniques. They will be discussed in detail in later chapters.

Distance

Imagine this scenario:

> Tough guy 1 is mad at tough guy 2. There are a lot of mean looks, posturing, finger-pointing, cursing, threatening, and chest puffing going on. To show how tough he is, and mimicking the military drill instructors he's seen in movies, tough guy 1 stands nose-to-nose with tough guy 2 and bumps chests. Tough guy 2, not wanting to look like he's afraid of tough guy 1, bumps chests too. This primal activity continues until one of them backs down, friends pull them apart allowing them to save face, or it escalates to shoving, grappling, strikes, and possibly worse.

It shouldn't be too hard to imagine this situation because we've all witnessed it several times—both in real life (as opposed to fake life) and on television. There are two knuckleheads in almost every bar in America reenacting this scenario almost every night. A number of police calls are responding to this type of situation. And what do the officers think when they arrive on scene? Probably something like, "Morons! Grab a beer, listen to the tunes, and just chill out."

The scenario outlined above in which two adults act like children is even more embarrassing and more dangerous when one of the two participants is an officer of the law. We've all seen it. Perhaps we've even been in it. It's stupid. It's really stupid for a law enforcement officer to behave this way. It's also very dangerous. We should never stand this close to someone who could hurt us.

You may be the best fighter in the world. You may be the fastest, deadliest, "my whole body is a weapon" cop ever. I don't care how good you are, if the other guy gets in the first lick, and it's a good lick, then you may never recover. If you doubt this, do this drill. Stand nose-to-nose with your buddy. Then have your pal attack you in any way he or she chooses. You should notice a few things. First, when you are that close to someone, it really restricts your peripheral vision. It's almost impossible to see what is happening, particularly below waist level. Second, everything they taught you in the academy about action beating reaction is true. Being so close to an opponent makes it incredibly difficult to respond effectively to an attack. Third, your buddy is probably having a great time punching you in the ribs, kicking you in the knee, and slapping you in the crotch.

Don't let people get that close to you. You should have a barrier around you that is a little farther out than your opponent can reach if he extended his rear leg toward you (Figure 5.12). If a bad guy wants to attack you, make sure he has to at least take a step to reach you. That gives you a little more time to react. You then have a large visual cue (the subject's whole body movement)

Figure 5.12 The minimum safe distance: a little farther than the subject can reach with his rear leg.

that he is moving your way. There are very few people that you should allow within this safety zone. For me, it's pretty much just my wife and son. Okay, I'd also make an exception for Salma Hayek, but that's it. If anyone else enters that space, alarms should be going off in your head that something bad is about to happen.

Try this: Go up to your good friends and casually begin talking to them and get so close you almost touch noses. What do they do? They probably get really uncomfortable and start inching away from you. Remember the Seinfeld episode on the "close talker?" It's just awkward, and we naturally don't like our personal space invaded. As a law enforcement officer, you should be even more aware of your personal space, and it should be larger. Anybody who you are not intimately close with doesn't belong in this space. Certainly no one on the street belongs in this zone.

So what do you do if someone tries to sneak up on you or step on your toes? Don't let them. Don't let them stand that close to you. As they begin to break your invisible barrier of safety, step back and maintain that safe distance. You can hear it now from the bad guy ("What's your problem? I'm not going to hurt you? Why are you being so uptight?). Don't fall for it. Don't let them sucker you in. As soon as someone begins to invade your space, step away and command, "Stay back!" As was mentioned in Chapter 2, anyone who attempts to get that close to you is a threat. If someone is insistent on closing the gap with you, you must consider them to be an aggressive resister (because they are) and be prepared to respond with a baton, pepper spray, TASER, or personal weapons. If they obey your commands and stay at an appropriate distance, then wonderful. If they later explain it's just a cultural thing where they feel more comfortable speaking to people at closer distances, great. You can then educate them on how best not to upset people in law enforcement. You can tell them that your training requires you to prevent anyone from getting that close to you, as they are then considered a threat. And to repeat myself, anyone who violates your personal safety zone *is* a threat.

It is a basic tactic that greater distance typically benefits the officer. The more distance between you and the potential bad guy, the more time you have to recognize an attack and respond appropriately. Always seek to maximize distance. When you close the distance, do it because you chose to do so at the tactically best time, not because you allowed the bad guy to dictate the encounter.

Having lived in large metropolitan areas, I also recognize it's not always possible to keep everyone more than a leg's length away. You're standing on a street corner, waiting for the crosswalk sign to change, and you are surrounded by a mass of humanity all within touching distance. Or you're waiting in line for a movie, waiting for a table at a popular restaurant, or many other possible situations in which a large number of people are all crammed into a small space. How bad can it get?

The worst situation I can imagine was one I experienced while suffering through a rush hour ride in Japan. It's difficult to adequately describe just how packed the trains become. A friend who was with me said a Japanese school girl literally fell asleep while smashed up against him. It was so crowded, the other people packed in against her kept her upright while she slept. I had another friend say he didn't want to exhale as he was afraid the crush of people would worsen and prevent him from inhaling and he would suffocate. I was squashed against the side of the train's interior with what felt like all of the bodies of Hades pressing against me. It was so crowded that if both of your arms were at your sides prior to the onslaught, they were stuck there until the crowd thinned out. Add to all of this the fact that I'm slightly claustrophobic and I was one miserable camper.

So what do you do in this situation? Prior to being encased in human bodies, I made sure I had one arm above my head and my other hand down at my side. If necessary, I could bring down the one arm and strike someone near me, most likely with an elbow. The hand by my side could block a low level attack and reach out and grab or strike. This may sound paranoid, but it's not unheard of for people to be attacked or pickpocketed in these situations. It is also known that women are groped and otherwise molested on the Japanese commuter trains. In response, Japan tried to have at least a few train cars that were for women only (the "pink" cars). If you are compressed into a small space on a Japanese train or standing on a crowded sidewalk in a big city, it may be impossible to maintain a safe space, but you can at least be aware that your zone of safety has shrunk considerably if not completely disappeared. You should then be even more alert and aware of those around you.

Almost always, distance favors those in law enforcement. We want as much distance as possible initially to give us time to survey the area, assess the situation, see any potential attacks, and respond appropriately. If we are forced into a close-proximity situation, we understand the nearness has made the world more dangerous and we have less time to react. Therefore, we are even more alert and prepared for something bad to happen. "Distance is our friend."

Drills

1. Stand on a mechanical scale and repeatedly practice dropping your weight. Experiment with different methods of relaxing your muscles until you can instantly and effortlessly increase the readout on the scale.
2. Standing in front of a mirror, practice transitioning smoothly and quickly from an interview stance to a response/survival stance. Are you balanced in all four directions?
3. Get in a response/survival stance and have a buddy try to push you from the primary four directions to ensure your stance is of proper width and depth. Then move out of the stance quickly to ensure you have maintained mobility.

Endnotes

1. Lee, B., *Tao of Jeet Kun Do*, Ohara Publications, Santa Clarita, CA, 1975, p. 47.

Get Out of the Way! 6

During your career, you will be attacked. If you complete a career in law enforcement, you will probably be physically assaulted multiple times. As reported in the FBI *Law Enforcement Officers Killed and Assaulted 2005* report, 11.9% of the officers from reporting agencies were assaulted in 2005. Of those, 27.4% were injured.[1] If you work in law enforcement long enough, you will be required to use force and you'll be required to use that force because the subject is trying to hurt you or get away.

Knowing you will be attacked, what is the best response to someone invading your personal space, trying to creep up on you and sucker punch you, or just launching an all-out violent attack? You have three general options if you are attacked. One possibility is you can panic and sit there like a bump on a log, but since that is obviously not a desirable outcome, we'll throw it out. The two remaining options are you can either engage or disengage. Whether you choose to engage may depend on your skill level. Please recognize, however, that even if you are highly skilled, you have a lot of things working against you. First, the bad guy gets the first move. The bad guy gets to launch a surprise attack, and he may use an unseen weapon against you. The odds are not in your favor. Typically, if you engage, the bad guy's action will beat your reaction. If you are working with a partner and you engage, you have also made the decision for your partner to engage. And it may not be a decision your partner will be particularly happy about. It also defeats the cover-contact strategy of having one officer approach while the second officer remains at the ready with a higher level of force. Once you're in a tussle, lots of bad things can happen. A weapon you didn't see previously may be pulled out of a pocket, and now you're going against a knife or gun in a fight for your life. If you initially engage, and you decide it was a bad idea and now want to disengage, you may no longer have that option.

What I strongly advocate is to disengage. It's always easier and safer to disengage and go to one of your weapons. If you disengage, you can always choose to engage later. You engage when you clearly have the tactical advantage.

I know what some of you are thinking, "But, Chuck, you don't understand! Disengaging is for wimps! You have to understand that I'm the meanest, toughest cat on the planet and I can take anyone!" My response would be, "Cool, I'm glad you're on our side." But even if this is true, would you recommend this approach to all officers? Sometimes defensive tactics (DT) instructors get caught up in the machismo. They can fall into the mindset that only the biggest and baddest should be cops. That's fine, but what are you going to do without 99% of your department—you know, the ones who aren't as tough as you? We have a responsibility to teach *all* officers how to safely do their job. There are several officers that seek self-defense training on their own and constantly work on improving their skills. God bless them. But they are definitely a minority, and we need to concentrate on the vast majority who don't.

Let's assume you are the best fighter in the world. That doesn't mean you can't be sucker punched. That doesn't mean someone can't slip out a blade and stick you. That doesn't mean you're invincible. What if you get into a fight with a bad guy, you punch him in the nose, he bleeds a lot, and is rendered unconscious. All is good, right? Not necessarily. What if the bad guy is HIV positive or has hepatitis C and he bled into an open cut on your hand? You think you've won only to find out later you lost. Your goal was to survive. Even though you won the fight, you lost. My friends who work in corrections tell me there are plenty of bad guys who use their contaminated blood as a weapon. Those infected bad guys would be happy to share their diseases with you.

My job caused me to spend a lot of time in Cambodia. It seems as if every time I traveled there I would read in the local paper about another "acid attack." It was not uncommon for people in the villages to be attacked by someone throwing a container of acid into their face. How would you block such an attack? You couldn't. Your best response as the acid was flying toward your face would be to move out of the way.

So what happens if you disengage? First, you have thwarted the bad guy's initial attack. You also, at least temporarily, foiled the bad guy's strategy, as you are not where he wanted you to be. Let's look at the strategy of disengaging further.

If someone tries to punch you, what is your primary objective? Don't get punched. If someone tries to kick, stab, or tackle you, what is your primary objective? Don't get kicked, stabbed, or tackled, right? It seems simple enough, but how do you do that? The answer is not, "Well, if someone tries to stab me, I'll grab his wrist in a c-clamp fashion, twist it to the outside to disarm him, and sweep his leg to take him down. And if he tries to punch me with a right haymaker, I'd use my left arm to do a hard middle block and then …" The answer is much simpler. The answer is one word: move! You'll see that word a lot. It's the simplest and best answer to any attack. Move. If that's too simple of a concept for you, here's one that uses more words: Get out of the way! Same idea, just more words.

Move. Does that make you look weak or afraid? Absolutely not. It makes you look professional, alert, experienced, and very difficult to hurt. I know most officers are aggressive, hard-charging, type A personality types. That's why you went into law enforcement, right? You may have been hired for that trait, but you were also hired to be smart. One question you should constantly ask yourself as you are dealing with the public, making an arrest, participating in a raid, driving around town, is "Do I have the tactical advantage?" If the answer is no, I'd suggest you do what is necessary to get the tactical advantage. The job is dangerous enough without making it more dangerous unnecessarily. Imagine this: You are talking to a potential bad guy and this person is younger, stronger, bigger, and faster than you. If things broke bad right then, do you have the tactical advantage? I think not.

Furthermore, you can't tell by looking at someone if he is a threat. My wife is a petite, attractive female with a disarming smile. She is also an incredibly vicious fighter. I've trained with some very small and very old men. If you saw them on the street, you'd never think of them as being a threat. Yet these small, old men are some of the most dangerous fighters. Even if you think you are bigger, stronger, faster, and more skilled than the person you're dealing with, you never know. That person only has to get lucky once and you're dead. In a fight, not only are you trying to control him, but you are also trying to maintain control of all of the weapons you have on your belt. All of those wonderful tools are a liability if you lock up with someone and begin to grapple. All the bad guy has to do is access one of those weapons and your life gets more difficult (and possibly much shorter). If that's not bad enough, the bad guy always gets the first move! As a law enforcement officer, you are responding to the threat. The bad guy gets to launch a surprise attack, and you have to be good enough to recognize it and respond effectively. Obviously, initially disengaging from a surprise attack and moving out of the way has the highest probability of success.

I think we unwittingly short-change officers by having them spend countless hours attempting to learn complex DT techniques that require a high-degree of skill and extensive practice to do effectively. I strongly believe the majority of time in DT training should be spent on teaching officers to do two things really well. The first is to maintain proper distance. The second is to move properly. Now you just have to do those two things while maintaining proper balance. If you are capable of this simple physical feat, you will be significantly safer.

Getting out of the way is instinctive. As little kids we naturally dodge, duck, and run. Remember playing dodge ball on the playground? We grew up learning how to get out of the way. It's interesting to watch hard-style karate training for beginners. As a punch is coming, people innately want to move out of the way. The instructor, with good intentions, tries to quash this natural survival instinct by having the student stand solidly in place and attempt to deliver a hard block against the punch. It may be okay if you are much bigger and stronger than your opponent to stand as if you are rooted into the ground, but even then I think it's a bad idea. For the martial arts practitioners out there, think of all of the sparring sessions you've seen. Did you ever see someone successfully execute a hard block against a reasonably well-matched opponent? In over thirty years I haven't. In all of the sparring I've seen, skilled fighters instinctively use soft, redirecting style of blocks as they try to move out of the way.

Remember, one of your first lessons at your academy was action beats reaction. It's true. As a law enforcement officer, how do you overcome this? We are almost always reacting to a threat. How can we possibly survive? The answer is in two words. Once again, they are *distance* and *move*. If we are standing an appropriate distance (at least a few inches farther than the bad guy can reach with his rear leg), then we give ourselves time to see the attack and respond. Rather than having thousands of possible responses to the attack, which may slow down our reaction time, we will do just one thing, and that is move. Move out of the way. We will simply be somewhere else when the attack arrives.

The second thing moving does for us is that we've now changed the action-reaction equation. What happens to the bad guy when we move and are no longer where he expected us to be? He has to react to our movement. He now has to reposition himself physically and mentally to launch another attack. We are now in control of the encounter because the bad guy is now reacting to our movement rather than vice versa.

Bruce Lee said good footwork will defeat any attack.[2] What he was saying was if you move effectively, if you get out the way, you can't be hurt. When I was kick boxing, the one style of fighter I hated to compete against most was the runner, the guy constantly moving. This is true for most fighters. It's really difficult to fight someone who won't stay still and constantly moves away from you. It causes you to chase and overextend your strikes in an attempt to catch up to him. The reason you don't see more of this in competition is because eventually the runner has to stop running and throw some punches and kicks if he has any hope of winning the fight. Fighters earn points from the judges for demonstrated aggression. The other reason is the ring is only so big and eventually you can catch up to him. But if you're not looking to outpoint the bad guy, if your interest is to survive, then you can move and consistently get out of his way. This is true if you've learned to move correctly, which is not that hard. However, your goal is not to dance the night away until the bad guy drops from exhaustion. Eventually you have to make the arrest. And eventually you will get nailed if you just keep dancing around.

As you are moving away from an attack, you will also simultaneously draw an appropriate tool (e.g., pepper spray, TASER, baton, handgun). To summarize your strategy, you maintain at least a minimum safe distance between you and the subject, allowing you to see the attack in time to respond. Your initial response is to avoid the attack by moving and thereby reversing the action-reaction equation. As you continue to move, you draw the appropriate tool and subdue your attacker.

It's important you don't get in the mindset of moving out of the way of the initial attack one time and think, "Whew! Glad that's over." You must continue to move because the attacker will continue to attack. As you are avoiding the attack, you must draw a weapon and continue to move. Regardless of the weapon you now have in your hand, still move. You'll be more effective and harder to hurt if you remain a moving target.

Moving out of the way does not require size or strength to be effective. Moving is easy to teach and easy to learn. Moving doesn't require constant training and repetition to be effective. We move every day of our lives. Moving is effective regardless of the type of attack. I may have the best punch, kick, baseball bat swing, or ax chop in the world, but if you move out of the way, I can't hurt you. Even if you are in a worst-case scenario and the bad guy has drawn a handgun, your best strategy is still to move. You become a moving target, which is harder to hit, and you are moving to cover as you draw your weapon.

How do you move? The short answer is move out of the way, any way, and with balance. Most fighting arts list ten general directions of movement, although the directions you can move are infinite (Figure 6.1).

Some directions of movement are better than others, though. For example, I'd never have an officer move straight back. No matter how fast you can move backwards, the bad guy can move forwards a whole lot faster. Also, if

Figure 6.1 The ten general directions of movement.

you move straight back, you're not changing the action-reaction dynamic. The attacker just needs to move quicker on the attack to reach you. If you move straight back, the attacker doesn't have to reposition his body to reengage you.

I'd also choose not to move straight into my attacker. I'm going into his strength, where he has all of his personal weapons (and possibly weapons I don't see) available to him. Even when moving forward to engage, it's best to move in at an angle. Moving at an angle is a higher concept of footwork used successfully by experienced fighters for centuries. Moving in at an angle puts you in a position of tactical advantage and greater survivability (Figure 6.2).

You don't want to be too close to your attacker, nor do you want to be directly in front of the attacker. As one of my former DT instructors used to say, "Never kiss a crook!" It's a dangerous place to be.

Jumping up is only a good move against a low-level attack that is coming in at knee height or lower. It takes timing, coordination, and athleticism. You may be wearing so much heavy gear that it feels like you're carrying around a kitchen sink. All of this hampers your jumping ability. I, for one, can say my jumping days are behind me (if they ever existed). There are better options than jumping up, so we'll discard that choice also.

Ducking down is sometimes a good response if you get caught flat-footed (which you shouldn't be) and don't have time to step away from a high-level, horizontal attack such as a baseball swing. The problem is once you've ducked, now what (Figure 6.3)? How good are you fighting from a kneeling position? Some folks are very effective fighting in this position. For the other 99.99% of the population, I'd recommend against ducking.

Figure 6.2 Moving at an angle to a better position outside of your opponent's strength.

Figure 6.3 The position after ducking. I've avoided the attack, but now what?

So, of the ten possible directions of movement, we're left with six. All six are some variation of moving to the side, either directly to the side, or at a 45° angle toward the opponent and to the side, or at a 45° degree angle away from the opponent and to the side. To simplify things, let's just say the best way to avoid an attack is to step to the side. The exact angle of the side step I'll leave up to you, but be aware the most effective method to get out of the way is to sidestep—either at a 45° angle or straight to the side (Figure 6.4).

I like to use visualization when I practice footwork. Imagine this, you are standing on railroad tracks and a train is coming. Woo woooo—you hear the train's whistle blow. You don't want to get hit by the train, so what do you do? The simplest method to avoid getting crushed is to simply step off of the tracks. When a resister attacks you, simply step out of line of the attack, or off of the tracks (Figure 6.5).

If you are standing in an appropriate interview stance or survival/response stance, you should first move the foot nearest in the direction you want to go. In other words, if you are moving to your left, your left foot would step out first and then your right foot would follow. If you are stepping to your right to get off the tracks, step with your right foot first off of the tracks and then move your left foot. As you do this, you should pivot your body so

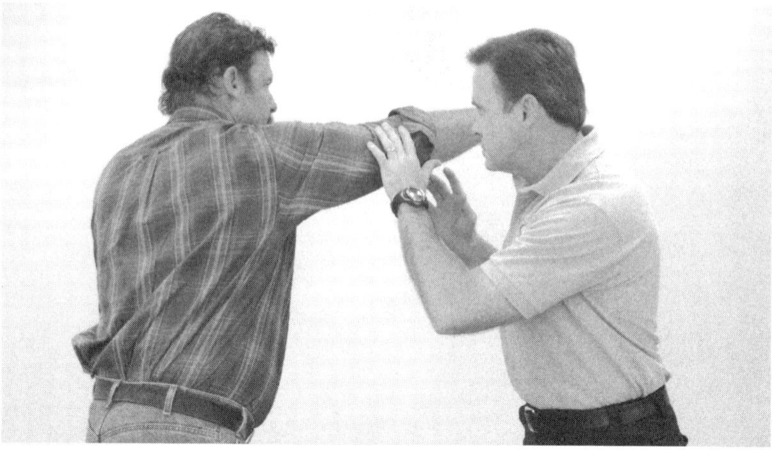

Figure 6.4 A sidestep to the outside of the subject to avoid an attack.

Figure 6.5 I need to get off the tracks to avoid getting hit by the train.

Refer to Video 6.1 at www.SurvivalSciences.com to see a properly executed side step. As was mentioned near the end of the introduction, go to the "videos" page at www.SurvivalSciences.com and type in *access@SurvivalSciences.com* as the user and *dtconcepts* as the password to gain access to the video section.

you are always in a bladed position and facing your attacker. Always face your threat. Moving in this manner is the quickest way to get off-line and out of the way of the attack. What if you make a mistake and step with your left foot first when moving to your right? It's no big deal. It will just mean you may be a microsecond slower getting your body out of harm's way. The main thing is to move and to continue to move.

Following is a drill I use to reinforce moving out of the way. I have students line up in two columns facing each other. One line is the officers. The other line is designated as the bad guys. The officers stand at the appropriate distance to conduct a field interview of an individual. On my signal, the bad folks attack by rushing forward and attempting to stab the officer with a rubber knife. The officers simply step out of the way (get off the tracks) when they recognize an attack is coming. What is interesting is the officers always easily avoid the attack with little effort and then appropriately go to a secondary weapon (in this case, a red rubber safety gun). Not once did the attackers come close to being successful. If you maintain proper distance, you remain alert to the potential for attack, and if your first reaction is to move out of the way, you become very difficult to hurt.

The side step, at any angle, is the most effective and simplest footwork to move to safety. We sidestep every day of our lives. If you walk down a crowded grocery aisle and someone is pushing a grocery cart your way, you instinctively sidestep to avoid it. If you are walking down the sidewalk and the person in front of you stops unexpectedly, again, you instinctively step to the side to avoid running into that person. Almost any sport you can think of that involves moving in an upright position entails stepping to the side. It's very natural to all of us.

Although there are many types of footwork of varying degrees of complexity, I only teach two to law enforcement officers. The first is the side step and the second is the lunge step. The lunge step can also be performed in a variety of directions. Again, I would recommend against lunging straight toward an attacker or straight back from an attacker. Just like the side step, the leg closest to the direction you want to go moves first. If you want to lunge forward, the forward leg moves first. If you want to go backwards (but not straight back, back at a 45° angle), the rear leg moves first. If you want to lunge to the right, the right leg moves first. If you want to lunge to the left, the left leg moves first.

Refer to Video 6.2 at www.SurvivalSciences.com to view examples of the lunge step.

If you are lunging in a forward direction (again at an angle to the resister), you explosively push off with your rear leg as your lead leg moves forward. The primary difference on this type of footwork is the dynamic push off from the rear leg to quickly propel you in the direction you want to go. The lunge step is effective for covering short distances very quickly. I've heard some instructors incorrectly describe a lunge step as hopping over a log. This is a bad analogy for several reasons. You don't want to go up; you want to go forward at an angle as quickly as possible. You always want your head to stay the same level or height when you move. If your head bobs up and down, it's a large visual cue to your opponent and it will tip him off you are moving. It's also bad for balance, as you now have a tendency to bounce up and down rather than moving smoothly and gracefully.

A good drill you can do on your own is to stand in a good interview or survival/response stance. Then, as vividly as possible, visualize someone attacking you with a kick, tackle, punch, or weapon. React appropriately to the visualized attack by getting off the line of attack and automatically reaching for a secondary weapon. Another way to think of a lunge step is as a fast side step.

I've given countless demonstrations to law enforcement, military, and civilian groups. I spend the majority of teaching time on simply getting out of the way of an attack. As a demonstration, I will attack an assistant instructor with a wide variety of full-speed, full-power attacks. I haven't hurt a single assistant instructor yet. This is because they know how to move. As long as they keep moving effectively, they can't be hurt. If you try this drill, I can tell you when you will get hit. You will get hit the instant you start thinking about a counterattack, or block, or anything other than getting out of the way. It's exciting to see how even the most inexperienced neophyte can avoid the attacks of highly skilled fighters by focusing on nothing more than getting out of the way.

In the late 1990s, I developed a training video on prisoner processing for the FBI. My wife was working in private industry at the time and few agents would recognize her, so I used her in the role of a white-collar subject being booked. My wife is petite. She is 5 feet 1 inch (but she'll lie and tell you she's 5 feet 2 inches), about 110 pounds, and has a cheerful disposition. She definitely is not someone you'd find threatening. During the booking process, she would "break bad" and attack the agents on scene and flee to make her escape. Knowing that they would be kicked or punched, the other agents in the training video wore martial arts chest protectors under their raid jackets to soften the blow. My wife also performed the kicks at half power. The agent role players later said they didn't have to pretend they were hurt. They were in pain from my wife's kicks even with the protective padding. The point is, you can't tell what someone's skill level is by looking at him or her. Don't take anyone lightly. Don't take chances. Avoid the attack and deal with the situation on your terms.

Movement Drills

1. Stand in front of a full-length mirror in an interview stance. Vividly visualize a variety of attacks and respond by moving out of the way (side stepping).
2. Practice side steps and lunge steps directly to the side (90° angle), to the side and forward (45° angle forward), and to the side and to the rear (45° angle to the rear). Practice moving to the right and to the left.
3. With a partner, practice moving out of the way of one attack (punch, kick, stab, or tackle attempt). Once you feel comfortable with this drill, increase the speed and intensity of the attack.
4. Using safe weapon replicas (e.g., rubber red gun or soft baton), have a partner attack you as you simultaneously move out of the way and draw the weapon. Continue to move and deploy the replica weapon as you would in reality.

Endnotes

1. FBI Uniform Crime Reporting Program, *Law Enforcement Officers Killed and Assaulted 2005*, Table 68, www.fbi.gov/ucr/killed/2005/index.htm (accessed February 9, 2010).
2. Lee, B., *The Tao of Jeet Kune Do*, Ohara Publications, Santa Clarita, CA, 1975, p. 143.

7 Handcuffing and Searching

As a law enforcement officer, what is the most dangerous thing you do? As was mentioned in Chapter 1, most injuries and deaths occur when you are arresting someone, when you have to put your hands on him and take away his freedom. Knowing this, we always need to be hyperalert when handcuffing and searching subjects. It's like the fox chasing the rabbit. For the fox (you), it's just another day earning a living and finding the next meal. For the rabbit (bad guy), it's a life-or-death chase. So which one is more motivated? Which one is more alert? More importantly, which one is more desperate?

If you have a (currently) compliant subject and are moving in to handcuff, stop, slow down, and think about what you're doing. There is no need to rush in and make a mistake. If the subject is compliant, take full advantage of it. Recognize proximity gets us killed and we are getting ready to close the distance. Recognize the inherent danger in closing that gap and treat this situation with the respect and caution it deserves.

For a standing subject, you want his hands up, elbows locked out and facing away from you. Pay particular attention to the hands and waistband area. Command the subject to slowly turn around once so you can see the entire waist area prior to leaving cover and approaching the subject. What? You're not behind cover? Why not? The only acceptable reason is no cover exists in the immediate area. If cover is present, recognize it, get behind it, and stay behind it until you're ready to make your approach. Once you have the subject facing away from you, take your handcuffs out and position them in your hand exactly like you want them so you can apply them quickly and smoothly. Keep your eyes on the subject at all times. Since the subject is complying, have him do as much of the work as possible. Command the subject to place his hands in a position that makes it easiest for you to use the handcuffing method taught to you.

Next, how do you want the subject to stand? You don't want him to be balanced and comfortable. If you allow the subject to stand normally, it takes very little skill for the subject to drive his foot back into your knee. At best, you may be good enough to overcome this attack and still get control quickly. But even then, you may have just suffered a lifelong debilitating injury that keeps you from doing the job you love. At worst, your knee will snap, the bad guy will take advantage of the situation, and kill you. Before approaching the subject, have him stand with his feet as wide apart as possible (Figure 7.1). As mentioned in Chapter 5 regarding proper distance, you want to keep a subject a little farther away than he can reach with his rear leg. He will have

Figure 7.1 A standing subject with his feet spread wide enough to disrupt his balance.

to take at least one step to reach you, and that gives you a large visual cue that an attack is on its way. Similarly, if you have the subject stand with his feet spread uncomfortably wide, he first has to bring his feet together to reestablish balance prior to launching an attack. This creates the large visual cue you want to give yourself time to react.

Approach the subject with the mindset he will turn at any second to engage you. Be prepared to let loose of the cuffs instantly as you draw a weapon. Approach forming a 45° angle to the subject's rear.

Now put yourself in the bad guy's shoes. You're being arrested, you don't want to go to jail, and you made up your mind you are going to make a break for it at the first opportunity. You may also have decided that the only person standing between you and freedom is this officer, so the officer has got to go. What is the best time for you to strike? When are your chances of success the best? The best time to attack or flee is as soon as the officer touches you. At that moment, you know the officer's weapon is holstered, you know exactly where the officer is positioned, and you know the officer's attention may be directed toward the handcuffs and not on your attack. So as soon as you are touched, you spin violently into the officer and attack.

Knowing this, what should you do to protect yourself? The answer is in your attitude and preparation. Don't get lazy when you are putting on the handcuffs. Don't think the threat is over. It's not. The danger is just beginning. Every time I put handcuffs on someone, I expect him to attack me. As soon as I touch him, I expect him to attempt to turn, push, pull, or engage me in some way. So if the bad guy does one of these things, I'm not surprised. I expect this action and I'm ready to react appropriately. As was discussed in the previous chapter, you can either engage or disengage at this point. Disengaging is probably your best option, as it allows you to reverse the action-reaction equation and gain tactical advantage. You are no longer where the attacker expected you to be. Only if you're certain you have the tactical advantage (such as you can contact the subject before he can regain balance) should you engage. Expecting an attack, you're ready to move, create distance, and draw the appropriate weapon to end the conflict and obtain control.

I don't want to discuss all of the different handcuffing methods, as there are several good techniques, and you should use what has been taught at your academy. I would suggest the technique should allow you to cuff quickly and without the need to switch hands or having to regrip the subject's wrist once you've made contact. The FBI teaches a method of grabbing the back of the subject's near hand and twisting the wrist slightly toward you to further imbalance the subject (Figures 7.2 and 7.3).

A quick note about control holds used with handcuffing. If you have a compliant subject, recognize he may become noncompliant in a hurry, but don't you do something to cause that change to noncompliance. You even see it in handcuffing practice with fellow officers. The officer with the cuffs comes up to the compliant partner and wrenches the wrist or shoulder. The other officer instinctively reacts to the pain, which is to turn abruptly and angrily toward the source of that pain. You get the same result with bad guys.

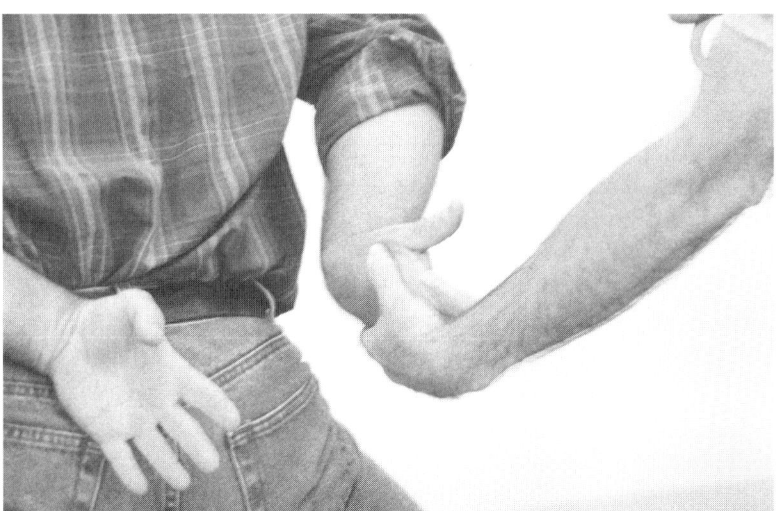

Figure 7.2 A close-up of the grab.

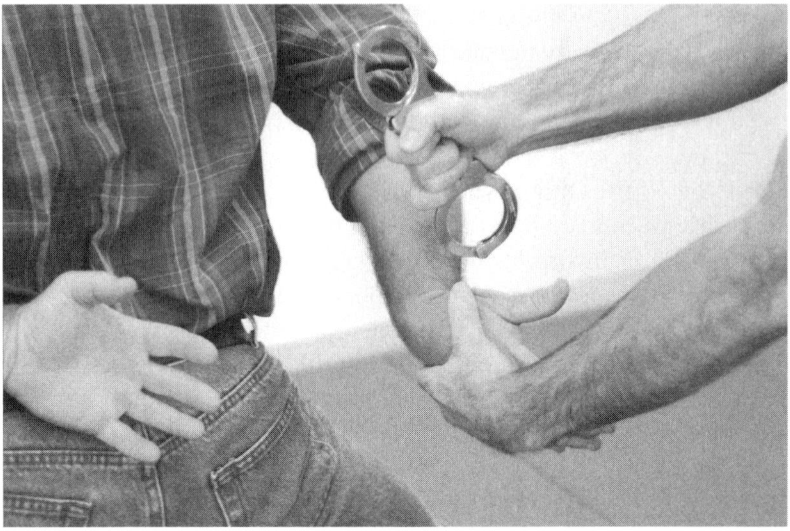

Figure 7.3 The slight twist of the wrist to drop the subject's shoulder slightly and to further imbalance the subject. This is done as the handcuffs are being applied.

Also, it will be difficult to explain in court why you separated the shoulder or broke the wrist of someone who was obeying all of your commands.

Another side note about control holds. I'll let you in on a secret that took decades of training to find out. They don't exist. There is no full-proof control hold. At best, they are a temporary control. For every technique, there is a counter. And for every counter, there is another counter, ad infinitum. For example, one technique many officers use is to have a subject interlace his fingers on the top of his head. The officer approaches a subject from the rear, grabs several of the subject's fingers and hair, and pins the subject's hands to his head. I can guarantee every one of you reading this can get out of this hold in seconds. If you truly believed you'd be given a million dollars if you could get out of that hold, and if you didn't you would be killed on the spot, all would be running free in seconds. If you are willing to lose some hair and have a broken finger or two, it's not that difficult to twist free. The bad guys can have that type of commitment—and more. So when you are using a control hold, recognize its effects are temporary and don't dally. Get the handcuffs on quickly.

Some departments teach a "speed cuffing" technique in which they have the subject place his hands together. The officer then approaches, grabs fingers from both hands, and places the handcuffs straight down onto the wrists (Figure 7.4).

No matter what technique you use, it is best to handcuff the subject with the backs of his hands together. If you handcuff someone with his palms facing, you really haven't limited his ability to grab and manipulate tools (such as

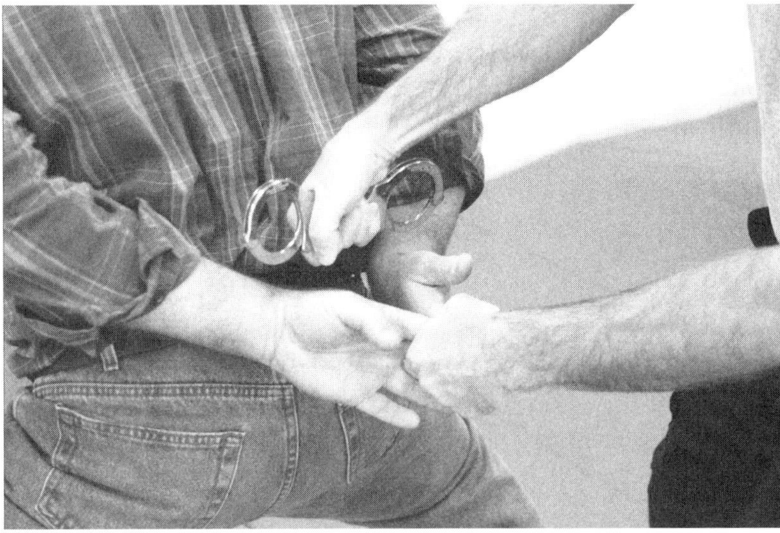

Figure 7.4 The positioning for speed cuffing.

a hidden handcuff key or pick). With palms facing inward, a person with good flexibility can bring his cuffed hands underneath his butt and legs. Now he has his hands in front of him and could use them effectively to fight. Worse, he now has the ability to pick up a weapon and use it. Try it yourself. Place your hands back to back and see how limited you are in manipulating any item. Now try it with your palms facing each other. It's a much more natural and comfortable position. As many an experienced officer has said to a bad guy who was complaining about the handcuffs, "They weren't designed to be comfortable."

The next point is never handcuff in the front. A person handcuffed in the front has too much mobility and it's too easy for him to hurt you. The only time you should ever handcuff someone to the front is when it is accompanied by a belly chain or belt. Of course, if you are ordered by a judge to handcuff a prisoner in the front, you have to comply. If you are forced to handcuff in the front due to judge's orders, watch the bad guy like a hawk. But you were doing that anyway, weren't you? It cannot be stressed enough that handcuffs are a *temporary* restraining device. Yet it is not unusual to see officers handcuff subjects, then turn their backs or leave the bad guys unattended. Don't do it.

See Video 7.1 at SurvivalSciences.com for a demonstration of a handcuffing method of a standing subject. As was mentioned near the end of the introduction, go to the "videos" page at www.SurvivalSciences.com, and type in *access@SurvivalSciences.com* as the user and *dtconcepts* as the password to gain access to the video.

If for any reason you think it will be safer to have the subject kneel prior to handcuffing, don't hesitate to have him go to a kneeling position. The same rules as handcuffing a standing subject apply to a kneeling subject. Some officers like to have the subject cross his ankles in the kneeling position. I don't. If you have a bad guy cross his ankles, you really haven't inhibited his fighting ability at all. He can still stand as quickly, and worse, he can roll into your legs to take out your knees. Just because the bad guy is kneeling doesn't mean you can relax. Another problem with having the subject cross ankles in a kneeling position is many people are physically unable to do it. They will struggle to cross their ankles, lose their balance, and then fall, causing you to lose sight of their hands. Prisoners have practiced doing just this. They fake fall forward while simultaneously drawing a weapon from the front of their waistband. Since you lose sight of their hands, you don't realize they have a weapon until they roll and bring the weapon up to fire.

Another problem is some officers like to have subjects cross their ankles and then the officers will stand on the ankles. This is a bad idea for a couple of reasons. First, as before, you haven't reduced the subject's ability to roll. It's actually worse now because your balance has become compromised. Instead of standing with both feet on the flat, stable ground, you now have one foot placed on an easily moving object (the subject's ankle), your feet are at different heights, and you are unable to balance your weight properly over both of your feet. If the subject moves in any direction, it will upset your balance. For the same reason, I hate to see officers stand over a prone subject with one foot placed on the subject's back. Trust me, you aren't keeping him pinned to the ground by standing on him with one foot. If you doubt this, try it with a friend. You'll see how easy it is to move from this position by rolling in one direction or the other. Once the bad guy does roll, your balance will be broken and lots of other very bad things could happen.

I prefer to have a kneeling subject spread his knees as wide as possible, just as I prefer to have a standing subject spread his feet. Once you approach the kneeling subject, you must stay balanced (as is true in all defensive tactics (DT) encounters). Don't reach forward off-balance to grab the subject's hand. Have the bad guy extend his hands toward you, then pull him back off-balance. As before, if he fights, just push away and draw a weapon to resolve the confrontation.

For a prone subject, it is important that you have him go to a prone position facing you. Get behind and stay behind cover if it's available. If

> See Video 7.2 at www.SurvivalSciences.com for a demonstration of handcuffing a kneeling subject.

you prone someone out facing away from you, you lose sight of at least one of his hands, and that hand could be accessing a hidden weapon. Once the subject is in a prone position, order the subject to look away from you. Approach from a 45° angle toward one of the subject's shoulders and away from his line of sight. Have the subject lift both hands off the ground, then grasp the hand nearest you, pulling it slightly toward the subject's head while ensuring the arm stays locked out. Place a cuff on this hand and then bend the arm into your handcuffing position. As you step toward the subject's feet and bring the subject's arm to his back for handcuffing, lock the subject's arm with the handcuff to his side with your knee. Place your other knee on the subject's shoulder to pin him to the ground. A better option is to use your second knee to pin the subject's neck and head to the ground. Some departments may not allow this, as damage could occur if you drop your knee into position on the subject's neck rather than place the knee in proper position. Ask for the subject's second hand. If the subject doesn't comply, you can begin running the subject's cuffed hand up his back toward his head until he complies. Grab the second hand as you simultaneously bring the handcuffed hand to meet the second hand. Handcuff and double-lock.

What happens if you get one handcuff on the subject and the subject breaks free before you get the second handcuff in place? You now have a subject armed with a dangerous weapon. The single strand of the free handcuff can now be used as a hook to cut you. Move, make distance, and draw the appropriate weapon to resolve the confrontation.

Once you get both handcuffs in place, immediately double-lock. For some reason, some officers get lazy on this and don't double-lock. You need to for two reasons. First, it's much easier to disengage a handcuff that is not double-locked. Bear in mind handcuffs are considered a temporary restraining device and you are required to closely monitor a subject even when handcuffed. The second reason is if you don't double-lock, the handcuffs can cinch down more tightly, perhaps cutting off the circulation and causing physical damage. You are responsible for the safety and well-being of your prisoner.

Okay, you have succeeded in handcuffing your subject. Now what? Now is the time to conduct a thorough, systematic search. In a U.S. Department of Justice FBI study of felonious assaults on law enforcement officers, only three out of forty-two offenders thought law enforcement searches were always thorough. I think the offenders were being generous. From what I've seen,

Video 7.3 at www.SurvivalSciences.com demonstrates handcuffing a prone subject.

very few officers conduct a thorough search. If there is one thing that will get you killed, it's failing to do a comprehensive search.

While conducting tactical, force-on-force training for FBI agents and other agencies, I would always warn the students at the beginning of the day that the bad guy role players will be armed and they will have concealed weapons. I would also tell them that if they missed a gun on a search, I promise that they and their partners would be shot in the back by the role player. During the exercises, I would randomly pick a role player to conceal a large frame revolver in the back of the waistband. This should not be a difficult weapon to find even in a sloppily conducted search. After the role player was handcuffed, I would instruct her (I usually used a female for this role) to place her cuffed hands over the concealed revolver, necessitating the searcher to physically lift the role player's hands away from the waistband and to the side to conduct a proper search. Sure enough, I had at least one team miss the gun every day of training. One team member would do a cursory high-risk area search, pass off the "cleared" role player to another student, and off they would go down a hallway. After they were out of sight of the team that was still clearing the building, the role player would draw the weapon (although handcuffed in the back) and blast the escorting officer. Being true to my word, I would then have the role player return to the search team, sneak up behind them, and shoot as many as she could with paintballs. My hope was that if agents and officers missed the concealed gun in training, the sting of the paintball and the embarrassment would be enough to ensure they would never miss a weapon when it was for real.

In a notorious incident in San Bernardino County, California, a deputy sheriff had been shot during a routine traffic stop. The subject had an extensive criminal history. When other deputies arrived on the scene, neighbors in the area pointed out the shooter. The subject was arrested, but the handgun used in the shooting of the officer was not found. The subject was taken to an interview room equipped with a video camera. In the video, one officer is initially viewed in the room with the subject and later brings the subject a bottle of water. As the subject sits in a chair submissively drinking his water, the officer steps out of the room. After the officers leave, the subject puts down his water, removes a .45 caliber handgun from his waistband, places the muzzle against his head, and shoots himself. The officer is then seen rushing into the room at the sound of the gunshot, yelling some expletives, and then states, "Nobody shook (searched) him." The first time I saw this video and upon hearing that statement, my first thought was, "Yeah, nobody searched him … including you." This event could have been much more tragic if the subject had decided to shoot a number of other people in the station prior to turning the gun on himself. He had already demonstrated he had no hesitation in shooting a deputy. Reportedly, the deputies who accepted the subject from another agency were told the subject had been searched and did not search the subject themselves prior to transporting him.

On SWAT, we had a saying: "If you bag him, you tag him." What we meant was once you encountered a subject, it was your responsibility to handcuff, search, and properly hand off the subject to a transport agent. Whenever you touched a subject, from that moment onward he became "yours" and you were responsible for re-searching and ensuring the handcuffs were still properly secured and double-locked. I don't care if the most experienced, crustiest officer in your department hands you a prisoner for you to transport and says in an authoritative manner, "You don't have to search him. I already did it." Still search the subject yourself. I don't care if the crusty veteran becomes angry or ridicules you. Search the subject again. When you accept that prisoner, he is *your* responsibility and it is *your* life.

If you succumb to the pressure of the older officer, I can tell you what will happen. If you're lucky, you won't be killed. If you're lucky, you will only be embarrassed when you hand off your prisoner to the jailer and he finds the weapons and contraband you should have found. Then your name becomes mud. I will guarantee you the seasoned veteran won't step forward to clear your name and claim responsibility for giving you bad (and potentially fatal) directions.

I used to try to trick new agents by handing off a prisoner and telling them not to worry about searching, because I already did it. If they fell for it (and few did because we specifically covered this point in tactical training), I would chew on them a little. I would then ensure they did a proper search before putting the subject in their car.

What is a proper search? It's exactly the way you were taught to do a search in your academy, but very few officers do it that way because that was "just BS training and this is the street, man!" Why do we become complacent? I discussed it in Chapter 3 on the warrior/survival mindset. Don't fall into the trap. Stay on the path of the warrior. Be professional.

A high-risk search is just that. It's a search of any area where a weapon can be reached, or any area the bad guy can access a weapon even while handcuffed. Usually this means the waistband area and pockets. If you have the subject in a kneeling position, this also includes areas around the feet, ankles, and legs. The idea behind a high-risk search is that you are in the middle of a building search or similar event, and this is just one of several possible subjects. The idea is to get him handcuffed and out of the area quickly so the rest of the team can continue with the operation. Knowing a subject is only high-risk searched means everyone has to be hypervigilant. It also means the subject has to be thoroughly searched prior to being transported.

While searching, be aware of your weapons' location at all times and ensure they are not within reach of the subject's grasp. Always keep one hand on the subject to control him, while you search him with your other hand. Always search the subject at a 45° angle to the rear of the subject if he is standing.

It's incredibly dangerous to search anyone from the front. I'm amazed how many times I see officers on reality television shows search or "pat down" someone while standing directly in front of the subject. The officer is in the worst tactical position possible, usually bent over at the waist, off-balance, and distracted as he checks the subject's pockets and legs. It wouldn't take much skill for the subject to seriously hurt the officer in this position. I cringe every time I see it happen and hold my breath hoping nothing bad happens to the officer. Please don't do it. It's just not smart.

Prior to searching, always ask if there is anything on the subject that may hurt you (e.g., weapons, syringe, or sharp objects). It's a good investment to buy a pair of cut-proof gloves. It only takes one puncture to catch an infectious disease. When you search, don't pat or just slide your hands over the subject's body. Use a methodic kneading motion and take your time. To conduct a thorough search, mentally divide the subject's body into segments. These segments are the head and neck, upper right torso, lower right extremities, upper left torso, and lower left extremities.

When searching the head, look through the hair; remove any hats, scarves, or headbands; inspect jewelry (some earrings have been modified into blades); check behind and in the ears; and check inside of the mouth. One inmate had fashioned a pocket of flesh inside his mouth in which he secreted a handcuff key. For the neck area, pay particular attention to the collar and any necklaces or chains.

In 1998, a suspect was arrested in Tampa, Florida, for shooting his four-year-old son in the face with a semiautomatic rifle. As the subject was being transported by two detectives, the subject accessed a handcuff key he wore on a chain around his neck. He had been searched earlier, but the key had not been discovered. The subject was also handcuffed in front. After surreptitiously removing the handcuffs, the subject grabbed the gun of the detective driving the car and quickly killed both detectives. The subject then retrieved the rifle he used to shoot his son from the trunk of the detective's car. He later killed a state trooper with the rifle.

What exactly are you looking for when conducting a search? It's much more than a handgun or edged weapon. You are looking for something as small as a handcuff key, or even smaller—a thin piece of plastic or metal that can be used to insert between the teeth and locking mechanism to pick the handcuff's lock. This must be your mindset as you conduct a search. If you miss something that small, you have given the bad guy an opportunity to kill you, fellow officers, and members of the public.

After conducting a thorough search of the head and neck area, move on to the body. Check all pockets, armpit areas, hands, natural body crevices, belts, belt buckles, and groin area. Always remove belts, personal property, and jewelry and keep them separate in a property bag. A special note about the groin area: Check it and then check it again. The bad guy will cast aspersions about your masculinity/femininity or sexuality, but don't fall for it. Don't fall into his trap. Be professional and meticulous. Recognize the groin area is the favorite hiding place for weapons and contraband because bad guys know officers are squeamish about thoroughly searching the groin.

Whenever you conduct a search, do it in a systematic, overlapping fashion. As you search the upper torso, go beyond the midline of the subject's body. When you search the opposite side, again you cross over the midline to make certain you have considerable overlap and avoid missing any areas. The key to being a good sniper is consistency in your preparation and actions. The same is true for being a good searcher. Do it in a consistent, thorough, and systematic fashion.

Conduct a detailed search of the legs and feet. Don't forget to check the shoes, socks, and feet of the subject. Obviously, to search these areas effectively, you must remove the subject's shoes.

What about searching subjects of the opposite gender? If possible, it's preferable to have an officer of the same sex conduct the search if he or she happens to be present. If not, search the subject as thoroughly and professionally as you always would. If you have a partner, have your partner witness the search to save you from false allegations and problems later. If you work alone but have a dash cam, then conduct the search in view of the camera if it is safe to do so.

If you have another officer search your subject because of gender issues, you are still responsible for ensuring the search is complete. Make sure you watch as the officer conducts the search. If you believe an area has been missed, don't hesitate to ask the other officer to search that area again. A San Diego county sheriff's deputy was responsible for transporting a female prisoner who had been searched by a female officer from another agency. During the drive to the jail, the prisoner had removed her handcuffs and accessed a hidden handgun. The deputy and a ride-along bailed out of the vehicle to avoid getting shot. It was later determined the prisoner had tried to shoot the deputy, but the gun had malfunctioned.

This should be a review of everything you've been taught at your academy, but when is the last time you saw an officer remove a subject's shoes as part of the search? If a handcuffed subject is in a kneeling position, doesn't that subject have access to the ankle and feet area? Why do we insist on being complacent? Why do we take shortcuts that endanger our lives and the lives of others? Don't be careless. Expect to find something. Be the one officer that others on your department look to for the right way, the professional way, to do things.

Please visit www.SurvivalSciences.com and view Video 7.4 to view proper searching of a subject.

Video 7.5 at www.SurvivalSciences.com depicts the large number of weapons that can be easily concealed.

Subject Control

8

Subject control techniques are best used on passive resisters. It is difficult (and therefore dangerous) to attempt to use a control technique on an aggressive resister. It is possible to successfully use a control technique against someone who is actively trying to hurt you, but it requires a higher level of skill and training—a level of skill many officers do not possess. Given the option, it is safer to use nonlethal weapons such as the TASER, impact weapon, or pepper spray against an aggressive resister. I also recognize that subjects can instantly go from passively resistant to aggressively resistant or even deadly resistant. In those moments, it is typically best to create distance and go to the appropriate weapon. Sometimes you may not have that option because the subject successfully locked you up before you could react. In that situation, you can use the techniques discussed in this chapter to break free of your attacker, move away, and go to the appropriate weapon as soon as possible.

Although a variety of throws, trips, and joint manipulations are typically taught in law enforcement academies, a simpler and more effective response is to focus on core principles. One overriding DT rule is to always maintain your balance while you disrupt the resister's balance. This can be done in a number of ways, but the most direct approach is to attach and move. The concept is for you to attach to the resister in a safe position (preferably to the resister's rear at a 45° angle) and then drop your weight out and down at a 45° angle (where the resister's balance is at its weakest).

Since there may be some confusion about what is meant by "out and down," let me explain it further. Standing in a neutral stance (feet side by side at shoulder's width), point your right arm out at a 45° angle to your front right. Your right arm should be extended, parallel to the ground, halfway between directly in front of you and directly to your right side. That is the 45° angle. Step with your right foot in the direction your arm is pointing. You have now stepped out at a 45° angle. Next, think of your center of gravity or belt buckle area. Previously as you stepped, your belt buckle remained the same height. Step again in the same direction as before, but this time make sure as you are stepping out you also ensure your belt buckle is steadily dropping in height as you step by bending your knees. This results in you moving in two directions at once. Your weight is moving outwards and down toward the ground. Moving in two directions makes it very difficult for an attacker to counter the move. Moving in two directions makes it easier for you to take your attacker's balance.

Going back to Chapter 5 on fundamentals, we want to use our bodyweight efficiently and typically move at a 45° angle to the resister. Almost all defensive tactics (DT) programs teach approaching a resister from the 45° angle to the rear of the resister. If you can get to this position, great. If you can't, the techniques described will work at any angle, but you want to avoid being directly in front of the resister. A typical law enforcement approach is to grab the resister's wrist with your rear hand and simultaneously grab the resister's elbow area with your hand nearest the resister (some departments refer to this as a c-clamp). Since almost all officers were taught this position, it is a natural place to begin.

Option 1 (Attach and Move)

Visualize this: A person is standing normally and with good balance. What would happen if you could sneak up and invisibly attach a 100-pound weight to his side? He would lose his balance and would fall. That is the same concept for attach and move. The attach and move technique is effective if you only weigh 100 pounds. It's even better if you weigh more. Physical therapists will tell you improperly lifting even a few pounds can wrench your back. This is why you don't need to push or pull and exert a great amount of energy. You simply attach your body weight to the resister and step out in a direction he doesn't expect.

You need to step close to the resister to latch on properly. Don't try to do this technique from a distance. If you grab an opponent while you are reaching, you are likely to be off-balance. Your goal is always to maintain your balance while upsetting the balance of your resister. Step close to the resister and apply the c-clamp, two-handed grip to his arm. Once you've latched on to the resister, immediately step away from the resister at a 45° angle from which he is facing, either to the front or the rear (depending on if you want the resister to fall on his face or his back). Let your body weight drop, as was mentioned in Chapter 5 and as mentioned above in this chapter. Remember the drill at the end of Chapter 5 to practice relaxing and increasing your weight on the mechanical scale? The key is not to pull the arm or attempt to "muscle" the technique. Simply use your body weight in a relaxed fashion by stepping out and down, lowering your center of gravity to allow gravity and your dead weight to assist you. Don't cross your feet as you step. Step out and down with the foot closest to the direction you want to go. Think of changing your opponent's balance, not fighting (Figures 8.1 and 8.2).

That's it! It may seem too simple (and it is simple), but it relies on the proper fundamentals and body mechanics described earlier. The key is to

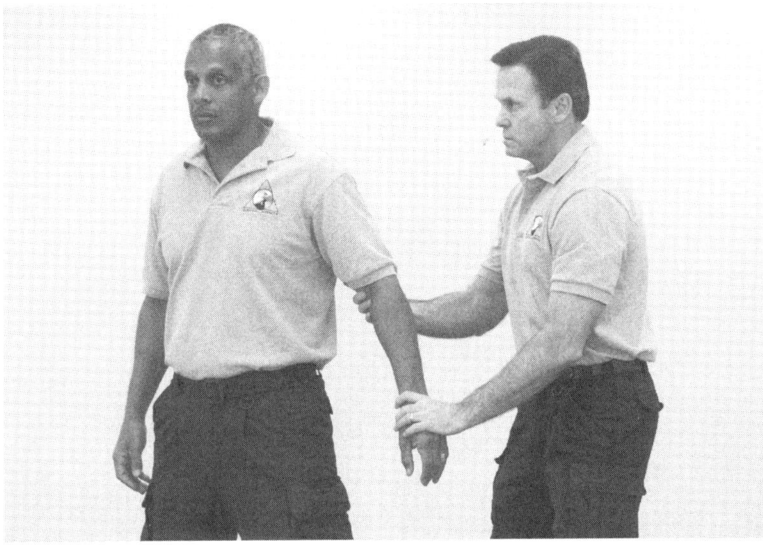

Figure 8.1 The proper position as you first attach to the resister.

Figure 8.2 The movement down and out at a 45° angle, taking the resister's balance.

latch on and step (don't pull) at a 45° angle while simultaneously dropping your body weight. You don't even have to grab the resister's wrist and elbow. It works equally well if you grab the resister's bicep, belt, shoulder, or best of all, collar. You can usually grab the collar even if you can't get completely behind the subject. When you grab the collar, first pull back to get the bad

Figure 8.3 The knee press to take the subject's balance, which would be followed by the officer stepping out and down.

Please see Video 8.1 at www.SurvivalSciences.com to view the attach and move technique. Use the user name and pass code listed in the introduction.

guy on his heels, then drop your weight down. If you feel the need to supplement the move, you can first break the resister's balance by pushing on his knee with your foot just prior to stepping out (Figure 8.3).

Option 2 (Arm Bar)

An arm bar technique can be used to supplement option 1, or it can be used as a separate technique. Anytime the resister offers you a straight arm (such as to fend you off, push you away, etc.), an arm bar is a viable option. As before, your rear hand grabs the resister's wrist as your hand nearest to the resister is placed on the straight arm of the resister just above his elbow. Don't attempt to pull the resister to you; it won't work if he is bigger or stronger. Simply step toward the resister to get in the proper position. Lock the resister's hand to your hip and then use the knife edge of your other hand to apply downward and forward pressure on the resister's elbow in a cutting motion. The resister's elbow should be at your center of gravity, or belt buckle area. Almost every technique should be brought to your center/belt buckle. Think of it this way: If you were to carry a heavy box, you wouldn't do it with your arms extended. You carry a heavy object by bringing it close to your body, arms relaxed, and placed near your belt buckle.

As always, don't think of using strength to take the resister down. Lock the elbow in place, drop your body weight while maintaining pressure on the resister's elbow, and take him to the ground face first. Drop straight down to minimize the resister's ability to counter. Step out and lower the resister more gradually if you choose to be more gentle. Once the resister is on the ground, continue to apply pressure to the elbow area while simultaneously levering upwards on his captured hand.

Once the resister is on the ground, rotate the resister's elbow forwards toward his head to force it to bend into a proper position for handcuffing. Immediately block the resister's bent arm against his body by assuming a kneeling position. One of your knees is against the resister's head and the other knee is against the resister's elbow, locking it into his side and preventing him from rolling. Pressure can be applied by directing the resister's hand toward his head. Handcuff this hand first, then ask for the second hand. If the resister is unwilling to bring the second hand to a handcuffing position at the small of his back, you can increase the pressure by continuing to drive the handcuffed hand toward his head until the resister complies (Figure 8.4).

Please see Video 8.2 at www.SurvivalSciences.com to view the arm bar technique in its entirety.

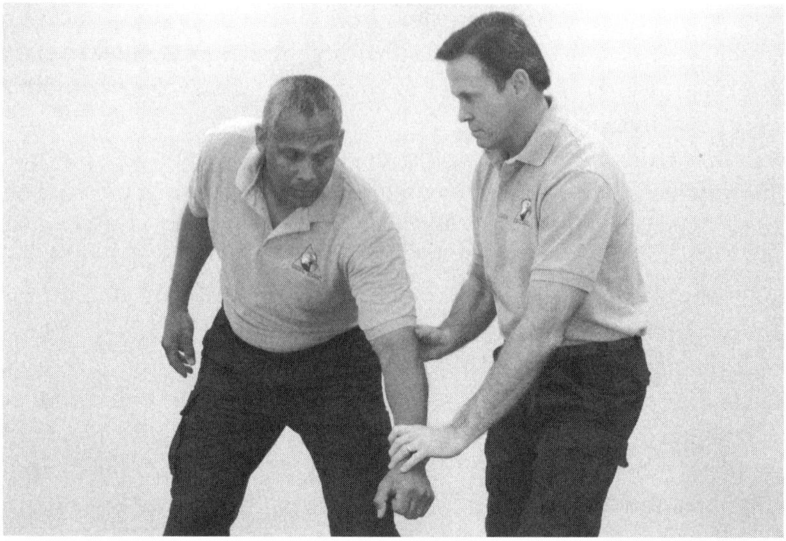

(A)

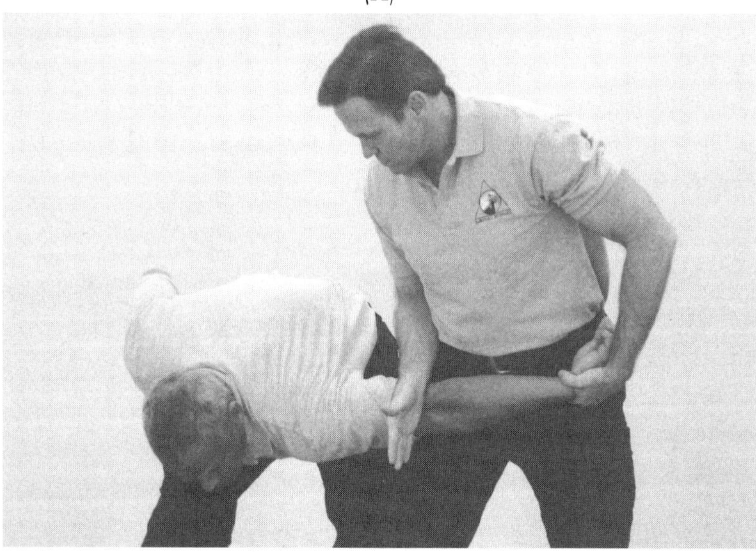

(B)

Figure 8.4 (A) The initial position for the application of the arm bar. (B) A view of the hand position of the arm bar and of bringing the resister's elbow to the officer's belt buckle area. (Continued)

(C)

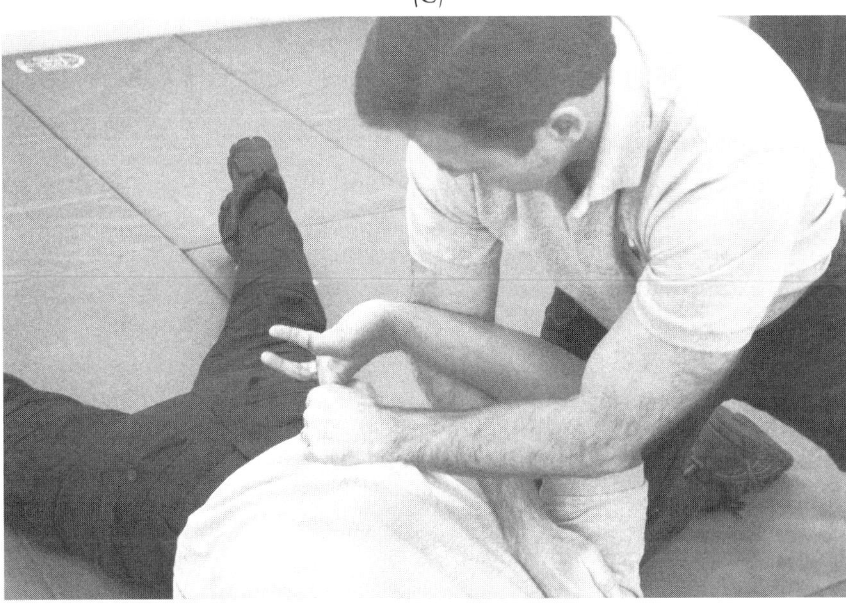

(D)

Figure 8.4 (Continued) (C) The resister being forced to the ground using the arm bar. (D) The position to lock the resister's arm in place in preparation of handcuffing.

Option 3 (Chin-Neck Takedown)

This option is based on the simple principle of "where the head goes, the body goes." The actual technique involves grabbing the resister's chin with one hand while your other hand grabs the back of the resister's head. You then rotate the resister's head around and down.

Safety was mentioned in Chapter 4, but this technique requires a special warning. When practicing this technique with a partner, you **must** perform it slowly and gently. Your partner is in a vulnerable position and injury is likely if you jerk or snap your partner's head into position.

The chin-neck takedown is a simple technique, but you aren't likely to be successful if you reach out for the resister's head. People instinctively protect the head, so the resister is likely to block or push your arm away if you reach toward him. You have to be more subtle to be successful. You may want to first distract the resister by lightly grabbing one of his hands or arms. He will tend to focus on releasing his hand by pulling away or toward you. As always, you are constantly moving. After touching the resister's hand, slide your hand up the midline of the resister's body to the chin and place your other hand behind the resister's head. Or you can step in and run your hand up the midline of the resister's body. Most people don't see this move or don't recognize it as threatening. Once your hand is in position on the resister's chin, you can now do the technique.

Rotate the resister's chin up and around at a 45° angle. You reinforce this motion with your other hand by pulling the back of the resister's head down and around as you push the chin up and around. Think of it as rolling a ball.

You can also successfully perform the chin-neck takedown with one hand. If necessary, the hand on the chin is sufficient to take the resister's balance if you use your body weight properly by stepping into the resister. To repeat myself, be very careful when practicing this move, as it is easy to tweak someone's neck. Practice the technique at a slow, smooth, gentle speed (Figure 8.5).

A slight variation of the chin-neck takedown is to use the subject's shoulders as your attachment point rather than the chin. To take the subject's balance, you use your body weight as described in performing an o-soto-gari as described in Chapter 5 on the essential fundamentals. Think of pivoting the subject's shoulders around on a central axis as you simultaneously drive or drop (depending on the direction you are taking the subject) your weight

Video 8.3 at www.SurvivalSciences.com shows the chin-neck takedown from the initial contact with the resister to completion.

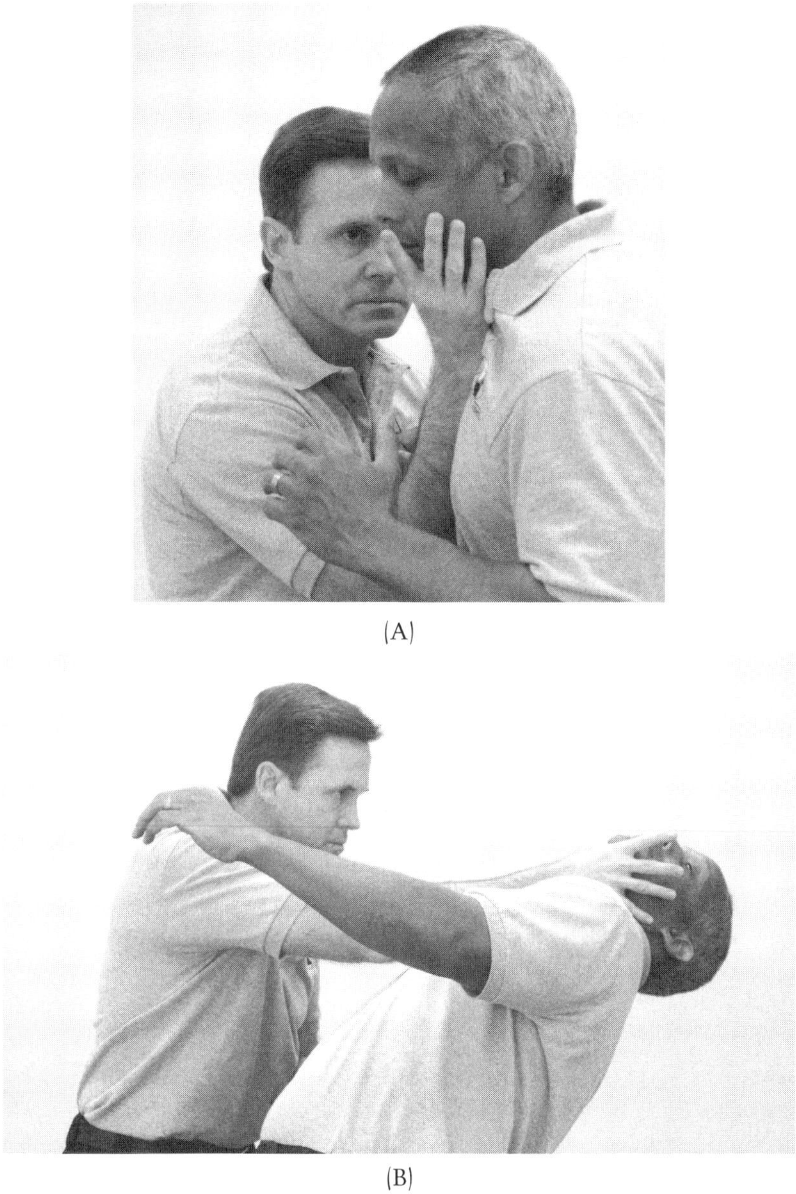

(A)

(B)

Figure 8.5 (A) The initial setup position for the chin-neck takedown. Note that you never stand directly in front of the resister. (B) The rotating movement used to break the resister's balance and take him to the rear.

Video 8.4 at www.SurvivalSciences.com shows the shoulder twist variation.

down at a 45° angle. It is important that you also think of moving the subject down at an angle rather than just spinning him in place.

Option 4 (Resister Actions)

Once you make initial physical contact with a resister, he may stay in place, turn toward you (and possibly attempt to strike you), pull his arm away from you, or turn and attempt to flee. If the resister remains stationary and doesn't make any overt moves, apply the techniques as described.

If the resister turns toward you, remember to constantly move. In this case you will rotate away from the resister as you apply the technique. A note of caution is necessary. The reason you chose to apply a control hold is you determined the person is a passive resister. If the person turns toward you to strike you, he is now clearly an aggressive resister. If you feel that the control hold is properly in place and you are confident you can safely take the resister to the ground, then do so. However, don't get locked into doing the takedown. Don't think that since you started the technique, you have to finish it to completion. You don't. Don't fight. If the resister has escalated the confrontation, you always have the option of pushing away and going to an appropriate weapon. I've repeatedly seen officers get tunnel vision while trying to force a technique to work. Never insist on a technique, or you will get hit (or worse) as you continuously try to muscle the technique and make it work. If it doesn't work, that's okay. Break away, maintain a safe distance, and reassess.

If the resister pulls his arm away from you but his feet remain in place, then you can step in the direction of his movement and continue to apply pressure with the technique. Sticking to the general concepts, don't resist his movements, don't fight, don't "chase" after a technique, and don't try to force the technique to work. This is a great time to use redirection of force. As the resister tries to pull his arm in one direction, don't pull in the opposite direction (force against force), but instead step and use your body weight to go in the same direction as his pull (Figure 8.6).

If the resister pulls away from you as if he is attempting to flee, don't chase after his arm. Step with him as he pulls his shoulder nearest you away. To do so, he is rotating his body away from you and shifting his balance. Instead of trying to reengage the same side, simply place your hand on the resister's opposite shoulder (the one that is now rotating toward you as he

(A)

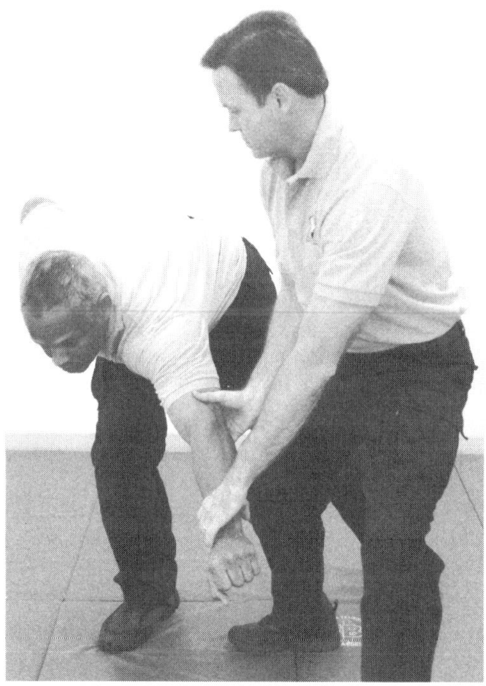

(B)

Figure 8.6 (A) The resister pulling his arm away as you make contact. (B) The officer using redirection of force, stepping in the direction the resister is pulling, and applying the technique.

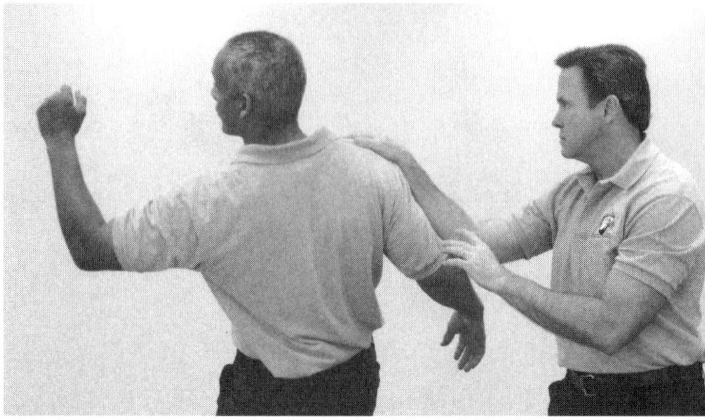

Figure 8.7 The officer rotating the resister's far shoulder down and at an angle as the resister attempts to flee.

At www.SurvivalSciences.com, Video 8.5a depicts the proper response to the resister turning toward you. Video 8.5b depicts the resister pulling his arm up after the officer has first made contact. In Video 8.5c, the resister attempts to pull his arm away. In Video 8.5d, the resister attempts to turn and run away.

attempts to step away), and use your body weight to rotate the resister down and to the ground at a 45° angle (Figure 8.7).

Never attempt to force a technique or chase after a technique. If you are using strength rather than proper movement and body weight, then you are not doing the technique correctly. You are also wasting a lot of energy needlessly. If the resister pulls away, let him. Just step with him, grab the opposite shoulder, and rotate him to the ground.

Option 5 (Resister on the Ground)

What if the resister is on the ground and you were unable to control him and put him into a position suitable for handcuffing? How do you immobilize the resister on the ground who is still moving and resisting? First, let's talk about what not to do, but is commonly done. Do not jump on top of him. If you are sprawled on top of the resister (even if you are in a good mount position), you have to worry about the security of all the weapons on your duty belt. You are also vulnerable to attack by other subjects since you are now locked up with the one subject and can't extricate yourself quickly if necessary. Finally, your visual field is limited because you are face-to-face with the bad guy in close proximity.

Another bad idea is a dog pile maneuver. Usually the ones who get hurt in a dog pile are the officers. Let's look at a typical approach in attempting to control a bad guy with a dog pile. Officers swarm the subject, everyone grabs a limb or any body part available, and a massive struggle takes place until the bad guy is finally handcuffed. Afterwards, the officers are all breathing heavily, sweating like goats, and thinking how tough the bad guy was to control. Some officers may be nursing sprains and bruises suffered when another officer jumped into the fray or from the impact from swirling, random appendages. What happened? Whenever you resort to a dog pile maneuver, you're ignoring basic physics. It works great if you all have trained together extensively and each officer has a clear understanding of specific roles and responsibilities. But this is typically not the case. Officer Brown is pulling on bad guy's left arm. Officer Jones is pulling in the opposite direction on bad guy's right arm. Officer Smith is trying to roll bad guy to his left, while Officer Johnson is trying to pin bad guy's legs together. The bad guy just needs to relax as the officers strain and struggle, never realizing they're working against each other.

A friend from a large department said it was common practice for officers to be told by a sergeant during a struggle, "You'd better get in there and grab something!" The intention was good, as the idea was to reinforce the idea of teamwork and helping your partner. Particularly today, many officers have never been in a fight and they're hesitant to get involved. The supervisor's attitude is you better get your hands dirty. You better learn how to handle a physical confrontation. But the results were poor because officers jump in not having a clue what to do. Their participation actually becomes counterproductive to controlling the bad guy.

So going back to the original question, what is the best way to control a resistive subject who is on the ground? The key is to lock the resister's hip and shoulder to the ground. This is actually fairly easy to do. You kneel on the resister, placing one knee on his shoulder and the other on his hip. Pressure should be directed straight down through the resister's shoulders and hips to the ground. Do not apply pressure at an angle, as this will allow the resister to roll. If the resister's hips and shoulders are pinned, he is unable to roll or get up. In a kneeling posture, you are able to scan for additional threats and both of your hands are free. If the resister attempts to grab your leg or arms, let him. It's no big deal. The key is to think about **moving**, not **fighting**. If the resister grabs your arm or hand, that's great. Just apply pressure downwards using gravity and your body weight to pin his hands (Figure 8.8).

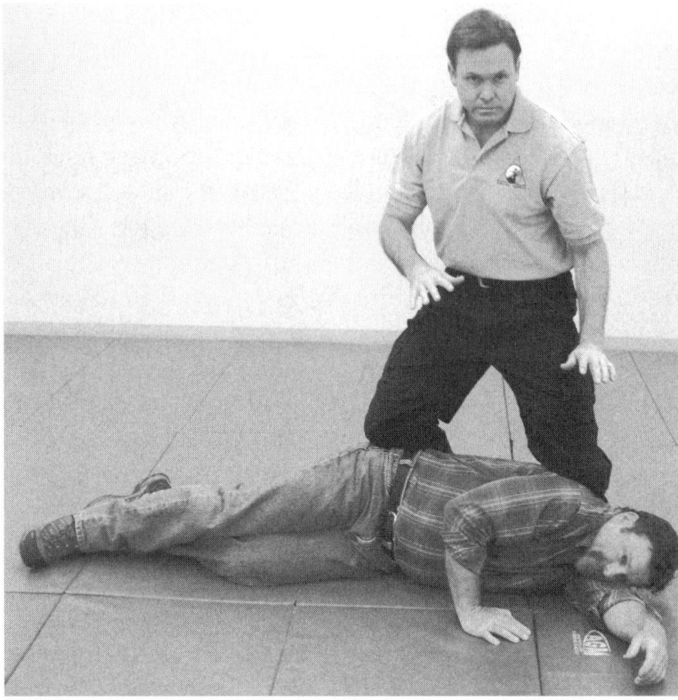

Figure 8.8 The proper position of this ground immobilization. Notice my knees are directly over the resister's shoulders, locking them in place. The same is done to lock the resister's hips.

Please review Video 8.6 at www.SurvivalSciences.com for a demonstration of the ground immobilization technique.

Drills

1. Approach a partner and attach using the grip as shown in Figure 8.1. Practice smoothly stepping out and down at a 45° angle to bring your partner to the ground. The key element to this drill is finding your partner's balance and learning to effectively change and disrupt that balance.
2. Practice the arm bar technique as demonstrated in Video 8.2. At times, have your partner bend his elbow to prevent the arm bar. What you should discover is you can easily transition to the "attach and move" to take your partner to the ground. You already have a grip on your partner, so don't be overly concerned if you lose the arm

bar position. Continue to move down and out at a 45° angle and you will take your partner to the ground.

3. Practice reaching directly toward your partner's chin and see how easily your partner is able to slap your hand away. Experiment with running your hand up your partner's midline as shown in Video 8.3 to set up the chin-neck takedown. Also, experiment with distracting your partner with a touch elsewhere to the body followed by your hand flowing up to the chin. Remember to apply the chin-neck takedown slowly and smoothly to avoid injuring your partner.
4. Once you are comfortable with the techniques listed above, have your partner attempt to break free of your grip by turning toward you or away from you. Remember not to insist on the technique or try to fight force with force. Move with your partner's actions and use redirection of force to take your partner to the ground.
5. Have your partner lie on the ground as you stand. Position yourself so that you are able to place one knee over your partner's hips and the other knee over the shoulder. Apply pressure straight down to the ground by dropping your weight and remaining in an upright position. From this position, practice rotating one of your partner's arms to the rear to a handcuffing position.

The Art of Not Getting Hit

9

The most important skill in ensuring your survival is your defensive capabilities. Fortunately, obtaining a high level of defensive skill is relatively easy, particularly if your primary concern is getting out of the way of an attack. As discussed in Chapter 6 on getting out of the way, the best defensive technique is to simply move. Move out of the way. Move out of the line of attack. Get off the tracks. Go to a weapon to thwart continued attacks.

Defense is also about your mindset. In *The Art of War,* Sun Tzu wrote, "Supreme excellence is not winning every battle, supreme excellence is breaking your enemy's resistance without going to battle."[1] It's the same for us. We don't want to fight every person we arrest. I think it's safe to say almost all law enforcement officers prefer to have every subject comply with our commands. Bad guys aren't looking for a challenge. Neither should you. If you're professional, if you're competent, if you're alert, you greatly reduce the odds of a bad guy trying to fight you. Remember, we are not paid to fight. We are paid to win. We are paid to put bad people in jail as efficiently and safely as possible.

I think we all know that one rogue officer with a chip on his shoulder and a personality defect. The one with the inferiority complex who has to show everyone how tough and macho he is. (I use the masculine term because females typically don't suffer from this defect.) We had an FBI agent in the late 1980s I'll call X who met this description. It seemed as if every arrest he was on resulted in a confrontation. Was it just because he was unlucky and always ended up with the bad guy who just refused to go quietly? No, X always ended up in a scuffle because he was a jerk. He delighted in provoking fights. Fortunately for X, he was a good fighter and he always won these confrontations, which he seemed to initiate. Before long, other agents chose not to work with him, realizing no good could come from his behavior. They also recognized it as just being wrong. A friend of mine from the LAPD says they call officers with this trait "ankle biters." These are the ones who puff out their chests and want to get in the last lick as the subject is being led off in handcuffs. My LAPD friend says another word for an ankle biter is coward.

I believe in the axiom "Be polite. Be professional. Be prepared to kill everyone you meet." That may be a little harsh, and some will take offense to the wording, but let's explore it.

Be polite. It is not a sign of weakness to be polite. Hopefully our parents taught us this at the beginning of our lives. As someone who has taken an oath to protect and serve the public, it is your duty to be polite to those you serve.

As a warrior class, we serve the community. If you are polite and respectful, at least you will not be the instigator in any confrontation you may face.

Be professional. We must always strive to be professional. We represent ourselves, our agency, our community, our municipality, and our profession. One bad apple just makes a very difficult job that much harder for the rest. Being professional means looking sharp and acting sharp. It also means knowing the law, your department policies, and your department procedures—and abiding by them. Don't take shortcuts and don't become complacent.

Be prepared to kill everyone you meet. Please recognize the humor in this and don't take it too literally. It is a reminder to always be alert. I don't want you to become paranoid, but I also don't want you to think you can read people and let your guard down. Everyone you meet, who is not a friend, should not be allowed to invade your personal space. During every contact with the public you serve, you should be in a bladed stance, weight balanced over your feet, at a proper distance to allow you to react successfully to an attack, and alert to any signs of danger.

In defense, what are you looking at? In the academy, you were taught to watch the hands. It's still good advice. The hands will kill you. I remember one "expert" who was brought in to train our SWAT team over a two-day period. I'll call the expert Bubba. Bubba said we should watch the opponent's eyes to see if they were dilated. I almost laughed when he said that because I was certain he couldn't be serious. I was wrong—he was serious. If you are close enough to see if the subject's eyes are dilated, you are way too close. Obviously, Bubba had never worked in law enforcement. Watch the hands, watch the hands, and oh yeah, don't forget to watch the hands.

The simpler and more practiced your response to an attack, the less thought it requires and the quicker you'll be. We already discussed your first instinct upon being attacked should be to move. If that has become your muscle memory (and I hope it becomes so soon if it isn't already), then it requires very little thought. This means all of the rest of your brain cells can now concentrate on monitoring the resister and successfully deploying a weapon.

Now let's discuss the actual technique (beyond moving out of the way). First, never reach out to block an attack that can't reach you. We've all seen photos in martial arts magazines and self-defense books in which the defender is shown blocking a punch or a kick that is at full extension and is clearly still a foot short of even touching the defender (Figure 9.1). Worse, you will see some photos of the defender reaching forward, obviously off-balance in an attempt to block a strike (Figure 9.2).

Why? If the attack can't reach me, I'm not interested in reaching out, upsetting my balance, and exposing vital organs to a follow-up attack. If I moved properly, the attack will fall short and there is no need to block. Good defense is not waving your arms around and intercepting an attack. Good defense is using your legs to get out of the way.

Figure 9.1 The officer blocking an attack that will clearly fall short of its target.

Figure 9.2 The officer giving up his balance to reach to make a block.

If for some reason you failed to move (e.g., you're in a corner, you were sleeping, you forgot to maintain proper distance, etc.) and are forced to block, think about catching a baseball. Most of us have caught a ball repeatedly in our lives. It shouldn't take too much thought. You simply put both hands up and catch the ball. You see boxers do this all of the time. A jab

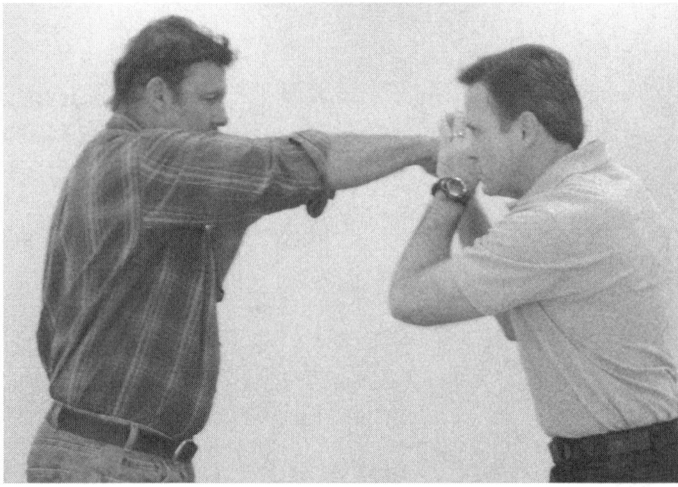

Figure 9.3 Catching a punch.

or cross will come screaming in at their head and the boxer will simply "catch" the punch with both hands (Figure 9.3). Just like you don't reach out to catch a ball in baseball (unless you're playing first base), don't reach out for the strike. Let it come, catch it, and then deflect it to the side. It should be a relaxed motion with your elbows at your sides rather than flailing or reaching out.

GET 1 (Guard, Extract, Tactical Advantage)

If you really got caught off-guard, another defensive technique used very effectively by fighters is a guard position. You drop your center of gravity into a very low, wide stance and bring both hands up to protect your head. Your elbows should be along the sides of your rib cage and your body bladed to protect your vital organs. Your head is down, eyes are up, and your chin buried in your chest (Figure 9.4 and 9.5).

> Video 9.1 at www.SurvivalSciences.com shows moving away from an attacker using GET 1 while striking. Use the user name and pass code listed in the introduction to access the video.

Figure 9.4 A side view of GET 1.

Figure 9.5 A front view of GET 1.

GET 2

Another version is to use the same deep, wide stance, but now bring your lead arm up with your elbow pointing toward your attacker. The lead arm is wrapped around your head. Your rear arm is wrapped around your body as if you are hugging yourself. Your chin is down and you look over your lead elbow. Joe Frazier, Ken Norton, and George Foreman used this defensive position with great effectiveness throughout their boxing careers. You can also reverse the arm position and have your rear arm wrap around your head and your lead arm wrap around your body (Figures 9.6 and 9.7).

The key to both of the above defensive positions is you must continue to move! If you stay in place and pretend to be a turtle, your attacker will pummel you. Don't be a punching bag. The two defensive positions are simply to buy you a moment of protection until you can move off-line and deploy another weapon. When you think of GET, think of covering up and GET-ting out of the way. Your objective is to **guard** against the attack, immediately **extract** yourself from the dangerous position (MOVE), and get to a position of **tactical** advantage so you can effectively deploy a weapon. The position of tactical advantage, as mentioned earlier in Chapter 5 on fundamentals, is off-line to your attacker, forcing the attacker to turn and reposition to continue the attack.

Figure 9.6 A side view of GET 2.

Figure 9.7 A front view of GET 2.

You can extract yourself more safely by adding a personal weapon strike as you move away from your attacker. If using GET 1, a strike that flows smoothly as you step out at an angle is a hook to the attacker's floating rib or jaw area. From the GET 1 position, step to the side while simultaneously rotating your body and striking with a hook. Continue to move at an angle to your attacker as you draw a weapon.

If you're using GET 2, and your lead arm is wrapped around your head, you are set up to deliver a brachial strike to your attacker. A brachial strike is delivered by raising your lead arm and striking downward at a 45° angle into the side of the attacker's neck. To increase the power of the strike, drop your weight as you strike. (How to generate power will be discussed in Chapter 11.) Immediately after you strike, step away at an angle from the attacker as you draw a weapon.

In summary, be professional, but alert. The best block for defense is not being forced to block. Use your legs to get you out of the way of an attack. Failing that, use GET 1 or GET 2 for protection against the initial barrage, get out of the way as quickly as possible, and deploy another weapon that is best for the situation (e.g., personal weapons, pepper spray, TASER, baton, handgun, etc.) and within your department's policy.

Video 9.2 at www.SurvivalSciences.com shows moving away from an attacker using GET 2 while striking.

Drills

1. Recognizing good defense is primarily using your legs to get out of the way of an attack; "shadowbox" your defense. Stand in front of a mirror in an interview or response stance, visualize a variety of attacks, and then quickly move to the side to avoid the attack.
2. Shadowbox "catching" a strike as you simultaneously deflect the strike and step to the side.
3. Shadowbox GET 1 or GET 2 (one will probably feel more natural and comfortable to you—stick with that one), as well as a strike to your attacker as you sidestep at an angle away from your attacker and draw a weapon.
4. With a partner and appropriate safety gear, practice the GET 1 or GET 2. Remember never to stand there and take a beating. As soon as possible, move to a position of tactical advantage.

Endnotes

1. Tzu, S., *The Art of War,* edited by James Clavell, Delacorte Press, New York, 2003.

Countering Common Attacks 10

The most common types of attacks against law enforcement officers were discussed in Chapter 1 based upon recent studies. The expected attacks are to be punched, kicked, pushed, tackled, or bitten. Chapter 6 provided the best response to all of these attacks: simply move out of the way and draw the appropriate weapon to stop the attack and obtain control and compliance. However, many officers and instructors I have taught often ask for defensive tactics (DT) techniques to counter other attacks commonly seen in the street. Typically, they include grabs, bear hugs, headlocks, and chokes. As was mentioned before, please be aware you should never find yourself in a situation in which someone can put you in a headlock, bear hug, etc. If you do, you most likely violated the guideline on distance and weren't alert to the potential threat. But since we are human and sometimes make mistakes, we'll cover these areas now. All of the responses will continue the same theme throughout this book—proper use of your body weight combined with moving by stepping out and down at a 45° angle. Chapter 8 on subject control explained the concept of stepping out and down in detail.

If you do find yourself in one of the attacks to be covered in this chapter and you failed to move out of the way, the appropriate response doesn't change. No matter what is happening, if you continue to move and do it with balance, you are likely to survive. If instead you freeze up, remain in place, and attempt to use force against force, then things will probably go badly. Always remember to move.

As mentioned in Chapter 5 on fundamentals, every technique described involves upsetting your attacker's balance while maintaining your balance. Once you take the attacker's balance, he must either release his grip on you or injure himself as he falls.

Grab

One of the simplest attacks to defeat is a grab. It doesn't matter if someone grabs your wrist, forearm, elbow, upper arm, shoulder, etc. Your response will be the same. You want to immediately lower your center of gravity and bring your arms up in a defensive position (the survival/response stance described in Chapter 5). Your hands should be in a protective position near your head with your palms facing you ("look at your palms") as you simultaneously step out and down at a 45° angle to your attacker. If the attacker has grabbed

Figure 10.1 A close-up of the result of an officer looking at her palm. The attacker must either let go or have his wrist injured.

your hand, wrist, elbow, or arm, by bringing your hands up with your palms facing inwards, you automatically torque the attacker's wrist. Stepping out and down will cause the attacker to lose his balance if he insists on maintaining his grip (Figures 10.1 and 10.2).

It's that simple. Don't try to stand in place and fight the grab. If you are stationary, you are not changing the action-reaction equation. You are right where the attacker wants you, and he is likely to follow up the grab with a punch, kick, knife thrust, or worse. You must move instinctively and immediately upon someone invading your space or being touched. Don't stand in place waiting to see what will happen next. If you do, I can almost guarantee you won't like what you see.

Many years ago, I was with another agent and our dates in Santa Monica. While standing on a busy, crowded street corner waiting for the light to change, a homeless man approached me from the rear and touched me. Instinctively, upon being touched, I swung away from the touch, forcefully knocked his hand away, and said, "Don't touch me again." I was angry and I was poised for an attack. I was angry at myself for being so engrossed

Video 10.1 at www.SurvivalSciences.com depicts the defense against a grab. Use the user name and pass code listed in the introduction to access the video.

Figure 10.2 The officer responding to a grab by bringing her hands up in a protective position, the grabbed palm facing inward, while simultaneously stepping out and down at a 45° angle. The grab is already being broken, as is the attacker's balance.

in the social aspects of my date that I didn't sense the man's approach. I was angry at the man for daring to touch me. My agent friend seemed embarrassed at my actions and even made a sarcastic comment about how I was spreading good cheer and good will toward mankind. I think my response was appropriate. No one has the right to invade your space without your consent, and certainly no one should touch you without your consent. If touched, move immediately.

Bear Hug

The initial defense to a bear hug attempt is the same as to a tackle. As was demonstrated in Chapter 6, the proper response is simply to move out of the way. Assuming you failed to do that and now your attacker has wrapped his arm around you in a bear hug, the response is still the same; you want to move out of the way. The only difference is now the attacker is attached to your body. This doesn't make it any more difficult for you. It should make it more painful for the attacker. Regardless of if you are in a rear bear hug or front bear hug, you will rotate your body as you step out and down. Are you getting tired of hearing step out and down yet? I hope not, because it's a basic, but incredibly effective counter to almost any attack. In this case, think of your footwork as either opening a door or closing a door. You are opening a door and creating enough space for your attacker to fall without landing on you.

The direction you step is determined by the attacker. Following the philosophy of redirection of force rather than meeting force head-on, step in the direction the attacker is trying to push you. It's the same principle as mentioned in Chapter 5 on essential fundamentals. You push when pulled and pull when pushed. You are adding to the attacker's power in a direction he wasn't intending, so he loses his balance. If the attacker has grabbed you from the rear and is trying to force you forward, you step forward (open the door). If the attacker has grabbed you from the front and is trying to force you backward, you step backwards. Almost any defense can be broken down into "move" and "change." As always, don't force your body in any direction; just relax and let your body weight fall naturally. If you are tense, it may not work. If you are relaxed, you will generate tremendous power.

If you are in a rear bear hug, your right foot will swing out to your left front and down simultaneously. Or you can step with your left foot out to your right front. It doesn't matter which foot you step with. It does matter that your use your body weight effectively by throwing it out and down. The move should feel very relaxed and heavy, almost as if you are a lumbering bear. If the attacker maintains a grip on you throughout the technique, he will wrench his back as well as being thrown to the ground. It doesn't matter if your arms are pinned or not. The technique is exactly the same and equally effective (Figure 10.3).

If you are in a front bear hug (how did that happen?), the technique is the exact reverse of the above explanation. Your foot (it doesn't matter which one) will swing back behind you and out as you drop your weight. This technique actually works better if your arms are pinned, as you will be able to lever your opponent's upper body under his arm as you step. If your arms are not pinned, you'll wrap your outside arm around the subject's head or neck area as you step. Again, to simplify, just step in the direction your attacker is trying to force you (Figure 10.4).

Video 10.2 at www.SurvivalSciences.com depicts the defense against a rear bear hug.

(A)

(B)

Figure 10.3 (A) The officer grabbed from behind in a rear bear hug. (B) The officer stepping out while simultaneously dropping her weight to send the attacker flying.

(A)

(B)

Figure 10.4 (A) The officer swinging her foot out to defeat a front bear hug. (B) The end of the technique for defeating a front bear hug.

Video 10.3 at www.SurvivalSciences.com depicts the defense against a front bear hug.

Headlock

To identify an escape from a headlock, first recognize where the lock gets its strength. The successful headlock involves pulling an opponent's head tightly against the body as the attacker attempts to bring the squeezing arm's elbow as close to his body as possible. To weaken this technique, you must change the position of the attacker's elbow so that it is away from, and in front of, the attacker's body (Figure 10.5).

Once more, why are you in this position? How asleep were you? Okay, you were sound asleep again and got caught in a headlock. The defense is (drum roll …) step out and forward at a 45° angle. By stepping forward and using your body weight, you have changed the position of the attacker's elbow so it is now away from his body in a weak position. As you step out, you simultaneously push the attacker's elbow forward as you continue to move by pivoting and release your head (Figure 10.6).

Figure 10.5 A headlock in which the victim's head is secured tightly.

Video 10.4 at www.SurvivalSciences.com shows the escape from a side headlock.

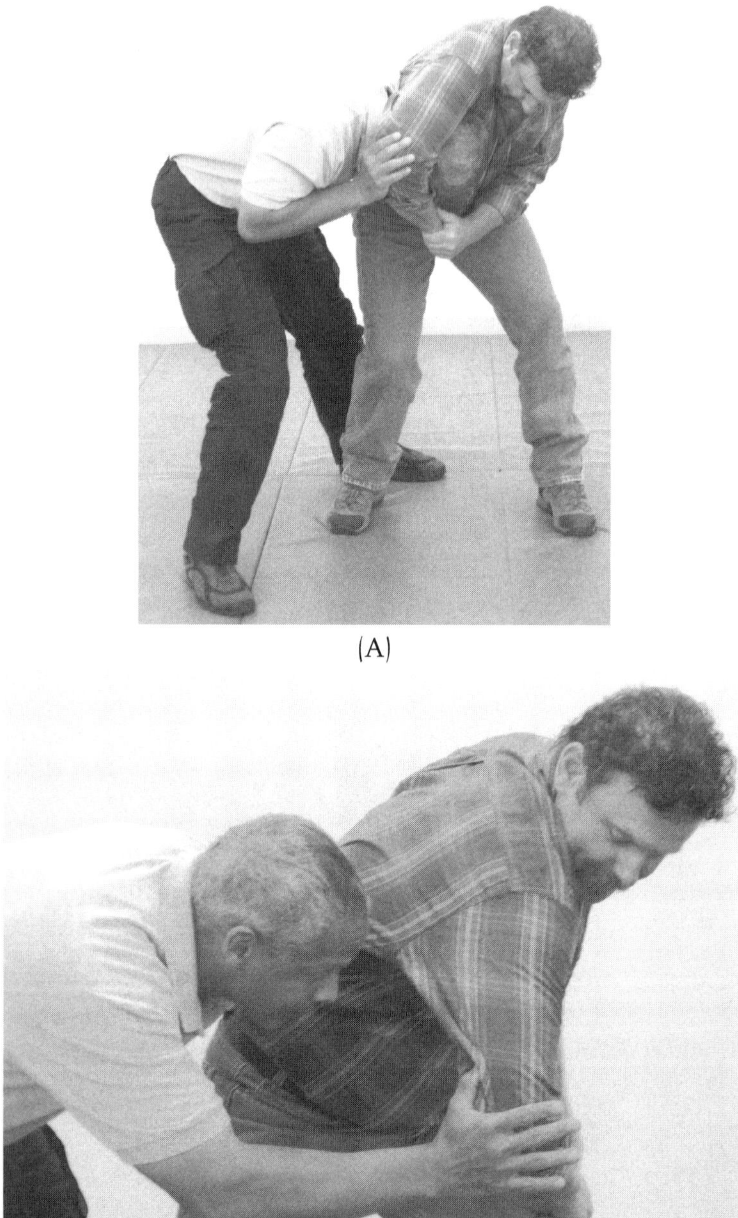

(A)

(B)

Figure 10.6 (A) The officer bracing the attacker's elbow forward as he begins to step forward with his body weight to weaken the headlock.(B) The completion of the defensive technique as the officer breaks free of the hold and is now able to move behind the attacker.

Choke

A defense against the Frankenstein choke is exceedingly simple. Just turn to the side and walk away. There are plenty of offensive techniques you can use if someone is stupid enough to reach out with both hands and grab you by the throat. Take your pick of all of the available personal weapons and then step away to draw a weapon and obtain compliance.

Even if you are pinned against a wall, it's the same concept. Turn and step to the side. Don't try to push back against the attacker (force vs. force). Redirect the choke to the side and escape (Figure 10.7).

More realistically, people will try to come from behind and choke you. As will be mentioned in Chapter 13 on the bilateral vascular restraint (BVR), a blood choke involves compression of the sides of the neck, and an air choke involves compressing the windpipe so it is difficult to breathe. The defense for either technique is the same, but since the bad guy is not limited by law, policies, or other niceties, assume he'll will attempt the air choke and try to crush your trachea. For any choke, you must first protect your throat. If possible, you want to tuck your chin to prevent the attacker's arm from encircling your throat area. You also want to get a hand up next to your face between your neck and the attacker's encircling arm. You will instinctively bring both hands up to grab the attacker's arm that is choking you and that is a good reaction. If possible, try to get one hand in between the attacker's arm and your neck. Don't stress about it if you can't, and don't waste time trying to force your hand into this position. If you can place your hand in this position, then great. If not, it's not a big deal. What is a big deal is that you move immediately upon being touched. By doing this, you greatly reduce the chance of the attacker "setting" the choke into place. You also begin to change the action-reaction equation as the attacker is now reacting to your movement and trying to maintain his balance.

If you find yourself standing and being choked from behind, you want to step out and down. You will step with the same foot as the attacker's arm that is choking you. For example, if the attacker is choking you with his right arm, step out with your right foot and swing it in front of your left. Don't twist at your waist. Maintain proper posture and keep your body aligned as you swing your weight around and down. If the attacker is choking you with his left arm, step out with your left foot. Once free, immediately create distance and draw a weapon to obtain compliance (Figure 10.8).

Video 10.5 at www.SurvivalSciences.com shows the escape from a rear standing choke.

(A)

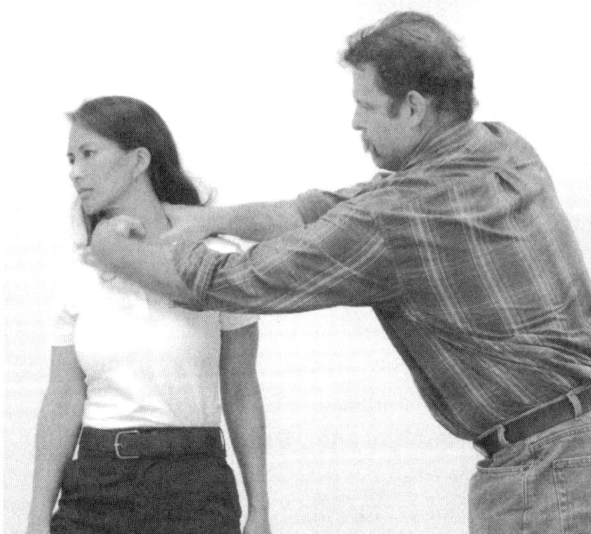

(B)

Figure 10.7 (A) A forward, standing choke in which the attacker has begun to force the officer back. (B) The officer simply "going" with the force by turning and walking away.

(A)

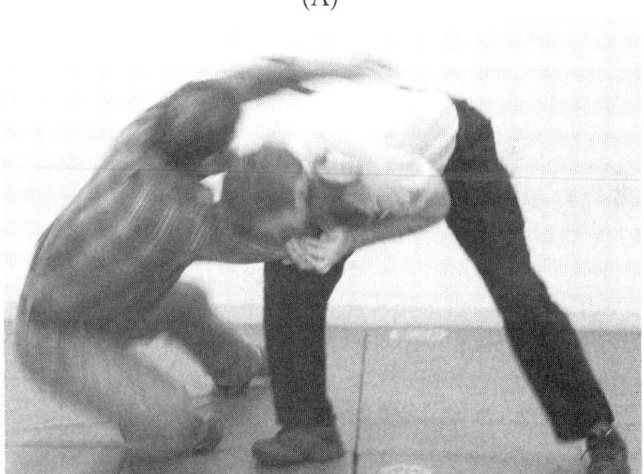

(B)

Figure 10.8 (A) Stepping forward and down to escape from a rear standing choke. (B) The attacker losing his balance and beginning to fall as the officer continues to drop his weight out and down. (Continued)

(C)

Figure 10.8 (Continued) (C) The completion of the escape from a rear standing choke as the attacker falls away from the officer.

If you are being choked from behind and the attacker has taken your balance to the rear, you will be unable to step forward. Don't resist the attacker who is pulling you backwards off-balance (force vs. force); go with it (redirection of force). As the attacker pulls you to the rear, swing your leg nearest to the attacker down and across. It works best if you drop your weight by taking a kneeling position, which further upsets your attacker's balance. If the attacker continues to hold onto you, the sudden change in your position and body weight will take him to the ground (Figure 10.9).

Chokes on the ground will be discussed in Chapter 12 on surviving the ground war.

If the preceding techniques sound exceedingly simple, it's because they are. There are hundreds of counters with a wide range of complexity and effectiveness. I chose the above techniques specifically because they all use the identical principle of stepping out and down. They are easy to remember, easy to apply, and are incredibly effective. If they are too simple for you, let me know. I can demonstrate a multitude of other techniques that are much more complex, much more difficult to master, require many hours of practice, but look really cool. I'm being facetious, but cool can get you killed. For DT training, success derives from sticking to the core concepts and fundamentals. The techniques explained above remain consistent with the

Video 10.6 at www.SurvivalSciences.com shows the escape from a rear standing choke in which the officer's balance has been taken to the rear.

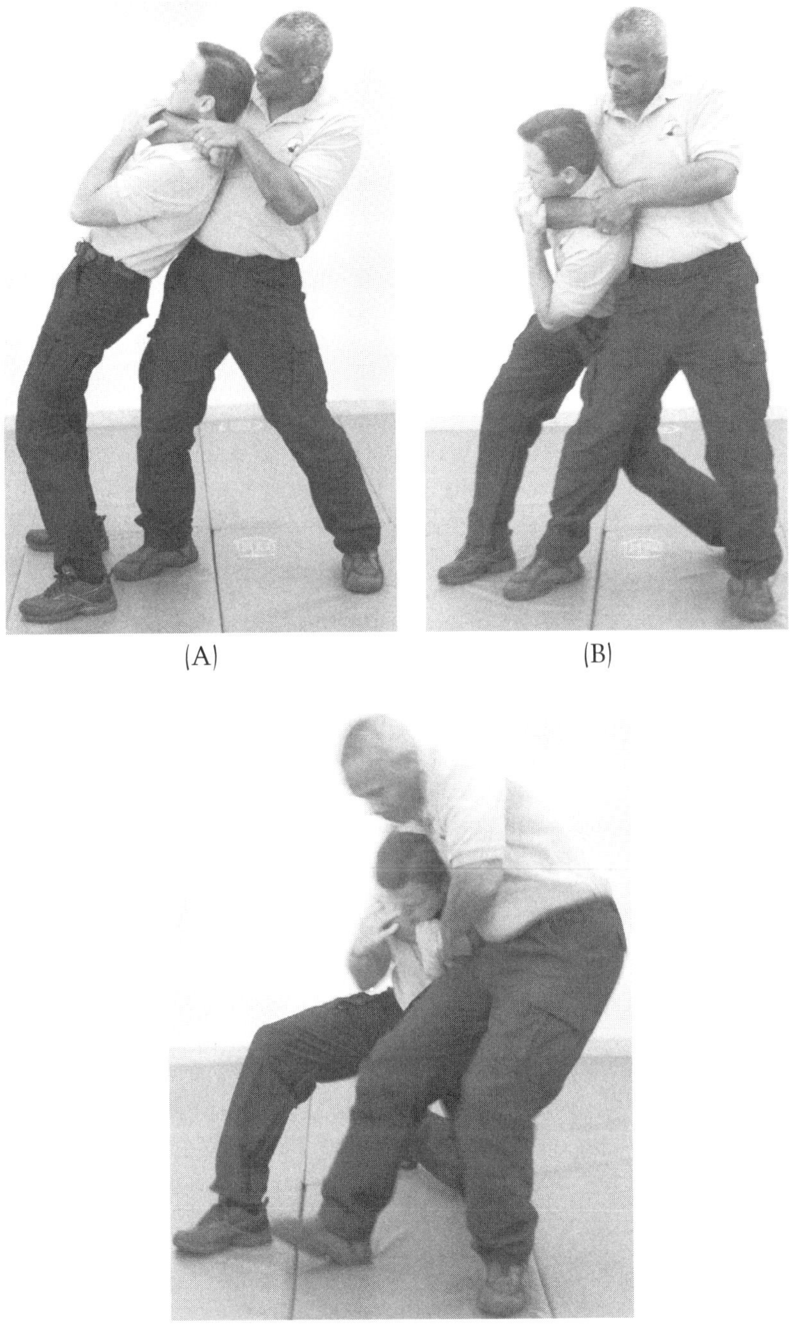

(A) (B) (C)

Figure 10.9 (A) The officer caught in a rear standing choke and his balance has been broken to the rear. (B) The officer stepping back to regain balance and take the attacker's balance. (C) The officer going to a kneeling position as he continues back and the attacker beginning to fall.

principles mentioned throughout the book. Relax, use your body weight, and step out and down to change your attacker's balance. Don't fight, don't resist, don't try to muscle a technique. Relax and use proper fundamentals and you will survive.

Drills

All of the above techniques can be shadowboxed in front of a mirror using visualization, but it is better, and builds confidence more quickly, if you practice with a partner. Go through each of the attacks above, practicing moving and dropping your body weight. Don't be too concerned initially with the exact direction of the step. Don't fight your partner/attacker; simply redirect the force. After a few practice sessions it should become evident it is a simple process of continuously moving, not resisting, and redirecting the force of your partner/attacker. Good things typically happen if you have the proper fundamentals.

1. Have your partner attempt to grab you. Your first response is to move out of the way. You should quickly discover it is almost impossible for your partner to successfully grab you if you maintain proper distance and move correctly.
2. Try drill 1 again, but with your partner attempting to bear hug, choke, or get you in a headlock. Again, by moving properly, your partner should never have the opportunity to "set" the technique.
3. Next, allow your partner to set one of the techniques mentioned above. By moving effectively and dropping your weight down and out, break free from each attack.
4. Stand stationary and allow your partner to approach you from any angle. Allow your partner to use any of the techniques mentioned above. Then react appropriately to defeat the attack.
5. "The circle of terror." This drill works better with multiple partners. Have your training partners form a circle around you. You are required to stand with your eyes closed. Partners will approach you silently from any direction and attempt to place you in any type of hold. Move and use your body weight appropriately as soon as you are touched or aware of the attack.

Generating Power with Your Personal Weapons

11

What is the key to success in using personal weapons (i.e., punches, kicks, elbow strikes, etc.)? What makes a personal weapon strike effective or ineffective? The answer is your ability to generate power with the strike. If you strike someone and it doesn't land with enough force to hurt or, at a minimum, distract the aggressive resister, then you just wasted your time throwing the strike. Even worse, you opened yourself up to a counterstrike. Every time you use a personal weapon, it must land with all of the power you are capable of generating. And the power you generate must be sufficient to have a significant impact on the aggressive resister.

There is much law enforcement officers can learn from the Rodney King event in 1991 to ensure it doesn't happen again. I recognize this is a controversial statement, but I believe one of several key components that led to the Rodney King incident was the ineffectual side-handle baton strikes. In Sgt. Stacey Koon's book, *Presumed Guilty: The Tragedy of the Rodney King Affair*,[1] he described Officer Powell's baton strikes (prior to the Rodney King incident) as weak and ineffective. When the general public viewed the video on the news, they witnessed several police officers (but primarily Officer Powell) repeatedly striking a man on his hands and knees. Ask yourself this question, "If I'm allowed by law and policy to strike this subject with a baton, am I better off hitting him once and breaking bones, or am I better off lightly striking the resister fifty times with ineffective blows?" I think the answer is clear. It is much better to strike an aggressive resister once or twice with immediate results than striking the resister multiple times with no effect. It's certainly safer for you, and it's also safer for the aggressive resister. If you are permitted to strike, then strike! How hard should you strike? As hard as you can.

I remember years ago watching a Court TV episode in which one young man (who we'll call Karate Guy) was being cross-examined about a confrontation with another young man (who we will call Bully Guy). Karate Guy has a black belt in karate and his father was his instructor. Karate Guy is at the mall with his friends when he is approached by Bully Guy and some of his friends. Bully Guy is trying to give Karate Guy a hard time and is generally being verbally abusive. To his credit, Karate Guy ignores it and walks away. Later, Bully Guy again approaches Karate Guy and continues his verbal assault. Bully Guy eventually becomes physical and braces Karate Guy up against a wall. After being slammed against a wall, Karate Guy hits Bully Guy with a right hook. Bully Guy slumps to the ground striking his head on the hard floor and dies. Karate Guy is prosecuted for manslaughter.

As I watched the show, I saw the district attorney feed the Karate Guy's ego. "So you're a black belt in karate?" asked the DA. "Yes," said the Karate Guy with pride. "You must be very skilled," continued the DA. I saw where this was going, but unfortunately for Karate Guy, he did not. The DA continued to puff up Karate Guys ego and got him to admit to his great fighting skills. The DA mentioned the incredible control it must require to obtain the rank of black belt. Karate Guy agreed that he possessed super-human control. Finally, the DA dropped the bomb. "If you have such control, why did you strike Bully Guy hard enough to kill him?" Karate Guy was a victim of his ego and was convicted.

I've exaggerated the story quite a bit and took some literary license, but hopefully you can see how a law enforcement officer could be asked the same questions. If I had the opportunity to talk to Karate Guy prior to his testimony, I would have told him to tell the truth. And the truth is he is not a superhero. The truth is he does not have mystical skills. The truth is he had some additional self-defense training (much more so than most police officers), but he cannot control how an attacker will respond to a punch. It amazes me how many so-called martial arts experts will say if they hit someone with a particular technique, the attacker will immediately be incapacitated. How can anyone say that? People don't react the same way to being shot in the chest with a .45. Some may collapse and drop dead on the spot, some may gasp and continue to fight, and some may not even blink. The point of this is if I'm legally justified in hitting someone, I'm going to hit him as hard as I can. I don't know how he will react. I just know I'm physically threatened and if I don't hurt him and get him off of me, I risk serious injury at a minimum. So, if you are justified in using a specific level of force, use it! Use it to the best of your ability. And as soon as the resister becomes compliant or you obtain control, stop using it.

Can you learn to strike with more power? Some people say no. The great boxing commentator Ferdie Pacheco once said a boxer is born with power and it can't be taught. Mr. Pacheco said trying to teach power in boxing is like trying to teach height in basketball. I think it's a funny statement and one of the reasons I enjoyed listening to Mr. Pacheco was his colorful analogies, but it isn't true.

You can teach power and you can learn to strike with more power. Here's an example: My dream was to play professional baseball. Actually, it was my dad's dream (he played semiprofessional ball), but I adopted the dream as my own when I was young. If I were to pursue that goal now and my objective was to first learn to throw a 90 mph fastball, there are several things I'd need to do. First, I'd hire the best pitching coach I could find, a strength trainer, and maybe a kinesiologist to teach me the most effective throwing motion.

I would then do nothing but train and practice and study for an entire year. At the end of that year, would I be throwing a 90 mph fastball and pitching in the major leagues? No and no. For one reason, I'm old. For another reason, professional ball players are operating on an entirely different athletic plane than the rest of us mere mortals. But would I be a much better pitcher than when I started? Absolutely. Would I be able to impress friends and family with my newfound pitching skills? Maybe so.

Here's another real-life example. While attending graduate school, I was the chief instructor for a Goju karate school that met on campus. One of my students was a rather small female named Gerry. Our martial arts training center was located in a large university gymnasium and across the hall was a weight room. Several of us were stretching and warming up prior to class. A huge body builder type from the weight room walked in and strutted over to the heavy bags. He began punching the bag, stopping occasionally to admire himself in the mirror. When the big, muscled guy hit the bag, it hardly moved. After several minutes of this, Gerry walked over to the bag next to his, looked at him, and smiled. She then began to hit the bag with thundering blows, making it jump with every strike. The body builder dropped his head in shame and immediately walked out. The body builder was about 6 feet 4 inches and at least 240 pounds. Gerry was 5 feet 2 inches and weighed no more than 120 pounds. How is it possible for a much smaller, much weaker female to punch harder than a much larger, much stronger male? I recognize the inherent sexism in the preceding question, but generally males have greater upper body strength than do females. The answer is physics. The answer is proper body mechanics.

Following is the magic formula for generating power:

$$Ke = \frac{1}{2} M \times V^2$$

It's a secret, so don't tell anyone. Okay, it's not really a secret. It's a well-known physics formula routinely taught in high school physics classes. It states **kinetic energy** is equal to half the **mass** multiplied by **velocity** to the second power. If there are any physics professors reading this, I'll apologize now as I'm going to take a few liberties for the sake of simplification. Kinetic energy is a measure of energy that defines the ability to do work. The work we want to do is strike, hurt, or distract our attacker so we can gain control and make an arrest. Kinetic energy is measured in joules and expressed in foot/pounds, but again, for our purpose, we'll just refer to it as units. Mass is not the same as weight, but for our objective it is close enough. What $Ke = \frac{1}{2} M \times V^2$ tells us is that the heavier the object and the faster it moves, then the more kinetic energy, or power, is generated. That's truly a magic formula because if you understand that principle and can apply it, you will be able to generate more power in any physical endeavor—to include striking someone.

Let's go back to the example of Gerry and the body builder. How was she able to punch significantly harder than the body builder? She could do this because she understood, either consciously or subconsciously, the physics behind generating power. First, Gerry was punching at a much greater speed than was the body builder. His tight muscles and the fact he was performing a physical act that he was not proficient at actually caused him to move quite slowly. Gerry had good hand speed. But wait, you say. The body builder weighed twice as much as Gerry, so that should have compensated for the difference in speed. Not so. Gerry was effectively using her entire body weight. The body builder was doing what is commonly referred to as arm punching. He stood flat-footed and slowly propelled his fist toward the bag using only his arm. Gerry struck with speed and moved her entire body to strike the bag. Assuming Gerry weighed 120 pounds and her fist was moving at 75 mph and Mr. Body Builder was using 20 pounds (his arm only) and his fist was moving at 25 mph, here are the results using our magical defensive tactics formula:

Gerry: $Ke = \frac{1}{2}(120) \times 75^2 = 60 \times 5{,}625 = 337{,}500$ units

Body builder: $Ke = \frac{1}{2}(20) \times 25^2 = 10 \times 625 = 6{,}250$ units

It's an extreme example, but an accurate one. It also shows how a small increase in the speed of the technique can greatly increase the power. Now, how do we generate power? How do we maximize the force we can generate? How do we maximize our weight and how do we maximize our speed? The answer is RRIP. As in "rest in peace," but with double emphasis on the R. What RRIP stands for is relaxation, rotation, (target) identification, and (target) penetration. Think RRIP.

Relaxation

Let's look at relaxation first. You increase your speed by relaxing your muscles. A tight muscle is a slow muscle. Think of any great athlete in any sport. Does he or she ever look tight and stiff? Or do the truly greats always look smooth and relaxed, as if everything they do is effortless? Think of Michael Jordan and how naturally and gracefully he moved at all times on the court. He made incredibly difficult and athletic movements look easy.

Tighten every muscle in your arms, chest, and back, and then throw a jab. It probably feels slow and weak. Now let your hand dangle loosely and snap out a jab like you're snapping someone with a towel. You should be able to feel the difference in speed and power.

When I was competing, I once had an opponent who would telegraph whenever he was about to move forward to throw a punch. I remember thinking I'd snap out a quick jab to stop my opponent's forward movement and then immediately follow up with a power right hand. I did just that, snapping out the jab with no thought as to the power of my jab. I just wanted to put something between him and me to stop him as he was coming in so I could connect with my right hand. The jab connected and, much to my surprise, my opponent dropped before I had a chance to hit him with a straight right. The relaxed, speedy jab resulted in a knockdown.

I later watched George Foreman when he won the heavyweight boxing championship at the age of forty-five. George was no longer the amazing physical specimen he once was, but his power seemed to be as strong, if not stronger, than it was as a young man. In an interview, George attributed his power to his newfound ability to relax.

Rotation

How do you increase your weight? You increase your power by perfecting your body mechanics. You increase your power by putting your whole body into a strike. This is accomplished by moving in the direction of your attack and rotating your hips sharply. If you are going to hit someone with your rear hand, your rear leg presses into the ground, sending your weight forward (not up), your hips rotate sharply in a popping motion, your abdomen tightens, your shoulders rotate (as the shoulder of the striking hand moves forward, the other shoulder moves back), and the hand shoots forward in a straight line to your target. Of all those elements of generating power, the most important is the rotation of the hips.

If you are a boxing enthusiast, you've heard of Jack Johnson. Jack Johnson became the first black heavyweight champion of the world when he defeated Tommy Burns in 1908. What is not as well known is the heavyweight title was vacant in 1905 and Mr. Johnson and another black fighter named Sam Langford were considered the top contenders. Many of the fighters of that time period, to include Jack Johnson, refused to fight Sam Langford because of his notable punching power. What makes this so remarkable is Mr. Langford was a middleweight. Mr. Langford was asked by reporters the secret to his incredible punching power. His reply was: "It's all in the hips."

The Learning Channel (TLC) once did a special on peak performance that highlighted Roy Jones Jr., who was then a world champion. Roy Jones Jr. was always one of my favorite fighters because of his incredible skill, his sense of humor, the uniqueness of his style, he's a native of Pensacola, Florida, and he was very nice to my mother when she met him. TLC wired Mr. Jones up to computers and EKG-type devices to monitor his physical responses as he threw a punch. The result of all of this scientific research determined Mr. Jones punched with such great power because of how he employed the muscles in his thighs, hips, and shoulders—with the key being the rotation of his hips. The result was the same thing Mr. Sam Langford had said almost one hundred years earlier. It's all in the hips.

Identification

Now we have relaxation and rotation, the next item is target identification. If we are talking about personal weapons, some targets are simply better than others. A strike to a joint will be more effective than a strike to an area covered by muscle or fat. A strike to an area containing a bundle of nerve fibers is better than a strike to an area without the prevalence of nerves. Simply stated, strike to the areas most likely to result in maximum effectiveness within the law and within policy.

The most common vulnerable areas of the body to be used by law enforcement as target areas are (Diagram 11.1):

Temples	
Eyes	(more about this target later)
Nose	
Ears	
Chin	
Base of the skull	(should only be struck in a case of deadly resistance)
Throat	(should only be struck in a case of deadly resistance)
Neck	
Elbows	
Solar plexus	
Floating ribs	
Groin	
Knees	
Shins	
Small bones of the hands and feet	

The target you hit will depend on which target is available. The point is to not strike out blindly, but hit something that is more likely to have an effect and get you closer to your goal of gaining control. Of the targets mentioned above, some require additional comment. The ears are susceptible to an open-hand strike, creating a pressure wave to cause pain to the eardrum. You can also grab and twist the ears.

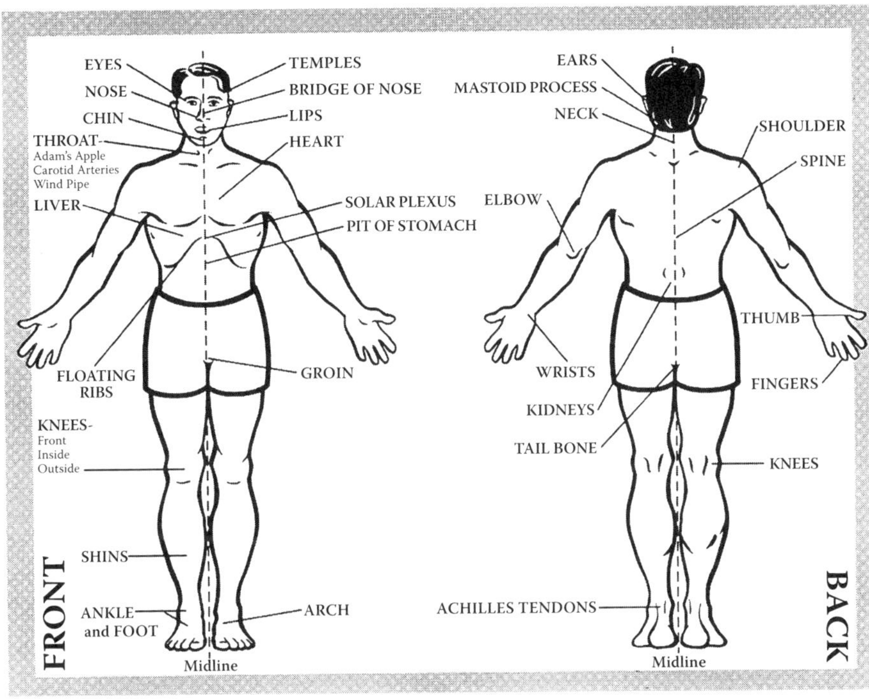

Diagram 11.1 The target areas listed in the text as well as others. This diagram was taken from an earlier version of the FBI *Defensive Tactics Manual.*

The nose is always a good target, as a solid blow to the nose causes the eyes to water, obstructing your attacker's vision. However, contrary to a popular myth, you can't drive the bones of the nose into the brain and kill someone. I know it sounds cool, but it just isn't medically possible. If it were possible, boxers would be dropping dead every time they got caught with an uppercut that landed on the nose.

Although it would require a considerable amount of force to kill someone with a strike to the base of a skull, it is best not to strike there unless you've encountered deadly resistance. There is a reason a blow to this area is outlawed by boxing and mixed martial arts (MMA). Similarly, a purposeful blow to the throat is only permitted if your attacker is in the deadly resistant category of the dynamic resistance-response model (DRM).

You obviously wouldn't try to punch someone in the elbow, but if he presents you with a straight arm (such as he is grabbing you or pushing you), a hard strike to the elbow may hyperextend it. The knees are always a great target, and we'll discuss the best way to attack them later in this chapter.

I've included the solar plexus just because someone would complain if I left it out. But it really isn't that great of a target. It's relatively small and difficult to hit effectively on a moving resister. The floating ribs, however, are a great target.

It is particularly effective if you can catch the bottom floating rib with a strike moving upwards at a 45° angle. Speaking from experience on the receiving end, if you get hit with a strong blow to this area at an upward angle, it makes breathing more difficult and makes you feel like you are going to vomit.

And now for the old standby—the groin. I hate to be the one to break it to you, but it's just not that great of a target. Sure, if you catch it just right, it will slow your attacker down. It's not the fight stopper people seem to think it is, particularly if your attacker is committed. Also, sorry guys, it really is not that big of a target. "But, Chuck," you say, "Speak for yourself! It's huge! It's huge, I say!" Sorry, but no it's not. We're actually talking about the testicles and, as a viable target, it's only a few inches of striking area. The male species have grown up instinctively protecting this area, and it only takes a small rotation of the hips to move the target area out of the way of an attack. If you are going to attack the groin, it's much more effective to grab, squeeze, and twist, rather than to simply strike.

Shins are best attacked by scraping them rather than striking them. It is more likely you would use this approach in a self-defense situation in which your attacker has grabbed you either from the front or the rear.

The small bones of the hand and feet are susceptible to breaking, but primarily by stomping on them.

In a law enforcement defensive tactics handbook, it stated that the "untrained" person typically directs blows to the opponent's head. It then went on to say that this is the location people expect to get hit, so it's an area they naturally protect. The manual was trying to encourage strikes to the body, which is not necessarily a bad thing. But I disagree with the manual's assessment. We are not preparing for a competition with rules. We are preparing for a dirty street fight in which you may die if you lose. Very few people protect the head well. Almost all nonprofessional fighters (and even some professional ones) carry their hands too low and leave their heads open. Particularly when fatigue sets in, the hands drop and the head becomes completely exposed.

Personally, given the choice of striking the body or striking the head, I'd choose the head. Even though it may be a smaller target and people are capable of moving the head more quickly than the body, very few do. Against the vast majority of the public, landing a blow to the head is not that difficult. From the receiver's standpoint, I've only been hurt by a blow to the body once—and that blow was delivered by a world champion kick boxer in a sparring session. Even then, it didn't stop me from fighting. It just made it difficult for me to breathe and I danced a lot. But I have been hurt by blows to the head. So, hit what is available, and it will probably be the head.

An often neglected target is the knees. Even skilled martial artists have trouble defending against kicks to the legs. Watch almost any MMA event and see how effectively a fighter scores with kicks to an opponent's legs. We'll look at how to strike the legs later in this chapter.

Penetration

Finally, the last element of RRIP is penetration. A strike is never *to* a target, it is *through* a target. If you are going to hit someone in the nose, don't try to hit him in the nose. Try to hit through the nose to an area at least several inches past your target.

In summary of RRIP, you generate power first by relaxing the muscles. The more you practice, the easier this becomes. Next, you want your feet to grip the floor and push forward toward your opponent. The most important element of maximizing your body rotation is a sharp pivot of the hips toward or through the resister. Sharply exhale as you strike, as in a "kiai" in martial arts or the grunt of a tennis player. Sit close to a boxing match and you'll hear the boxers forcefully exhale on every blow. Finally, pick your targets and hit through your targets.

Personal Weapon Techniques

As law enforcement officers, we aren't allowed to just walk up and slug someone. Generally, we are permitted to strike a subject under limited circumstances. Those circumstances are when the subject is aggressively resisting and we feel threatened by the subject's actions, as seen in Diagram 11.2.

Diagram 11.2 The DRM and the possible responses to aggressive resistance.

If we are faced with aggressive resistance, we have several tools available, to include personal weapons (punches, kicks, knee strikes, etc.), impact weapons (collapsible baton, straight baton, side-handle baton), pepper spray, and electronic control devices (ECDs). Given the choice when facing an aggressive resister, and authorized to do so by your department's policy, I would recommend you choose the most effective tool for your specific situation, the most readily available tool, and the one that allows you to obtain control or compliance at the greatest distance from the aggressive resister. The purpose of an entire chapter on movement was to drill the idea of getting out of the way and drawing a weapon. For an aggressive resister, the tools mentioned above are approved by the courts (your department may be another matter). Looking at the possibilities on the DRM for this category, the ranking in terms of my preference would be:

1. ECD (i.e., TASER)
2. Pepper spray
3. Impact weapon
4. Bilateral vascular restraint (BVR)
5. Personal weapons

The TASER has proven exceptionally effective and can be deployed from a safe distance. Pepper spray is slightly less effective, can also be deployed from a safe distance, but can become a problem if officers are affected by residual spray. Impact weapons require the officer to be much closer to the resister, but, if done correctly, remain out of reach of the subject. Impact weapons can be effective, depending upon the officer's skill level. The BVR (covered in Chapter 13 and similar to a carotid restraint) is extremely effective, but requires the officer to lock up with the resister, which is always a dangerous thing to do. However, when the BVR is used, it is because the officer has been successful in getting to the attacker's back and is in a good tactical position. Also, as discussed in Chapter 1, carotid types of restraints have proven to result in fewer injuries to the officers and subjects than do personal weapons. Finally, personal weapons require the officer to be within striking distance of the resister, and the effectiveness is certainly dependent upon the officer's skills and ability to generate power. The studies discussed in Chapter 1 also indicate a higher likelihood of injuries to the officers and subjects when personal weapons are used.

Given that other tools are more effective and can be used at a greater (and thereby safer) range, why would an officer use personal weapons? The answer is you wouldn't if given the choice. You'd use personal weapons because there is no other option. Sometimes an officer is in an unexpected confrontation as he or she approaches the subject to handcuff. The officer may not be able to deploy another tool as quickly. The one advantage of personal weapons is you always have them with you and ready to go. As mentioned earlier in this chapter, your success in using personal weapons is dependent upon developing the ability to generate considerable power.

The point of this chapter is not to discuss an endless variety of techniques. A multitude of personal weapon techniques are taught at every academy. Some techniques you probably liked and would use instinctively. Others you may have discarded, as they didn't work well for you. Use what you like and what you're comfortable with. This section is to discuss the concepts of striking and how to generate more power for those personal weapons specifically selected due to their broad range of application and effectiveness. Also, this is not a discussion of the sports application of strikes. This chapter is about the application of striking techniques in a street fight. There is a difference. In competition, you have to worry about scoring points and keeping enough stamina in reserve so you can make it to the end of the round. In the street, there are no points and everything you do is to survive.

Generating power, using proper body mechanics, and learning to strike effectively takes some effort and practice. But it can be done if you understand the core concepts and are willing to devote a little time to development of the basic striking skills.

Hand Strikes

Straight Hand Strikes

Please note that this section is called "hand strikes" and not "punches." We seem to forget (or never learned) that some of the most effective strikes that can be delivered are not necessarily with a closed fist. I would be reluctant to teach strikes with a closed fist to officers who are not regularly training on their own. Professional fighters have professional trainers wrap their hands prior to a fight. Gauze is wrapped tightly around the wrists and individual fingers. Padding is placed over the knuckles, and then taped. More layers of padding and more layers of tape are added. By the time the job is done, it's as if your hands are nothing more than two large rocks extending from your arms. In spite of all of the precautionary measures and in spite of all of the intense training and conditioning professional fighters endure, they still break their hands. Now take an officer with much less training and no protective hand wraps. That officer strikes a resister in the head or other hard part of the body and breaks his or her hand. This is bad—particularly if it's the gun hand. I've talked to several officers who did just that.

Unless an officer has trained regularly in boxing or martial arts, I would prefer the officer use open-hand strikes. Even for those who do train regularly,

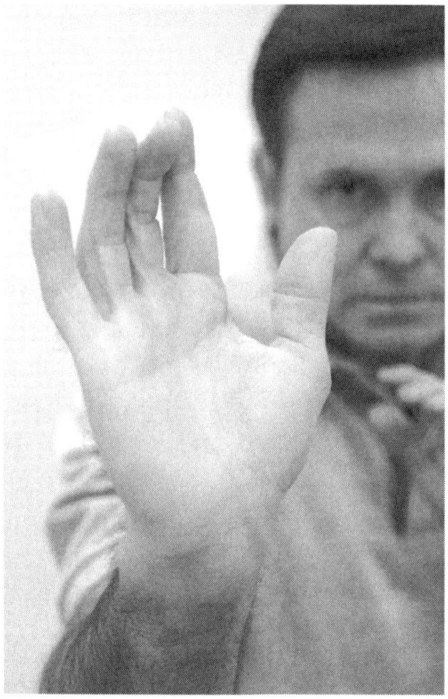

Figure 11.1 The striking surface and position of the hand for delivering a palm heel strike.

I would still suggest they use open-hand strikes. The open-hand strikes are performed exactly the same as punches, other than the officer is striking with the palm heel area of an open hand (Figure 11.1). The effectiveness of the strike suffers almost not at all, and the chances of injuring the hand and wrist are greatly reduced.

For simplicity's sake, I'll describe all techniques as if you are a right-hander. If you aren't, then shame on you. In ancient times, left-handed people were thought to be possessed by evil demons or witches and such, and were usually flogged or burned at the stake. If you left-handed folks would just learn to get along with the rest of the world, you'd make it a whole lot easier for DT instructors and firearms instructors. But since you refuse to be like everyone else and because you insist on being "individuals," I'll try valiantly to explain things by saying "lead hand" or "rear hand." Please recognize that for "normal" (i.e., right-handed) people, the lead hand is their left, and their rear hand is their right. You lefties reverse that. Before I get letters from the "Be Nice to Lefties Committee," I concede that my mother and sister are left-handed. I also believe most left-handers, because throughout life they have had to adjust to a right-handed world, are more intellectually fluid.

The mechanics of a rear hand strike were covered earlier in this chapter, but I will go into more depth here. Some common errors I typically observed when coaching a fighter included hitting flat-footed, letting the elbow fly up and away from the body, and not pivoting the hips and shoulders fully. We'll address hitting flat-footed first. Going back to the magical physics formula, a key component is proper use of your body weight. If you are not moving into the strike, you are not maximizing your weight, and therefore, you are not hitting with as much power as possible. If you are throwing a straight hand strike, your entire body should be moving forward at the time the strike lands. For some reason, many fighters have a bad habit of lunging toward their opponent, braking to a stop, and then hitting. This is like driving a car at a high rate of speed, slamming on the brakes, and then hopping out of the car to push over a wall. Don't do it. Hit as your body weight is moving forward. You maximize your body weight and you increase your speed. Think how fast you can punch. Now think about how fast you can lunge forward. If you combine the two, you have increased the speed of your strike because you have added the speed of your body going forward to the speed of your strike. To repeat, don't hit while you're standing still—move!

Next, let's look at the flying elbow syndrome. If throwing a straight hand strike, you do not want the elbow to fly up and away from your body. If this happens, you are not using proper body mechanics and you are not optimizing your weight. Raise your rear hand to shoulder level, arm bent at a 90° angle and parallel to the ground, and the point of your elbow pointing out to the side (Figure 11.2). If you should punch right now, how much of your body can you put behind the punch? Very little because the only thing behind your arm is air. Now hold your arm in a natural fighting position—arm bent, hand near your face, elbow tucked against your ribs, and the point of your elbow

Figure 11.2 The elbow in the incorrect "chicken wing" configuration.

Figure 11.3 The elbow tucked correctly into position to ensure your bodyweight is behind the strike.

pointing down toward the ground (Figure 11.3). If you threw a strike from this position, ensuring the point of your elbow continued to face the ground throughout the strike, how much of your body could you put behind the punch? The answer is all of it.

Next, you must pivot your hips and shoulders into the strike. Remember, "it's all in the hips." As you strike with your rear hand, your hips should rotate quickly and violently. Think of throwing the same side hip as your punching hand into the strike. Your hip should move just prior to the hand moving, as if by throwing the hip first, it's propelling your hand into the strike. Your lead shoulder rotates back away from your opponent as your rear shoulder drives forward.

To summarize, drive with the legs, rotate or "pop" your hips, rotate the shoulders, and strike as your body is still moving toward your opponent. Remember, this is not sport sparring. You are trying to hit as hard as possible, then move away on an angle to deploy another weapon. Or, if the strike was completely effective, immobilize your attacker and handcuff.

The lead hand strike, or jab, is simply a straight punch thrown with the lead hand. Some people have described the jab as nothing more than a distraction technique or a precursor to the real, power technique (such as the straight rear hand punch). I disagree. For one reason, I have knocked people out with nothing more than a jab. Admittedly, they assisted me greatly by moving toward me and were nice enough to meet my jab with their face as my jab was coming out, but I still believe that a properly thrown jab can also

Video 11.1 at www.SurvivalSciences.com shows the proper body mechanics of a rear hand strike. Use the user name and pass code listed in the introduction to access the video.

be a power technique. As any good boxer will tell you, a good jab is an indispensable tool in a fighter's toolbox.

The lead hand can be thrown from any position you may find yourself, but preferably from your interview stance or, better yet, your response/survival stance. Just like the rear hand strike, the key is to throw the lead hand in a straight line to your target. Imagine a taut piece of string that runs from your lead hand to your target (let's assume it's your aggressive resister's nose in this case). Your hand should travel in an absolute straight line from its on-guard or ready position to the resister's nose. Any deviation from that line will result in a loss of power, a loss of speed, and will telegraph the punch, making it easier for your opponent to defend against it. If you "loop" the punch, it's as if you just threw away some of the power. Think of a car rounding a curve at high speed. Centrifugal force wants to pull the car away from its direction of travel. The same thing happens to a punch. If the punch curves, power is "leaking" away.

There are two common mistakes I see when students are throwing the lead hand. The first is failing to rotate the hips into the punch. No hip, no power. The more hip, the more power. It's that simple. You can't rotate the hips as much when throwing the lead hand as you can the rear hand strike, because your hips are already angled in that direction. But take advantage of what little room you have to rotate them to maximize power.

The second mistake (and just the same as with the rear hand strike) is allowing the elbow of the punching hand to fly upwards instead of keeping it tucked under your hand. Like before, whenever your elbow flies outward (with the exception of throwing a hook), you lose power, speed, and telegraph the strike. We've all been taught the shortest distance between two points is a straight line. Nope, your elementary school teacher didn't lie to you. It's true. It's also true that the shortest distance happens to be the fastest. If you're a car enthusiast, imagine your arm is a piston. It starts in a bent position, straightens to throw the punch, and then bends again back into its original, defensive position.

If you're using proper body mechanics, your body, specifically the legs and hips, are driving the punch forward. Your arms are just along for the

Video 11.2 at www.SurvivalSciences.com depicts the execution of a lead hand strike.

ride. Think of the lead elbow as being locked to the lead hip. As you snap your hip forward, the hip propels the strike to the target.

Now for another visualization I'd like for you to try: Your lead arm is nothing more than a limp, wet towel and your hand is a bar of soap contained in the end of the towel (or a rock in a sock). You're going to snap the jab out there just like you would pop somebody with a towel. Your hand (the soap) is just dead weight at the end of the towel. Your arms don't do any of the work. Your body starts the whole process by pushing off the rear foot, a quick snap of the hips, and a sharp turn of the shoulders. Remember to *relaxxxxxxxzzzzzzzz*. There should be no tension in your arms. Your rear foot pushes against the ground, your weight moves forward, your hips rotate, and your hand snaps out to the target.

Another common error during the execution of a hand strike is to "cock" the hand prior to delivering the blow. Even some fairly good fighters have fallen prey to this mistake and are often unaware they are doing it. In a misguided attempt to add power to the blow, some people unknowingly bring the hand backwards a few inches just prior to launching it forward. Don't do it. For all of your hand strikes, there is no setup or preparation. The hand just flies straight out from wherever it is.

Many years ago when I was preparing for competition, I had the opportunity to spar with a particular fighter on a couple of occasions. He was a reasonably talented fighter with the exception he would cock his right hand ever so slightly just before throwing it, telegraphing his intention to land the big right hand. I immensely enjoyed sparring him as I gleefully would step in and pop him with a jab whenever I saw his right hand pull back. He thought I was psychic. I never told him he telegraphed his punch. Don't give your adversary the same advantage. Don't telegraph your techniques.

Two drills should be done: one to focus on speed (velocity), the other to focus on proper body mechanics (mass). The first drill is to stand in place with a loose, unclenched hand, and casually throw it out in front of you. Concentrate on relaxing your entire body and lazily throwing your hand in front of you. Your arm is a noodle with no muscle, tendons, or ligaments. It's just a towel, a piece of string, to which your hand is attached. Slowly increase the speed of the hand going outward and back in a jab-like motion, but your primary objective is relaxation.

The second drill, a "bag push drill," focuses on proper body mechanics in deploying maximum mass into a hand strike. Either using a heavy bag or a partner holding a striking shield, assume a survival/response stance. Your objective is to move the heavy bag or your partner with each strike. With your hips rotating in alignment with the strike, think of pushing your partner back. If you drive with your legs, rotate your hips and shoulders, and shift your body weight forward, you will be able to move your partner backwards with each strike. You can see the difference in power even in a still photo (Figures 11.4 and 11.5).

Figure 11.4 You can see a rear hand strike with no rotation of the shoulders and hips, the posture is upright, and the body weight is stationary. There is obviously very little power in this strike.

The first time I saw the bag push drill, I didn't like it. I enjoy watching people punch on the heavy bag to determine their effectiveness as a fighter. One of the many things I look for is if the bag sways and moves a lot, or if the bag jumps when struck. If I see the bag swinging back and forth, I know that person is "pushing" their punches as opposed to hitting with a sharp snap. A push is not as effective in a fight as is a sharp, violent strike. Think of it this way: Would you rather someone with a 6-foot pole place it on your chest and then push you, or that he quickly drive it into your chest? The first may knock you slightly off-balance, but it wouldn't hurt. The other method, because it is traveling faster than you can fall backwards, actually feels as if it is penetrating your body and is much more painful. I thought the bag push drill encouraged bad habits by causing people to push their punches. What I observed, however, is that people with poor body mechanics quickly began to understand how their body had to work to provide the necessary rotation and torque to generate power. Once a student understands that, then it's just a matter of speeding up the strike, snapping it out, and pulling it back into the proper on-guard position, to have an effective strike. I must credit two individuals for introducing me to this drill. They are former professional

Figure 11.5 You see the rotation of the hips and shoulders and the body weight is clearly moving through the bag.

kick boxer Sam Greco and MMA fighter Marco Calvacante, an incredibly accomplished Brazilian jiu-jitsu instructor who had instructed FBI agents in Los Angeles for many years.

Hooks and Uppercuts

Hooks and uppercuts are effective power techniques. Although they are traditionally done with a closed fist, they can also be thrown with an open hand, striking with the palm heel area. Hooks and uppercuts are not looping, arching strikes, but should actually travel in a straight line. A hook should drive straight through the target with the bent arm parallel to the floor. An uppercut travels straight upwards against an opponent who is leaning forward and exposing his chin, or drives upwards at an angle to drive the opponent's head up and back. Finally, a hook moving upwards at a 45° angle to the rib area is effective if delivered with sufficient power. Regardless of which of these techniques you use, your hand is moving in a straight line. If the strike begins to loop, you are losing power.

Particularly on the hook, it is imperative you drive with the hips. Your hips snap in the direction you want the hook to go, almost as if your body is

Figure 11.6 The proper position of a hook to the head.

pulling the strike through your attacker. The hips rotate quickly and propel the hand into the target (Figure 11.6).

The uppercut is not thrown by dropping your hand. Your hands remain in a protective position as you drop your entire body weight by bending your knees into a crouched position. Using your legs, you drive the punch upwards, putting as much body weight into the strike as possible (Figures 11.7 and 11.8).

Video 11.3 at www.SurvivalSciences.com demonstrates a hook.

Please see Video 11.4 at www.SurvivalSciences.com for the execution of the uppercut.

Figure 11.7 The incorrect way to begin the uppercut. Don't drop the hand!

Figure 11.8 The proper setup for the uppercut by bending your knees and dropping your weight.

Kicks

There are hundreds of kicks, but for law enforcement, I now only teach two. I used to teach the roundhouse kick to officers, as it is a highly effective kick with a good probability of landing when it's directed at your opponent's legs. The best target for the roundhouse kick is the knee area of your attacker or slightly higher to strike the common peroneal nerve. The striking surface is the top of your foot or your shin. The problem with the roundhouse kick is very few people can do it effectively without a great deal of practice. Even some accomplished martial artists have poor body mechanics for this kick. I'll discuss the roundhouse kick here primarily for illustrative purposes and to highlight some fundamental principles.

Roundhouse Kick

Following are three tips to increase the effectiveness of a roundhouse kick:

1. The beginning of any kick is the bending and lifting of the knee of the kicking leg. This was a very useful tip I received from Hapkido

Grand Master Bong Soo Han. I was fortunate to receive one-on-one instruction from Mr. Bong Soo Han. For some unknown reason he took a liking to me and we would meet early in the morning before I had to go to work. Even in his seventies he was a phenomenal kicker. Many people try to kick starting with a straight or nearly straight leg and wonder why they fail to develop sufficient power in their kicks. The first thing to do on any kick is to lift and bend the knee of the kicking leg (Figure 11.9).

2. Rotate your support foot 180° so the heel of the support foot (the one remaining in contact with the ground) is facing your target. I can almost guarantee 99% of the people will not rotate the foot sufficiently on a roundhouse kick. For beginners, they leave their support foot planted in place, toes facing their opponent, and then perform an awkward-looking movement trying to kick. If you don't open up your hips by fully rotating your support foot, your hips have no place to go and your body works against itself. This reminds me of another DT axiom. I call it the goofy rule. If you are doing a DT technique and you look goofy, you're doing it wrong. Trying to do a roundhouse kick without sufficiently pivoting your

Figure 11.9 The beginning of a roundhouse kick (or any kick, for that matter, as all kicks should start by raising the kicking knee).

support foot will cause you to look very goofy. Don't do it. Some prospective mate may be watching you and lose all interest once they see how goofy and unathletic you look. Even experienced kickers regularly fail to pivot properly. Again, this is not a sporting event where you are trying to score a point. You are trying to hit as hard as possible. So pivot fully and kick through your target (Figure 11.10).

3. Kick down at a 45° angle through your attacker's leg. Hitting through the leg is good. Hitting downward at this angle also puts gravity and acceleration on your side, increasing the power of the strike.

The roundhouse is a great technique for those who practice it. For the majority of officers who will not regularly train, attempting to use the roundhouse kick will just upset their balance and make them vulnerable to attack.

See Video 11.5 at www.SurvivalSciences.com for a demonstration of the roundhouse kick.

Figure 11.10 The full pivot of the support foot.

Front Kick

One of the simplest and most effective kicks is a front kick. It's a more natural movement and most people can do a reasonably good front kick with little practice. As with all kicks, start by bending the knee and bringing it up in front of you (Figure 11.11).

As with hand strikes, you want to have your body weight moving forward and through your opponent as you kick your foot through the target. For law enforcement, never kick above belt level. Unlike sports application, don't snap the kick to the target and back. Kick through your target with all of your body weight and step down with the kicking foot now in front. Drive the kick through your opponent.

What is your striking surface for the front kick? Traditional martial arts say the ball of the foot. This is not traditional martial arts. This is a fight with an aggressive resister who intends to hurt you. The reason traditional martial arts teach to strike with the ball of your foot is they practice in bare feet. On the job, you are probably wearing hard-toed shoes or boots. By minimizing the striking area, you maximize the effectiveness of the blow. Let's say your kick generates X power units. It is better to have those X power units concentrated on a small surface area of your opponent rather than dissipated over a

Figure 11.11 The proper "chambering" of a rear leg front kick.

Video 11.6 at www.SurvivalSciences.com illustrates a front kick.

large surface area. So don't kick with the ball of your boot. Kick with the edge of the toe of the boot. Your toes won't be injured because they are protected by your hard footwear.

Stomp

The last kick is the most effective and the easiest to learn. It can be called a kick, but it is more accurately a stomp. By now, it may be apparent that every strike you do should involve all of your body weight. The stomp is not a strength-driven technique. The stomp involves dropping your body weight downward at an angle. You don't use your muscles to drive the kick. You just set up the position and "fall" into the stomp. The striking surface is the entire bottom of your foot. This is not so much a strike as it is an unbalancing and crushing technique.

Notice the body weight is driving through the target for the groin-level stomp and dropping down through the target for lower-level targets. The stomp is particularly useful when attacking the legs of your opponent. It is much more damaging to your opponent to have you place your foot on the side of his knee and then drop your body weight against the knee, rather than it is to strike the knee with a roundhouse kick. The advantage of the roundhouse kick is it can be thrown from a greater distance. The stomp to the knee is particularly effective if you are close and your attacker has grabbed you.

What should your hands be doing when you kick? This is a trick question. The answer is absolutely nothing, other than remaining in a defensive position. Many inexperienced kickers think they have to throw their arms out, down, or generally flail their arms through the air on every kick. Don't. It looks goofy, it telegraphs your kick, and it exposes you to a counterstrike. Your upper body and arms have nothing to do with the kick, so they should be relaxed and in an on-guard position.

Video 11.7 at www.SurvivalSciences.com presents the stomp performed at the groin and knee levels.

Head Butts

Head butts can be extremely effective, but it's possible to knock yourself out if you're not careful. Your head was designed for better uses than as a battering ram. Personally, I need all of my few remaining brain cells so I make it a point not to bang my head against hard objects (such as another person's head). I wouldn't use a head butt as a technique of choice, but it's nice to have in your repertoire if you're really in tight. If you are going to use it, here are two safety precautions. First, when striking to the front, strike using the hairline area of your skull. For those of you whose hairline has receded or disappeared, use the area where your hairline used to be. Second, when striking to the rear, don't drive your head straight back into your attacker. There is a skull fissure there and it is a weaker spot in the skull. Instead, turn your head slightly to the left or right, and then drive it backwards.

Your target area should be an area that is somewhat soft. You don't want to drive your head into the skull of your attacker, as this is one of the hardest parts of the body. You want to direct the head butt into the face of your attacker, focusing primarily on the area of the nose.

The Best Personal Weapon Ever!

I saved the best for last. This is my favorite personal weapon and it can be effective for anyone regardless of their size or strength. It can be effective no matter how big or strong your attacker is. This personal weapon is often neglected because it is not legal in any fighting sport. In the photo image section of www.bullshido.net, I saw a photo with the following caption, "EYE POKE—When you're outmatched, it's really your only option." It's funny. It's true. The eye jab is a great technique that doesn't require a great deal of skill to deliver effectively. As a law enforcement officer, you are simply trying to get someone off you and make enough space to go to another weapon or control position. It makes it very difficult for your attacker to continue to close on you if you are driving a finger into his eye.

Although it is a simple technique, there are some things you can do to increase the finger jab's effectiveness and likelihood of landing. Don't attempt to do the three stooges two-finger poke. Also, don't try to do a single-finger poke. Maximize your chances of a finger finding its way home by using all of them. I generally think of snapping my middle finger to the center of my opponent's brow. Then the first and ring finger naturally fall into my opponent's eyes. If I can strike both eyes, that's great. If I can only get one, that's fine too (Figure 11.12).

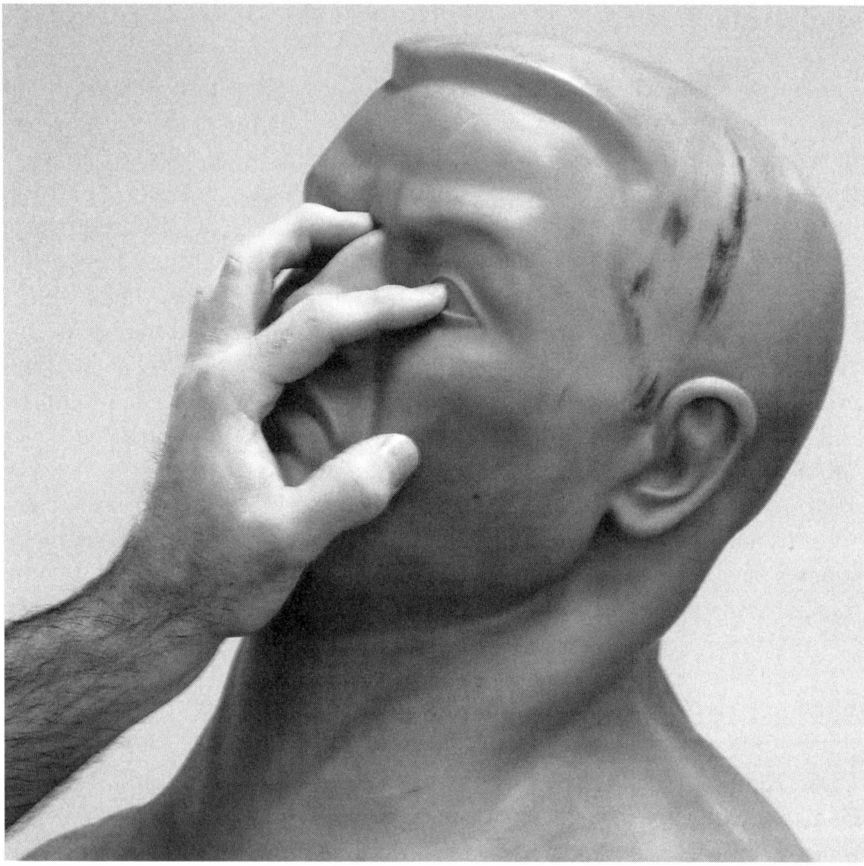

Figure 11.12 A close-up of the finger jab technique.

Tim Webb and I shared a special bond because we were promoted to black belt together in 1980. As strong as this bond was and as much as I liked Tim, he was one sneaky dude. I was the more talented fighter, but he certainly was the more cunning. We'd often get together on weekends to spar. During one session he laid out what appeared to be a weak lazy jab. I was already pivoting my body to hit him with a right hand over his left when he opened his fingers and raked them across my eyes. I was stunned. My eyes immediately began watering and I had trouble seeing. I was sputtering mad and Tim was smiling at me. When we sparred on weekends, it was just the two of us—no supervision and no rules. We had some knockdown fights,

Video 11.8 at www.SurvivalSciences.com depicts the execution of a finger jab.

but because we genuinely liked and respected each other, it never got out of hand. So I really couldn't cry foul at this unexpected technique (particularly since on more than one occasion I had bitten Tim during our sparring). Tim laughed, I laughed (much later), and it became a learning experience for me. A technique I misread as weak stopped me in my tracks and greatly diminished my ability to fight. I've been alert to finger jabs ever since.

As a reminder, personal weapons are an option of last resort. If you can, it is preferable to use a TASER, pepper spray, or impact weapon. It's safer for the bad guy and much safer for you. If you do use personal weapons, realize you are not trying to win a point competition; you are trying to survive a battle. Don't try to outfight your attacker. Hit as hard as you can, make distance, and now go to another tool to obtain compliance. And don't forget the finger jab is a really cool and effective technique.

Drills

1. Practice the drill mentioned earlier in this chapter to increase your relaxation and thereby increase your speed. The drill is to stand in a response stance and concentrate on relaxing your body as you practice throwing various hand strikes and kicks.
2. The second drill is the "bag push drill," also mentioned in this chapter. With a heavy bag or with a partner, practice using proper body mechanics and weight transference to push the bag or striking pad. After you are deploying the muscles properly (pushing off with the rear leg, body weight moving in the direction of the strike, hips rotating, and shoulders rotating), next speed up the drill to strike with greater and greater speed. Focus on striking while your body is still moving into the strike.
3. Using a "BOB" or other life-like striking dummy, practice instinctually flipping out a finger jab. You can also try this with a training partner wearing safety goggles. Practice the finger strike in various scenarios and positions.
4. Shadowbox your favorite personal weapon techniques focusing on relaxation. Concentrate on relaxing the muscles so you can deliver the technique effortlessly—no straining or tension.
5. Next, shadowbox your personal weapon techniques focusing on rotation and proper body mechanics. Pivot your hips sharply and see your body weight move in the direction of your strike.
6. Finally, shadowbox combining relaxation and rotation. Don't forget to constantly move as you shadowbox.

Endnotes

1. Koon, S. C., *Presumed Guilty: The Tragedy of the Rodney King Affair*, Regnery Publishing, Washington, DC, 1992.

Surviving the Ground War 12

There is a lot of controversy about the role of ground fighting in law enforcement. Let's be blunt. If you want to survive the ground war, don't go to the ground! Law enforcement officers should always avoid being on the ground, as it is a dangerous place to be. You lose sight of your opponent's hands, your weapons are easily accessible, and lots of bad things can happen very quickly. Even the courts have agreed it is dangerous for an officer to grapple with someone.[1] However, be aware there is a big difference in you taking a resister to the ground as opposed to purposely going to the ground and grappling.

Many ground-fighting experts have claimed "almost all" real fights go to the ground. Research has proven this is not necessarily true. What is true is the more talented and experienced fighter dictates the parameters of a fight. Therefore, a highly skilled grappler (such as someone from the famed Gracie family) will almost always take a fight to the ground since that is their strength. When I was younger, I was involved in many more street fights than I should have been. None of those fights went to the ground, as I was fortunate to be the more skilled fighter and I preferred to stand and strike.

I asked one of my first martial instructors, Keith Teller, about his thoughts on the then espoused theory that almost all fights go to the ground. In college, Keith was a third-degree black belt in Peter Urban's USA Goju Karate (he is now a tenth-degree black belt) and worked as a bouncer in a tough club to pay his college tuition. Keith said it was not unusual for him to get involved in several "altercations" a night. I asked him how many of those fights went to the ground. Keith's response was none of them. He said, "I knocked people to the ground and then dragged them out of the club, but I never grappled with anyone on the ground." This happened simply because Keith was the more skilled fighter and, as such, he determined the pattern of the fight.

In an article written by Bakari Akil II that appeared in *Black Belt Magazine*, he discussed a study he conducted of fight videos archived on YouTube.[2] Mr. Akil determined both fighters ended up on the ground in 42% of the fights he viewed and one of the fighters ended up on the ground 72% of the time. Mr. Akil further determined that of the people taken to the ground, 57% were taken there with a throw, trip, or by being pulled. Only 7% were pushed to the ground. Thirty-five percent of the fighters went to the ground as a result of being punched. In one out of three hundred fights reviewed, only one person fell because of a kick. Mr. Akil goes on to say that the person who went to the ground first lost 59% of the time, and there was no discernible victor in 33% of the fights.

There are several things to remember about these videos. They overwhelmingly involve untrained, unskilled fighters. The less skilled the fighters, the more likely it is to have one or both of the participants fall to the ground simply because of poor balance and poor footwork. The videos are still a wealth of information for officers to see how the general public typically behaves in a street fight. If you have good balance and move properly (as was explained in Chapter 6 on getting out of the way), you greatly decrease the chance of being taken to the ground. However, we would be remiss if we did not practice ground defense.

Much of what is taught today in grappling is extraordinary information with exceptional sports application. I believe in its value enough to have spent several years training with a Brazilian jiu-jitsu expert to better understand its strengths and weaknesses. It is a valuable addition to any fighter's repertoire. However, from a law enforcement perspective, we never want to be rolling around and grappling with a resister. We just have too many weapons on our belt (e.g., handguns, knives, pepper spray, etc.) that are in easy reach of the bad guy. A great deal of our training time in the academy is spent making us aware of the weapons we carry and ensuring we keep them out of reach of anyone who may want to use them against us. So why would we then purposely close the distance on a resister and allow his hands to roam over our bodies in search of something to hurt us? Furthermore, if we grapple with a subject, we have lost sight of the resister's hands. It would be easy for him to reach into his waistband or pocket and pull out a blade or handgun. In addition, what if the resister has several friends in the area? We can't afford to lock up with one subject as other bad guys arrive on the scene to beat us or kill us.

The first, and best, defense against being taken to the ground is avoiding the initial attack. As mentioned in Chapter 6, the simplest and most effective method is to maintain proper distance, have a balanced posture, stay alert, and move out of the line of attack. If they can't touch you, they can't take you to the ground.

So is any time spent practicing ground fighting a waste of time? We should be able to avoid almost any attack attempting to take us to the ground, but it can still happen and we should prepare for that possibility. Hopefully we can agree that being on the ground is not a good place for a law enforcement officer to be. Therefore, our mindset needs to be that if we are unfortunate enough to be in this position, our primary goals should be to initially assume a position of protection and get to our feet as quickly and safely as possible. If the attacker managed to grab you and is in the process of taking you to the ground (such as in a double-leg takedown), the best defense is still to move. If the attacker has wrapped you up, you can still simply sidestep, as discussed in Chapter 10 on countering common attacks (Figure 12.1).

(A)

(B)

Figure 12.1 (A) The attacker trying to tackle an officer and drive him back.(B) The officer's initial move to the side (opening the door) and down, even as the attacker continues the attempt to tackle. (continued)

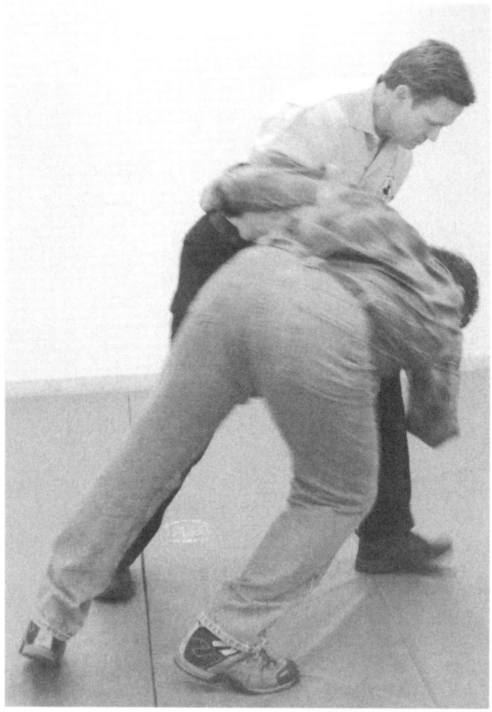

(C)

Figure 12.1 (Continued) (C) The continuation of the step that results in throwing the attacker to the ground.

In Video 12.1 at www.SurvivalSciences.com, I demonstrate defeating an attempted tackle by moving and shifting my body weight down and to the side. Use the user name and pass code listed in the introduction to access the video.

If you do get knocked, pushed, pulled, or tripped to the ground, the first concern is to not get hurt when you fall. Since this is a book on advanced concepts, I'll discuss the concepts of falling safely without belaboring the basics. To simplify, if you do fall, do *not* reach out for the ground to break your fall. Your weight, combined with gravity, is too much force for the bones of your wrists and arms to bear. If you fall and extend a straight arm toward the ground, you will likely break bones. That could be catastrophic in that it may now prevent you from using one of the tools on your duty belt to protect yourself.

Any falling body continues to accelerate until impact. Therefore, the greater the distance you fall, the greater the force will be upon your body (Figure 12.2). If possible, you want to minimize the distance you fall to lessen

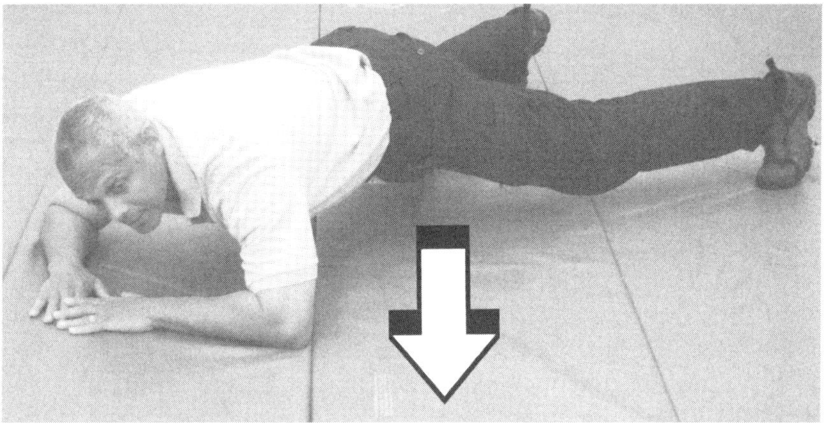

Figure 12.2 A fall with the force the body exerts upon the ground.

the potential damage to your body. How do you do this? This is accomplished by lowering your center of gravity as much as possible before falling. The more you can bend your knees and the lower you can place your butt to the ground prior to striking the ground, the less force the ground will exert upon your body. A roll is also preferable to a "break fall," as a roll disperses the impact among a greater surface area (Figure 12.3).

If you must "slap out," try to hit the ground with as much surface area of your body as possible. If you are falling forwards and don't have the space or

Figure 12.3 How the force of impact is lessened by rolling.

Please see Video 12.2a at www.SurvivalSciences.com for a demonstration of a front fall. For comparison, Video 12.2b depicts a forward roll. Note how a roll significantly reduces the impact on the body. Video 12.2c demonstrates a backwards roll.

time to roll, at least fall on the palms of your hands, your forearms, and feet (as opposed to only your hands). The more surface area in contact with the ground, the more the impact force is dispersed, and the less likely you are to get injured. When you practice falling, first do it from a sitting or kneeling position, then squatting, and finally standing. Don't progress to a higher level until you can fall with no discomfort at the previous level (Figures 12.4 to 12.6).

For either a roll or fall, ensure your head doesn't hit the ground. If your "brain housing unit" is damaged, then you are in bad shape. Protect your head at all times, particularly while falling.

Once you're on the ground, realize this is a really bad situation. As such, you want to get up as soon as you can do so safely. Once you're on the ground, one of three things will have happened: (1) the attacker immediately moved into a grappling/wrestling position (mount, side mount, etc.) and has joined you on the ground, (2) the attacker has remained standing and is too close for you to safely get to your feet (most likely the attacker is attempting to strike you while he is standing), or (3) the attacker remained standing and enough distance separates the two of you for you to safely get back up.

Video 12.3a depicts the progression of a front fall from kneeling to squatting to standing. Video 12.3b demonstrates a side fall performed while sitting, squatting, and standing. Video 12.3c depicts a back fall while sitting, squatting, and standing.

Figure 12.4 A side view of the proper position for a front fall, maximizing the surface area in contact with the ground. The officer's hands and forearms form a triangle, he has ensured his groin doesn't impact with the ground, and he has turned his head to the side to avoid smashing his nose into the ground.

Figure 12.5 The proper position for a back fall. The officer has rolled back onto his shoulder blades area and his head is up off of the ground.

Figure 12.6 The proper position for a side fall. The officer has landed on his right side, hip, and leg, protecting his spinal cord and head.

Let's look at the three possibilities and your strategy for each one:

1. **You and your attacker are on the ground and the attacker is on top of you.**

   This is the worst-case scenario. Your attacker may be in one of several possible configurations—mount, side mount, north-south mount (sometimes indelicately referred to as the 69 mount), or in your guard position. Regardless of the position of your attacker, your goal is the same—to escape, stand, move to a position of survival, and draw a weapon to avoid a continued attack.

The worst position to be in is prone (face down) with your attacker straddling you with his entire body weight while pummeling your unprotected head and spine. This is also referred to as the turtle position. Unfortunately, the turtle position doesn't work out too well for humans since we don't have a hard protective shell that we can pull our head into and protect our vital organs. If you assume the turtle position, you might as well say, "Yep, I'm a victim—do with me as you please." Recognize in sports competition (and yes, this includes mixed martial arts (MMA) competitions), it is against the rules to strike the back of your opponent's head. This is also true in boxing and is called a rabbit punch. The reason it is a rule violation is it is very dangerous. Please note your attacker in the street is not limited by the silly rules of sportsmanship or competition.

If you are on the ground, fight the temptation to go into the turtle defense. You will only succeed in getting your butt kicked faster. Once you turn your back on your opponent, you have exposed your sensitive spinal area and can offer no resistance. It may work in the animal kingdom to adopt this "submissive" posture, but I wouldn't bet my life it will work with a bad guy. Remember to always face your butt kicking. If you find yourself in this position, don't try to force your way up in a force-against-force attempt. This will only work if your attacker is much smaller and weaker than you. He also has gravity on his side assisting him in pinning you to the ground. Instead, try to create enough of a gap so that you can rotate/roll your body (as opposed to pushing upwards) and now face your attacker. This is not a great position, but at least you now have a better chance of surviving.

A slightly better position to be in (but still really, really bad) is to have your attacker mounted on top of you as you are supine (face up). You are still at an extreme disadvantage, but at least you can use your arms to protect yourself. If the attacker is on top of you in this manner (the mount), recognize his balance is based on your position. If you change your position (i.e., move), you can upset his balance and succeed in throwing him off of you. It takes a great deal of strength to push someone off of you. Going back to the chapter on fundamentals, please recall the ideal for law enforcement is always to use redirection of force, never applying force against force. The reason for this is in a force-against-force encounter, the stronger force wins.

This is great if you are the bigger and stronger person in the battle. Not so great otherwise. And I always assume the person who will attack me will be younger, stronger, bigger, and faster. Even if you are stronger than an attacker who has mounted you, brute strength will probably not be sufficient. If the attacker has mounted you, he now has gravity working in his favor and gravity is working against you. All the attacker has to do is sit on your chest, pin your arms to the ground, and begin what has become known in MMA parlance as a "ground and pound." In other words, the attacker will sit down on top of you and pummel you unless you manage to escape.

What is the easiest way to escape from the mount? Particularly if you are not in competition with an opponent of the same weight class and general fighting experience as you? The answer, again, is in the fundamentals. The answer is redirection of force. The answer is balance. The answer is movement. Using an analogy of viewing your opponent as a table with four legs, imagine your opponent is in the mount position, straddling your body, and pinning your arms by your head. Your opponent is in a balanced, solid, four-legged, square-table configuration. Life's pretty good for your attacker right now. It's not so good for you. Actually it sucks big time for you. The attacker's force and weight are pressing straight down, pinning you to the ground. The natural reaction is to try to push straight up against the downward pressure (force against force). Unless you are amazingly strong or your attacker is incredibly weak (and if that's the case, how did you get in this predicament?), pushing straight back toward the attacker is likely to be futile. How do you upset the attacker's balance? How do you redirect his force? As powerful as the attacker is pushing down on you, one thing he can't prevent you from doing is sliding your arms along the ground. Try it. Have a buddy mount you, pin your hands to the ground, and see how easily you can slide your arms above your head or down closer to your body. What you'll also discover is it's easiest to slide your hands along the ground up above your head like you're going to dive into water. As you do this, what happens to your attacker who was holding onto your wrists? First as your hands move above your head into the diving position, your opponent elongates his table position, making his balance narrower. As your hands come together, your opponent's table now only has three legs. A slight rotation of your body in one direction or the other (move) will now completely upset your attacker's table (balance) and redirect his force. It takes little strength to rotate your body to the side and unbalance an attacker—particularly if the attacker is attempting to strike or choke you at that moment (Figure 12.7).

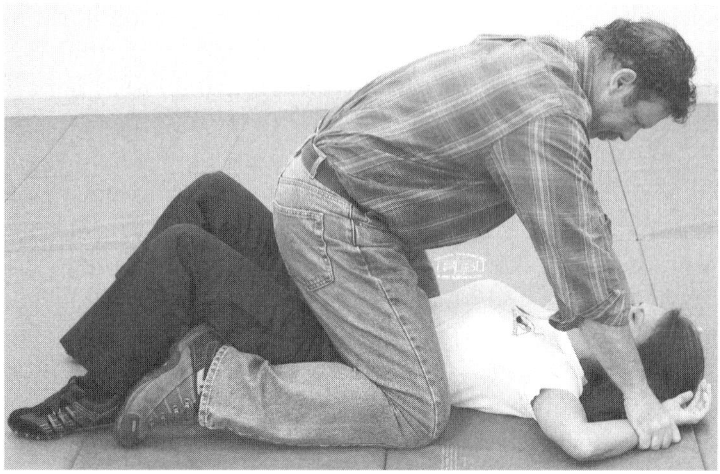

(A)

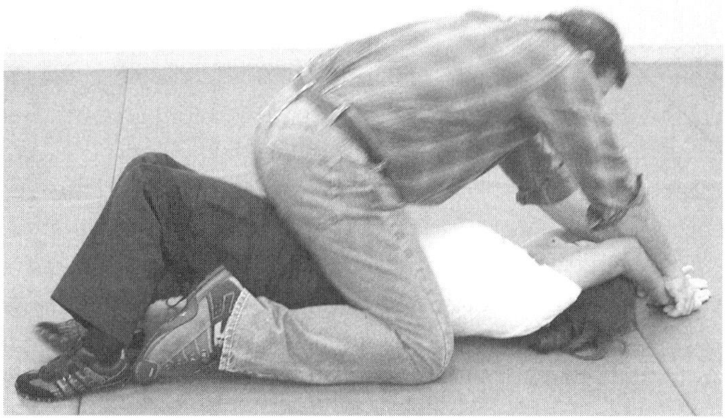

(B)

Figure 12.7 (A) The attacker in a balanced, four-point position as he pins the officer. (B) The officer has begun to slide her hands up and together, and is already beginning to take the attacker's balance. (Continued)

Rather than pinning your arms from the mount, let's now look at the attacker who is attempting to hit you while sitting on your chest. The principles of your escape response are the same as before. You will attempt to take the four-legged table and cut off a couple of legs. As the attacker throws a punch barreling down at your head, move your head out of the way. But don't just move your head, move your entire

Video 12.4 at www.SurvivalSciences.com demonstrates taking the balance of an attacker who has pinned you to the ground.

(C)

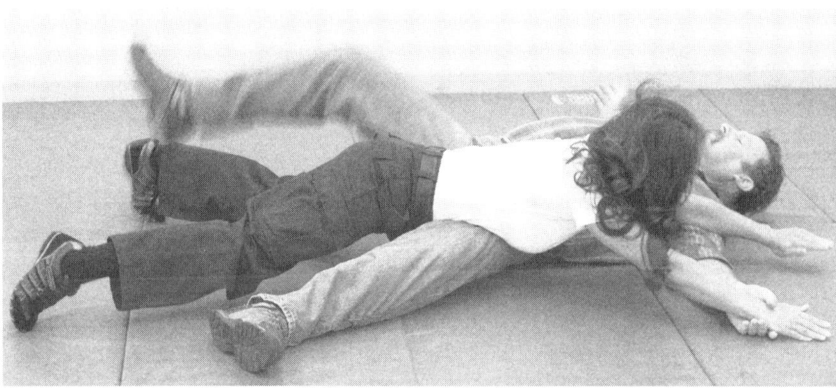

(D)

Figure 12.7 (Continued) (C) The officer is beginning to roll in the direction of her hands and the attacker's balance is now disrupted. (D) The officer has the attacker on his back and the officer is able to escape.

body. You should actually roll your body in one direction. Because your attacker has you pinned to the ground, you probably will only be able to roll your upper body. That's okay. That's enough. As you do this you will also extend your arm across your, and the attacker's, body. For example, if the attacker tries to punch down with a right hand, roll to your left as you extend your right arm across your body so your hand is near the attacker's right shoulder. It may not seem like it at first, but the attacker has upset his balance by punching at you. You now just roll to your right as your right hand guides the attacker's shoulder and the attacker will topple over. The key is not to try to lift your hips or push your body up. That takes a great deal of strength and won't work against a bigger, stronger opponent. Simply rolling, however, will take the attacker's balance (Figure 12.8).

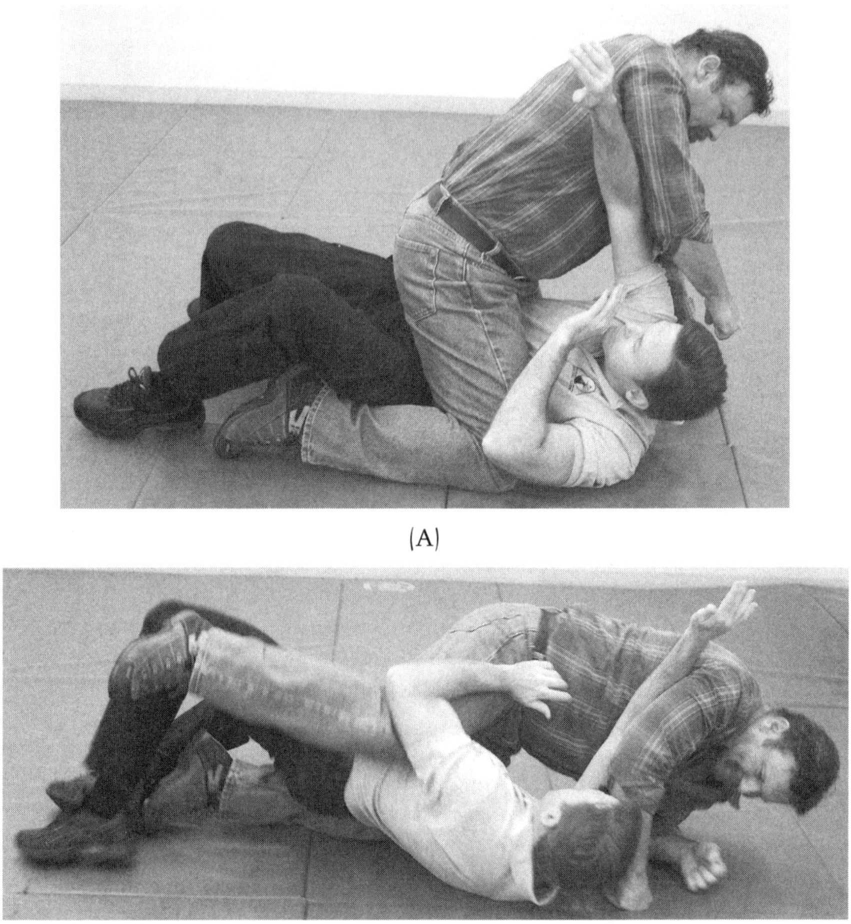

(A)

(B)

Figure 12.8 (A) Moving out of the way as the attacker strikes. In this example, the officer has rolled to his left and extended his right arm to get out of the way of the punch. (B) Taking the attacker's balance after the attempted punch by rolling in the opposite direction.

The next possibility is the attacker has mounted you and is attempting to choke you. This is simpler because the attacker has taken his four-legged table and made it a three-legged table by placing both hands on your throat. Reach across his wrists with one arm, brace his elbow with your other hand, and roll in the direction you are pushing his elbow. This is not a strength move, so don't think you

Video 12.5 at www.SurvivalSciences.com demonstrates a defense to a punch thrown by an attacker in the mount position.

Video 12.6 at www.SurvivalSciences.com demonstrates a defense to a choke while mounted.

have to exert a lot of effort to push the attacker's elbow. You don't. Your hand is there primarily as a guide. Your body rolling (not lifting) is what will take the attacker's balance (Figure 12.9).

Now what if the attacker is on top of you, but you have wrapped your legs around his waist in a guard position? This is better than having your attacker on top of you in a mount position, but not by much. Some people are effective at fighting from the guard, but it takes a great deal of training to become proficient. Again, as a law enforcement officer, you really don't want to be on the ground with a bad guy on top of you. You need to get up and draw a weapon as soon as it is safe to do so. You can use your hips to bring the attacker in close to you and wrap up his arms with you in a swimming motion (Figure 12.10). You can also use your hips to push the attacker away from you in an attempt to prevent him from hitting you (Figure 12.11). Realize either of these is a very short-term answer.

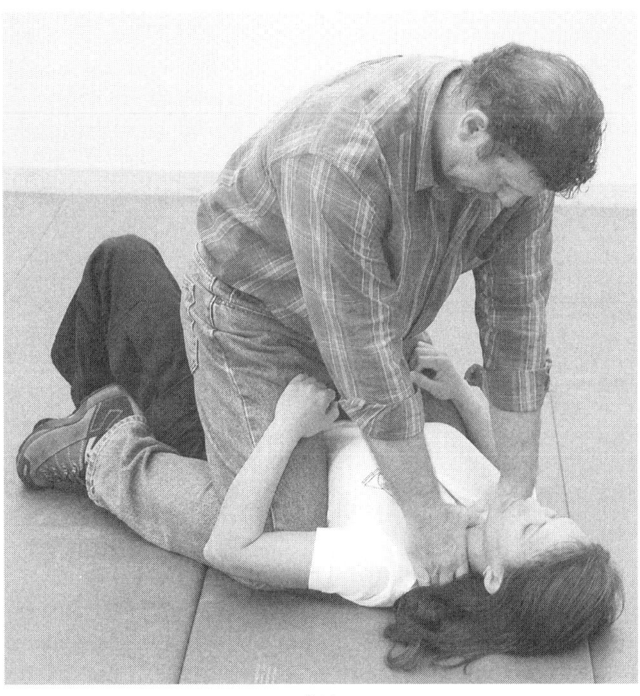

(A)

Figure 12.9 (A) The officer being choked while mounted. (Continued)

(B)

(C)

Figure 12.9 (Continued) (B) The officer has braced one of the choking arms while pinning the attacker's same-side hand. (C) The effect of the officer rolling to the side and taking the attacker's balance.

(D)

Figure 12.9 (Continued) (D) The attacker has been thrown off and the officer is free to escape.

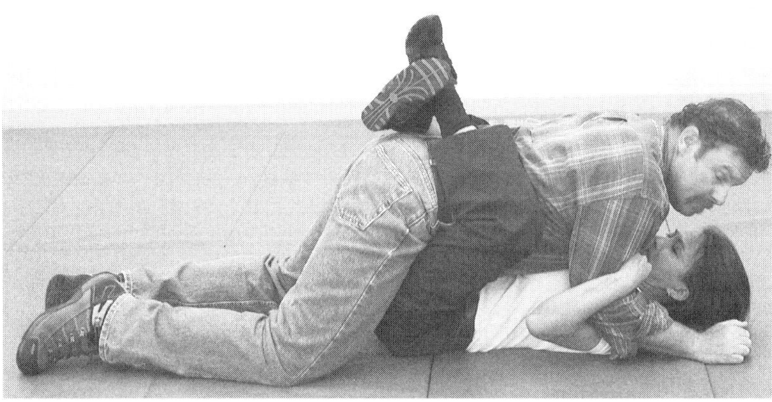

Figure 12.10 The officer bringing the attacker in close in her guard while controlling his arms.

Much like GET 1 and GET 2 presented in Chapter 9, these are temporary solutions. If you attempt to get a stalemate, you will eventually be destroyed. Worse, since you are tied up with your attacker, he has access to the weapons on your duty belt as well as any weapons he may have brought to the fight. As soon as possible, make enough space to drive your knee between you and your attacker's body. Then

Figure 12.11 The officer using her hips to push the attacker away from her while the attacker is in her guard to prevent being struck.

use the other leg to kick. Then continue to alternately kick with both legs until you create enough space to assume the ground defense position (described later in this chapter). From there, you want to draw a weapon as soon as it is safe to do so and stand up.

One way to make space or take your attacker's balance is by using your personal weapons. Don't forget the most useful personal weapon attack mentioned in Chapter 11. If one hand is free, a simple strike to the eyes of your attacker will likely create the necessary space and take his balance, allowing you to escape. This is another move that is not allowed in competition, and rightfully so. If you wanted to determine some of the most effective self-defense techniques, research the rules of boxing, wrestling, judo, etc. Everything that is against the rules in these sports is typically a violation because they are inherently too dangerous, and thus perfect for law enforcement in a life-or-death struggle. If you are able to place a finger in the eye of your attacker and push into the eye socket, you will take the attacker's balance away from you.

Video 12.7 at www.SurvivalSciences.com demonstrates a method to make space and kick out from the guard.

Video 12.8 demonstrates using body weight and driving your elbows into the attacker's thighs to break out of the guard.

Video 12.9 at www.SurvivalSciences.com demonstrates the ground defense position as well as rotating to face the threat.

What if somehow you ended up in the attacker's guard? Some MMA fighters like this position, but they aren't worried about the weapons they are carrying or the unseen/unknown weapons on their adversary. You don't want to be in this position for any length of time either. With your hands up protecting your head, drive your knee as hard as you can into the attacker's coccyx (tail bone) area. Place your elbows on the insides of his knees and apply pressure by leaning back with your body weight. Don't try to muscle his legs apart; use your body weight as you lean back to separate his legs. Once his lock has been broken, place your knee on top of one the subject's grounded legs. Your knee should be grinding into the inner thigh area of your attacker's leg. Stand up quickly, sweeping his other leg to the side to prevent being kicked.

As before, you have the option to attempt a finger jab to the attacker's eyes to disrupt him and create space and time for you to break away. A second personal weapon option is a strike to the groin. Particularly if you are in the attacker's guard, his groin is wide open and easily within range. As was mentioned in Chapter 11 regarding target areas, the most effective method of attacking the groin is not a strike, but a grab, squeeze, and twist. Anytime you are on the ground and tied up with an attacker, recognize how incredibly dangerous it is. Don't waste time looking for a sport's application solution. Fight dirty. Go for the eyes, groin, or bite to create a distraction, make space, get to your feet, and draw a weapon.

2. **The attacker has remained standing and is too close for you to safely get to your feet.**

Immediately assume a defensive position. You should have three points of contact with the ground. They are your support hand, your support forearm, and the same-side hip/buttock area. Your feet are facing your attacker and your knees should be bent so you have the ability to kick out. Your support hand helps you pivot and rotate on your hip so you can always face the threat. Your other hand is

Figure 12.12 The ground defense position. If possible, draw a weapon.

raised to protect your head and upper body, as well as grabbing an appropriate weapon for defense. Your primary defense will be to kick out toward your attacker, aiming primarily for his knees and lower extremities in an attempt to create enough space for you to safely stand. If enough distance exists between you and your attacker so that weapon retention isn't a concern, draw a weapon permitted by the law and your departmental policy. If deadly force is justified, I'd suggest drawing your handgun (Figure 12.12).

As soon as there is a safe distance between you and your attacker, get up! There are two ways to do this, depending upon if you have a weapon in your hand. If your hands are empty, quickly place both hands on the ground. One hand is placed next to your hip on the ground and the other farther back, away from your opponent. Next, forcefully swing both legs back so that you are moving away from your attacker. You should be in a crouched position as you move and simultaneously draw an appropriate weapon. Be alert, as your

Video 12.10 at www.SurvivalSciences.com demonstrates getting up from the ground defense position.

Video 12.11 at www.SurvivalSciences.com demonstrates getting up from the ground defense position while holding a weapon.

attacker will likely resume the attack as he sees you attempting to get to your feet.

The second method is used if you were successful in grasping a weapon in one hand. As before, you can place your empty hand on the ground for support as you swing your legs behind you to a standing position. Another option is slower, but it allows you to have two hands on your weapon as you get up. As you sit upright, bend one leg at a 90° angle so the knee is pointing outward and the outside of the leg is flat against the ground. The other leg is bent at the knee with the knee pointing to the sky and the foot flat on the floor. From this position you should be able to shift your weight forward to a standing position.

3. **The attacker remained standing and enough distance separates you to safely get back up.**

The thing to do in this situation is **get up!** The attacker knocked you down once, now go to the appropriate weapon and make sure it doesn't happen again. Use one of the two techniques mentioned above to get back on your feet and address the threat.

What if you were attacked and you were able to put your attacker on the ground while you remain standing. What do you do now? Jump on top of him and start to grapple? No! If you are in a position to mount a subject or straddle a subject's body, don't! It's too easy to break your balance and the fight for your gun is on once again. The best position as a law enforcement officer is not a mount, side mount, etc. Those positions lock you up with one subject (there may be more than one) and make everything on your duty belt too tempting for the bad guy to snatch. There is always at least one gun in the fight, and you brought it. Also, the bad guy can bring into play too many unseen weapons against you. You haven't searched him yet, so who knows what, and how many, weapons he has. Make distance, draw the appropriate weapon as justified by your policy, be absolutely prepared to use that weapon, and give appropriate commands.

Once you are sure you have the tactical advantage and choose to engage, the best position of control in these situations is to pin the subject's hip and shoulder with downward pressure with your knees while you keep both of your hands free, remaining in an upright position scanning for additional threats (Figure 12.13).

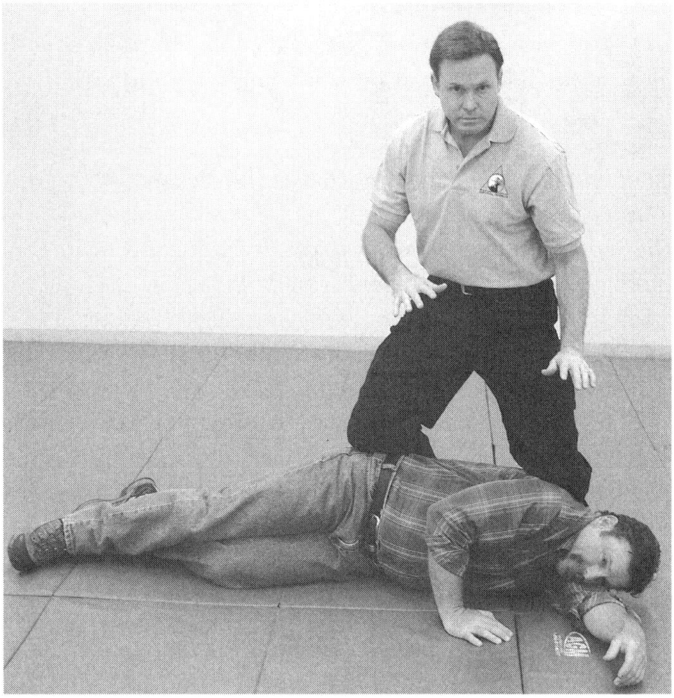

Figure 12.13 The proper pinning position. Notice the officer is erect, able to scan for additional threats, both hands are free, and the subject's shoulders and hips are pinned to the ground.

From this position, it's also easier to position the bad guy's hands for handcuffing.

In summary, the rules of the ground war are:

1. Don't go to the ground.
2. If you violate rule 1, get up as quickly as possible to a position of survival.
3. If you're in the ground defense position, attempt to keep your attacker at a distance by leg kicks and draw your handgun or appropriate weapon as soon as you can safely do so.

Video 12.12 at www.SurvivalSciences.com demonstrates the pinning technique. Note the focus is on applying force against the resister's shoulder and hip straight into the ground while remaining in an upright position.

4. You only ground fight long enough to find an opening to stand up and move to safety as you draw a weapon as soon as possible.
5. As always, the best defense and escape maneuver is to move.

Drills

Although a number of drills are listed below, you should be able to transition from one to the other quickly, creating a more realistic training environment. Use the falls and rolls to warm up, and then go directly to the ground defenses with a partner, switching roles frequently. Each of the ground drills should end with the person in the officer role breaking free, creating distance, and then simulating going to a weapon.

1. Using a soft mat and with appropriate safety considerations, practice forward, side, and back falls as demonstrated in Video 12.3a–c. Start from the lowest height initially and gradually progress to falling from a standing position when you can safely do so.
2. Practice forward and backward rolls as demonstrated in Video 12.2b and c.
3. Assume a ground defensive position with three points of contact with the ground, as depicted in Video 12.9. Practice rotating and moving while in this position to an imagined threat.
4. From the ground defensive position, practice quickly getting to your feet using the methods depicted in Videos 12.10 and 12.11 (while holding a weapon).
5. With a partner, assume a prone position (face down) and have your partner straddle you. Practice rotating your body so you are able to face your threat.
6. With your partner mounted on top of you, practice evading a punch and rolling your partner off of you, as shown in Video 12.5. Also, practice the defense from the mount position as your partner attempts to choke or pin you, as shown in Video 12.6.
7. With your partner in your guard position, practice kicking out, making distance, and quickly come to a standing position, as demonstrated in Video 12.7.
8. Get in your partner's guard and practice separating your partner's legs to break the lock, and then move to a standing position as you make distance, as shown in Video 12.8.
9. With your partner on the ground and you standing, practice moving to a position in which you can pin your partner's hip and shoulder, as demonstrated in Video 12.12.

Endnotes

1. *Carswell v. Borough of Homestead*, 381 F. 3d. 235 (3rd Cir. 2004).
2. Akil, B., "Grounded in Reality," *Black Belt Magazine*, 46, 92–96, 2008.

13 Bilateral Vascular Restraint

I was fortunate to be asked by Dr. John Pi to be part of a review group studying the effects and tactical application of the carotid restraint by law enforcement. Not only is Dr. Pi an accomplished emergency room physician and on the teaching staff at UCLA Medical School, but he is also an FBI agent. Dr. Pi coordinated and led a discussion group that consisted of medical doctors and personnel, most of whom volunteer their time to offer tactical medical support to local SWAT teams in the Southern California area. I was the only nonmedical person in the group. My role was to make suggestions based on the defensive tactics (DT) application of the technique.

This expert panel determined the vast majority of law enforcement personnel misunderstood, and had been incorrectly teaching, the physiological reasons for the effectiveness of a carotid technique. You may not care exactly why the technique works, as long as it works. However, by better understanding why it works, the better you may become at the application of the technique. The better you can apply the technique, the more effective it becomes. Also, a misunderstanding of the physiological responses can lead to improper application and unintended injuries to the resister. We all know what this leads to—lawsuits, administrative inquiries, and just generally bad stuff we'd rather not have to experience.

Recognizing the confusion on the physiological response and also acknowledging some of the "bad press" associated with a carotid technique, the panel first decided to develop a new name for the modified and correctly explained technique. It was determined a more accurate description of the technique is bilateral vascular restraint (BVR).[1] The goal of the panel was not only to educate the law enforcement community as to the actual physiological responses of a BVR, but also to develop a practical, safe technique to benefit officers and increase their safety. As was mentioned in Chapter 1, the use of a carotid type of technique was determined to be one of the safer force options and resulted in fewer injuries to the officer and to the resister. Therefore, with the modifications to the BVR increasing safety further, it was the panel's goal to encourage the inclusion of the BVR in DT training for all law enforcement agencies.

First, a carotid hold was never intended to be a choke. A choke works on an opponent by restricting the air passageway and can result in a collapsed trachea and possibly death. This is bad unless you are justified in using deadly force. If you are justified in using deadly force, you can use any tools at your disposal, including cars, bottles, manhole covers, etc. However, your department's policy may be more restrictive, so verify your policy first.

The problem was some officers were not properly trained on a carotid restraint and, in the heat of the battle, would apply pressure directly against the front of the subject's throat rather than the sides of the subject's neck. This led to unintentional deaths, which led to lawsuits, which led to massive settlements, which led to the restriction or elimination of the carotid as a viable tool in dealing with aggressive resisters. One attempt to remedy widespread prohibition of the carotid restraint was the creation of the lateral vascular neck restraint (LVNR), which proposed applying incrementally increasing pressure to the sides of a resister's neck while giving commands to the subject to stop resisting.

This was a commendable effort to resurrect the carotid restraint, but there are a few problems with the LVNR. I believe it potentially increases the danger to the officer and the resister. First, either you are legally justified in using a specific level of force or you are not. It's the same as using a firearm, a baton, a TASER, or personal weapons. Either you are legally and procedurally permitted to use it or you aren't. If you are permitted to use that level of force, then use it. You wouldn't attempt to shoot someone in the hand because once you fire the weapon, you are using deadly force. Similarly, you wouldn't "love tap" someone with a baton and gradually increase the intensity of the strikes in the hopes they would comply before you really had to get serious. So why would you do this with a carotid restraint? If you determine an immediate threat exists (i.e., the subject is an aggressive resister), then you are legally permitted to use the BVR, so use it. Of course, the one caveat to this is also to be certain the application of the BVR is approved by your department.

If you gradually increase pressure in stages, two bad things can happen. You have lost all surprise and the resister is now aware of what you are trying to do. Also, you allowed the resister to remain standing, you have not fully taken the resister's balance, and you still have not applied full pressure. This permits the resister a number of countermoves and endangers you and any bystanders. Second, by not applying maximum pressure to the sides of the resister's neck immediately, you have allowed the resister "wiggle room," which can now lead to an initially properly positioned restraint to become a potentially deadly choke that compresses the airway. Not only does properly applying maximum pressure and immediately taking the resister's balance result in quicker incapacitation (increased officer safety), but it also minimizes the risk of a proper BVR unintentionally sliding into an air choke (increased resister safety). When properly applied, the BVR is a valuable tool for an officer to achieve compliance of an aggressively resisting subject.

What did most of the law enforcement community (incorrectly) believe was the reason for the effectiveness of the carotid hold, that is, prior to the groundbreaking study by Dr. Pi's panel? It was believed the primary contributor to the desired effect (fainting) was the compression of the carotid arteries. Many in law enforcement believed, and taught, that the occlusion (blockage) of the carotid arteries resulted in a diminished flow of oxygenated blood to the brain, and this lack of oxygen was the sole mechanism for the success of the carotid restraint. This is partially, but not entirely, correct.

The panel determined the effectiveness of the BVR is due to several factors. The proper application of the BVR may trigger a spontaneous, temporary loss of consciousness. Three things are happening simultaneously that cause this loss of consciousness. They are the compression of the carotid arteries, compression of the jugular veins, and an automatic response of the vagus nerve. Through a literature search of clinical studies, the panel determined much less pressure is required to block the jugular veins (about 5 pounds) and cause unconsciousness, as opposed to approximately 11 pounds of pressure required on the carotid arteries. Jugular veins are a low-pressure system with easily compressed walls. The carotid arteries are part of a high-pressure system with much stronger walls and are therefore more resistant to pressure. If the jugular veins are even partially blocked, blood flow from the head is slowed and blood becomes congested in the head. Therefore, it is the pressure on the jugular veins that plays the larger role in causing the decreased flow of blood to the brain, rather than the carotid arteries.

It was also determined the primary cause for loss of consciousness was the stimulation of the vagus nerve. The vagus nerve controls involuntary body functions such as breathing and your heart beating. When in a confrontation, both the officer and the resister are likely experiencing fight or flight. Both individuals would be expected to have increased heart rate and increased blood pressure. In the BVR, as pressure is applied to the resister's mid-neck area, the carotid sinuses sense the increase in pressure and send a signal to the vagus nerve, which in turn responds to this threat to the body by slowing down the heart and lowering blood pressure—so much, in fact, the person faints. For the officer, this is a very good thing.

What this means from a practical perspective is not much size or strength is required to use the BVR effectively. A mere 5 pounds of pressure on the sides of the resister's neck in the mid-neck area is enough to start the blockage of the jugular veins and stimulate the vagus nerve to cause the resister to faint.

What is also important to note is that it is not necessary to elevate the chin of the resister to properly apply the BVR. Many officers have been taught they must elevate the subject's chin to apply the carotid. Based on the panel's research, and from officers' personal experiences, we know this is not required. The subject's chin would only need to be elevated to apply an air choke, which is prohibited by almost every department except in situations where deadly force is warranted. Since the effectiveness of the BVR is achieved by applying pressure to the sides of the neck, it is irrelevant if the resister drops his chin or not. People instinctively drop their chins when being choked, and this is a good survival reaction. However, dropping the chin doesn't impede the effectiveness of the BVR at all. It may give the resister a sense of security knowing his chin is tightly tucked into his chest, but it will be a false sense of security.

Chapters 5 and 6 covered balance, proper distance, the appropriate response to an attack (move), and footwork. All of those guidelines are still applicable in the application of a BVR. There are several additional fundamentals in the use of the BVR that distinguish it from other carotid-type holds. Adherence to the tactical elements of the BVR application should maximize the safety and effectiveness of the BVR.

In order to execute the BVR successfully, you need to maintain your balance while taking the subject's balance and exposing the sides of his neck so you can apply the technique. It is suggested the BVR be used with the officer's weapon side to the rear; however, this is not always possible and the officer should be trained to do the technique with either side forward. On your approach, it is best if you can apply the BVR from behind the subject if possible. If you are able to maneuver behind the subject, you first must break the subject's balance rearward.

To take the subject's balance in preparation for the BVR, pull the subject's hair, collar, clothing, or forehead backwards, causing his back to arch. If the resister is much taller than you, it is helpful to first apply pressure to the back of the resister's knee with your foot. Place your foot on the back of the resister's knee and push slightly forward and down on his upper calf to lower his center of gravity. Be careful when using this technique that he doesn't collapse on your foot or leg and possibly damage your knee. It is sometimes safer to block one of the subject's feet with your foot to prevent the subject from stepping back to regain balance. You may also apply pressure to the resister's lower back/tailbone area with your hand or hip as you take his balance and cause him to arch his back as you begin to slide your arm around his neck to apply the BVR (Figures 13.1 to 13.3).

The above methods work well when you are able to start from behind the resister. However, many times you will be unable to start from this position and will need to work your way behind the subject to apply the BVR. How do you get to the aggressive resister's back to properly apply the BVR if you begin face-to-face? There are several methods. Consistent among all of them is to first assume a response/survival stance with your body bladed and your hands up by your face in a "calm down" position. This is a great attack position because your elbows are bent to protect your body and your hands are up in a position where they can strike out quickly, but appear nonthreatening.

The first option is to quickly lunge toward the subject at an angle (never move straight into the subject), strike the subject's shoulder with one hand while simultaneously pulling and rotating the subject's other shoulder toward

Figure 13.1 The use of a hip thrust to take the subject's balance.

you. As you strike/push the shoulder, think of rotating a large ball at a 45° angle, or down and around. This will not only rotate the subject, but also cause him to bend his back, disrupting his balance further. This is exactly the same setup for taking an opponent's balance as was discussed for the o-soto-gari in Chapter 5 on the essential fundamentals.

A second option is the chin-neck takedown presented in Chapter 8 on subject control. Identical to the approach mentioned above, lunge toward the subject at an angle while placing one of your hands on the subject's chin and grabbing one of the subject's shoulders or the back of his head with your other hand. You will use a push-pull technique in which you rotate the chin up and outward in a circular motion as you pull on the subject's shoulder or head to face him away from you. The only difference from the chin-neck takedown

Figure 13.2 The use of a push to the lower back area of the subject.

technique mentioned earlier is instead of just using the technique to take the resister to the ground, you are now rotating the resister into the BVR.

If the subject attempts to punch or grab you, or is already in a side-facing position, step to the outside of the subject's arm. Simultaneously push the subject's extended arm away from you as you move to his rear. All of the above should be done in one smooth, continuous application (Figure 13.4).

Please refer to Video 13.1a and b at www.SurvivalSciences.com to see the above methods demonstrated. Use the user name and pass code listed in the introduction to access the videos.

Figure 13.3 The method of pushing the subject's knee with the officer's foot.

Using one of the above methods, you should now be in position for the BVR. The two primary terms we will use are encircling arm and support arm. The encircling arm is the one that wraps around the aggressive resister's neck and applies pressure. The support arm is placed behind the aggressive resister's head with the support hand preventing a head butt.

The setup for the technique is to slam or firmly press the side of your body into the aggressive resister's back. The subject's back is arched and his

Video 13.2 at www.SurvivalSciences.com depicts moving to the outside of the subject to apply the BVR.

Figure 13.4 Side-stepping out of the way of a punch while moving behind the subject.

balance has been broken rearward. Your center of gravity should be lower than the resister's to prevent possible counter takedown attempts.

Minimize the risk of injury to the aggressive resister when applying the BVR by immediately locking and applying maximum pressure to the sides of the subject's neck to prevent the possibility of your encircling arm slipping out of correct alignment and inadvertently applying pressure to the aggressive resister's airway during the struggle. As mentioned earlier, it is not necessary for your encircling arm to be under the resister's chin. The effectiveness of the BVR is due to the pressure applied to the sides of the neck—not the front of the throat. The pressure of the BVR must not be applied in incrementally increasing stages. Once you determine a threat exists that warrants the use of the BVR, it makes little sense to apply lesser force than is necessary for an effective restraint hold. Unless deadly force is justified, you must immediately cease applying pressure if your encircling arm has shifted and pressure is now being applied to the aggressive resister's throat area (Figure 13.5).

To ensure proper placement of the encircling arm, you must be certain your same side as your encircling arm is pressed firmly against the back of the aggressive resister at approximately a 90° angle. This is a key point: If you are facing in the same direction as the aggressive resister or if there is a gap between your body and the back of the bad guy, then it is likely your encircling arm is not in proper position and pressure will be improperly applied to the subject's airway. Make sure your elbow is directly over the aggressive resister's throat. Having your elbow in this position ensures you are not squeezing the subject's airway, and it ensures your arm is in proper position

Figure 13.5 The improper positioning of the encircling arm. The forearm area is covering the throat of the subject, which will result in an air choke. *Do not do this.*

to apply pressure to the sides of the neck. Next bring the bicep of your support arm up into the hand of your encircling arm. Place the support hand behind the head of the subject to lock him in tightly (Figures 13.6A and 13.6B).

Now that you have firmly locked the resister in the BVR, immediately and continuously take the aggressive resister all the way to the ground. Continue to keep the aggressive resister off-balance to minimize the opportunity for the subject to counter the BVR. If the resister is allowed to remain standing, a number of counter moves exist that would defeat a carotid-style restraint. As you go to the ground, maintain proper balance and proper posture while ensuring the resister is unable to execute a head butt.

Once you are on the ground, you have two options. I like to go all the way to the ground with my same-side hip as my encircling arm (e.g., right encircling arm and right hip) flat on the ground, and my legs spread in a bicycling fashion to lower and widen my base as much as possible (Figure 13.7). This makes it almost impossible for the bad guy, no matter how big or strong he may be, to move me or take my balance in an attempt to get out of the BVR.

Another option, if you believe other threats exist in the immediate environment, is to remain in a more upright position with your knees spread

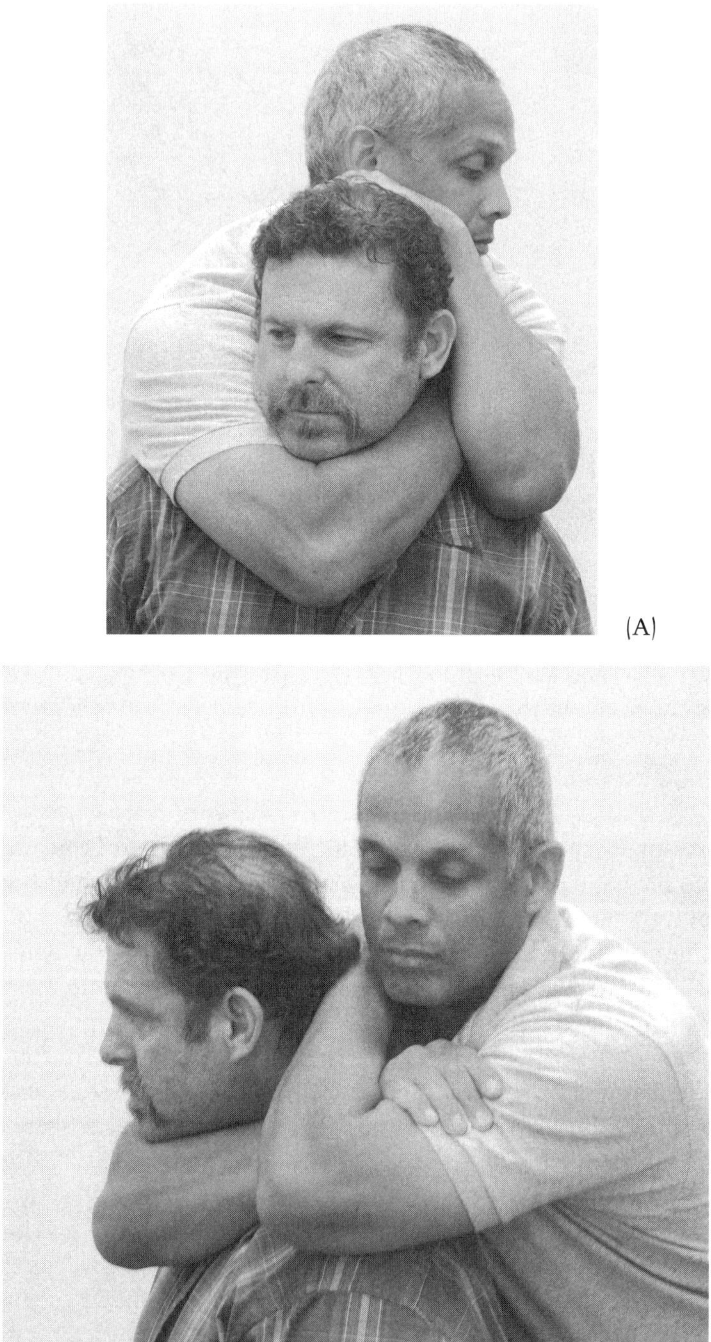

(A)

(B)

Figure 13.6 (A) The proper positioning of the encircling arm. Note the bend of the elbow is directly over the subject's throat, protecting it.(B) A side view of the proper positioning of the officer's arms.

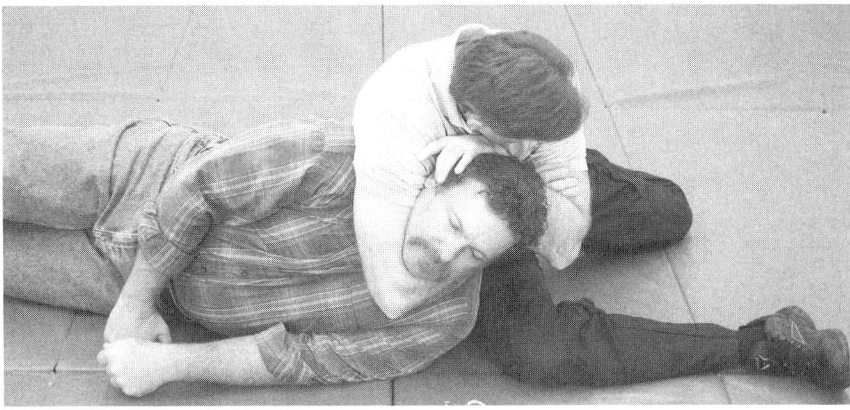

Figure 13.7 The proper body and arm position of the BVR. The officer's center of gravity is low and legs spread in a bicycle fashion to form a low, wide base and prevent being unbalanced.

wide to maximize your stability. The goal when you are kneeling is to have your knees form a wide triangle to establish a low, solid base (Figure 13.8).

Once you are in proper position on the ground with the subject, you can increase the pressure applied by the BVR by bringing your elbows together and down while simultaneously expanding your chest by arching your back.

An additional "handle" can be used during the application of the BVR to further immobilize the aggressive resister. The handle is applied by inserting

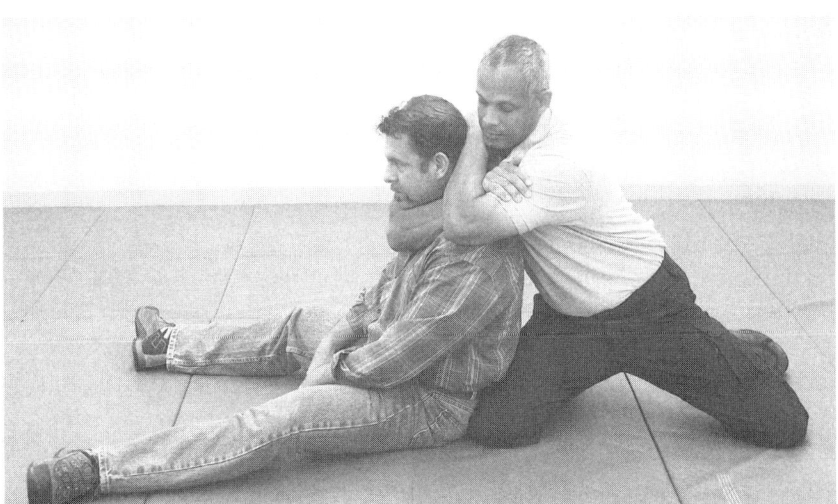

Figure 13.8 The officer's position while applying the BVR if he is concerned about other threats. In this position, the officer is upright so he can continue to scan for additional danger.

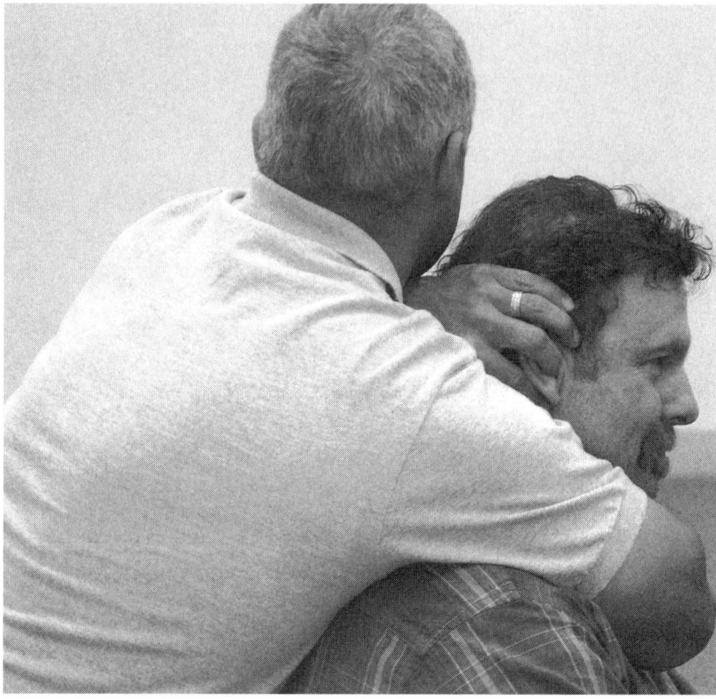

Figure 13.9 A close-up of the handle that can be use with the BVR.

one finger into the bad guy's ear canal to further restrict his head movements (Figure 13.9). It may sound silly, but try it with a partner. It is surprisingly effective and disconcerting to the bad guy. Not only does it help immobilize his head, but the pain caused by a finger in the ear canal distracts the subject from the application of the BVR. I'd like to claim credit for this technique, as I really like it, but it came from Bob Wall of *Enter the Dragon* fame. Bob said he got the idea from "Judo" Gene LeBell (whose daughter happens to be an FBI agent) and who is always experimenting with handles to increase the effectiveness of holds.

Maintain maximum, but relaxed (don't strain) pressure. As you apply the BVR, you should allow your body to relax and drop your weight. By bringing your elbows together, expanding your chest, and slightly arching your back, you will create more than the 5 pounds of pressure required to block the jugular veins and stimulate the vagus nerve. Continue to apply the BVR until the aggressive resister either complies and is handcuffed or is rendered unconscious and handcuffed.

Once you have controlled the subject, immediately handcuff and conduct a high-risk area search. There are some precautions after applying the BVR that should be heeded. First, once the subject is unconscious, don't continue to maintain the BVR for an extended amount of time. If you do, permanent damage or death can occur. I know what you're thinking. "What if he's playing possum? I'll keep the BVR on this rascal until I *know* he is out." Trust me. You'll know when he's unconscious. If you want to continue the BVR for a few seconds just to make sure, that's okay. Just be certain it's no more than a few seconds. Oh, it's useful to know that some of the after-effects of applying a BVR are the subject may vomit, defecate, and urinate. This will be a good time to use your buddy's patrol car for transport, especially if you just had yours detailed.

There are many counters to a carotid type of restraint. You should be aware of them so you apply the BVR correctly and avoid being countered. Some of the more common are discussed below with an explanation of how you can prevent them from occurring.

One possible counter is the subject will try to execute a hip throw. A hip throw can only be done if you allow the subject to remain standing in a balanced position. To throw you over his hip, the subject has to get below your center of gravity and bend forward. This cannot occur if you take the subject's balance to the rear and cause him to arch his back. So immediately take the subject's balance and don't allow him to remain standing.

Another counter is for the subject to step around your leg and execute a foot sweep. Even if you break the subject's balance to the rear, he can still position one of his feet around and behind one of your feet if you allow him to remain standing. Once he has accomplished this, he just needs to rotate his body and sweep your foot. To prevent this, don't allow the subject to remain standing or regain his balance. Immediately take him to the ground while applying the BVR.

If at any point the subject is able to turn and face you, the fight is on. We then go back to the strategy offered in Chapter 6 on getting out of the way. If you don't have the clear tactical advantage, don't engage. The subject has been successful in defeating your control attempt so far, so it's now time to get the tactical advantage back. Make distance by moving away at an angle and deploy the appropriate weapon to stop the attack.

Going back to my friend Dr. John Pi, what were his and the panel's recommendations for the BVR? First, officers should only use their arms while executing the BVR to apply pressure. If any other instruments are used (e.g., baton, flashlights, rope, etc.), then it is no longer a BVR. I don't know what you'd call the technique when you apply pressure with a baton, rope, etc., but it is not a BVR.

If a subject has significant pain or symptoms of an airway injury, he should be taken to a hospital for an evaluation. Most bad guys who require you to use the BVR are probably high risk for potential complications since they are likely under the influence. If in doubt, it's always best to have the subject cleared by medical personnel. Any time the BVR is used, the subject needs to be monitored. An unconscious subject should not be placed in an upright position since this may prevent him from getting proper blood flow to the brain. The subject also should not be hog-tied or placed face down.

In summary, the BVR is a great tool. The only problem with the carotid technique was, at times, it was improperly used, resulting in unintended deaths and injuries. That then led to the restriction or elimination of the technique for many departments. If the BVR is applied correctly and the safety guidelines are followed, this valuable tool can be used by law enforcement with confidence.

Drills

1. Have a partner kneel in front of you. Apply the BVR and gradually increase pressure until your partner taps out. Note the reason you are applying pressure gradually is to allow your partner the opportunity to tap out upon becoming uncomfortable or light-headed. The actual application of the BVR is to use maximum pressure immediately.
2. Practice approaching a partner from the front, side, and rear in the application of the BVR.
3. Once the BVR is set on a cooperative partner, gently practice taking your partner straight down to the rear by "laddering" your bodies together, as demonstrated in Video 13.2.
4. With your partner in the grounded BVR position, have your partner attempt to upset your balance as you gently hold the BVR in place. Refer to Figure 13.3 for the proper position. A deep, wide base will provide you with more stability.

Endnotes

1. Pi, J., Joyner, C., Lampert, N., Baldridge, R. T., Horowitz, T., Phillips, A., Uner, A., and Tang, D., "The Bilateral Vascular Restraint: Facts and Myths about a Carotid Restraint," submitted to *The Tactical Edge*, the official periodical of the National Tactical Officers Association (NTOA), Summer Issue, 2010.

Impact Weapons 14

This chapter will discuss the appropriate use of an impact weapon, the suitable striking targets, various impact weapons available, how to deploy an impact weapon effectively, how to generate power in impact weapon strikes, and tactical considerations.

When may you use an impact weapon? Clearly hitting a passive resister with a baton would not be appropriate due to the high risk of injury. Actually, if you are competent with the impact weapon, injury to a subject should almost be a certainty. Based on the DRM, and more importantly court decisions, impact weapon strikes may only be used on an aggressively resistant subject, or one who you can articulate is an immediate threat. As soon as the immediate threat ceases, you must also stop striking the subject.

What can you hit with your impact weapon? Check your department policy to ensure compliance, but generally you can strike any area other than the head, neck, genitalia, or spinal column/midline area unless, of course, deadly force is justified. Striking areas where the bone is closest to the skin (e.g., hand, elbow, forearms, shins) is more likely to be effective than striking soft body tissue such as the stomach or buttocks. When striking with the impact weapon, you can't just pound away and hope the bad guy gets a clue what you want him to do. You must give verbal commands as you strike, such as "Get down!" or "Stop resisting!" As soon as he obeys those commands or is no longer a threat, you must stop striking and make the arrest.

Obviously the impact weapon needs to be worn on your duty belt where it can be accessed with your strong hand. Few officers would be able to strike effectively with their weak hand. However, realize this will tie up your shooting hand. If the subject suddenly changes from aggressive resistance to deadly resistance, your best option will probably be to instantaneously release the baton and draw your handgun. Then again, if you are poised to deliver a strike and at that instant you notice the subject's hand is now reaching for a knife or handgun, you are permitted to use deadly force. In this situation, it would be reasonable to strike the subject's head with the impact weapon as deadly force is justified. I would select the option that you can complete the most quickly and effectively.

Are some impact weapons better than others? Of course. I've always preferred simple weapon systems—simple to understand and simple to use effectively. With that in mind, let's first look at an option popular with some departments today. The side-handle baton is an excellent weapon. It offers a number of applications that are not available when using a straight baton.

There are several useful deflections and control techniques that can be used with the side-handle baton. The problem is I know of very few officers who are capable of performing those techniques effectively because it requires a great deal of training time to become proficient. And training time is always a rare commodity. So what do most officers do? They use the multifaceted side-handle baton in a single-faceted manner—as a club. This is not necessarily a bad thing; it just would be simpler, and more effective, to use a straight baton.

After providing SWAT training at a local sheriff's academy many years ago, I was eating my lunch as new recruits were in a large open field practicing with straight batons, collapsible batons (the ASP), and side-handle batons. I had my back to the recruits as they repeatedly struck heavy bags with one of the three batons. Even though I couldn't see them, I easily could tell from the sounds if the recruits were hitting the bag with a side-handle baton. When the recruits were using a straight or expandable baton, the thuds emanating from the bags were indistinguishable. Wham! Wham! Wham! But I instantly knew when they were using the side-handle batons. Tap, tap, tap. I would then watch the recruits and see how they struggled with the awkwardness of using the side-handle baton. Could they eventually learn to use this tool effectively? Yes, with a great deal of practice. But they were instantly effective with the straight and expandable batons, because it was a natural, instinctive swing. If it were up to me, I would only issue expandable or straight batons to officers and then ensure they could strike effectively with them. By the way, the side-handle baton is nothing more than a revision of the tonfa, a martial arts weapon from Okinawa. The people of Okinawa used it as a weapon because they weren't allowed to have real weapons during the Japanese occupation. The tonfa's primary purpose was as a handle used to turn the grinding wheel on a mill. It's just a farm tool being marketed as a police weapon.

Now that I'm going to get hate mail from the makers and lovers of side-handle batons, let me add another group who can hate me. Police nunchaku (sometimes referred to as nunchucks). Nunchaku (two sticks connected with a string or chain) is another ancient farm tool used to flail rice. Can nunchaku be used effectively? Absolutely. I personally enjoy playing with nunchaku and have for years. If you don't know what you're doing, however, you are more likely to hurt yourself than your opponent. Again, there are countless nunchaku techniques that can be useful for law enforcement, but they require tremendous training time to gain any level of expertise.

Just so you don't think I'm a sourpuss who hates all tools used by law enforcement, I'm a big supporter of many being used today. There are a number of devices that were designed to make officers safer, and therefore resistant subjects safer. These tools are attempting to mitigate a lack of defensive tactics (DT) expertise with something that allows the officer to make an arrest and not get hurt. This is a noble mission and I applaud those companies that have succeeded in producing such tools. I count among these pepper spray, the expandable baton, and the TASER. I could also include the straight baton, but I wouldn't know who to give credit to. Perhaps the caveman who used the first stick?

The straight baton is a wonderful tool. Its only drawback is its size and the inability of officers to have it on their person while driving a car. This necessitates keeping the straight baton in a car door pocket or other easily accessible location so the officer can grab the baton when getting out of the car. The only problem is it becomes just one more device to carry on an already overcrowded belt and officers have a tendency to leave it behind.

To overcome this dilemma, Armament Systems and Procedures (ASP) developed and manufacture high-quality, reliable expandable batons. There are other manufacturers of expandable batons, and I don't mean to slight them. I'm just familiar with the ASP, as that was the baton first issued to me almost twenty years ago. Since the standard 26-inch-length ASP collapses down to only 9.5 inches, it is much easier for officers to carry. No weapon does you any good unless you have it with you.

Going back to dealing with an aggressive resister, you've recognized the threat and have drawn your impact weapon. How do you stand? Obviously you feel threatened, so you should be in your response/survival stance, lowered center of gravity, body bladed at a 45° angle to the threat, and your hands up in a defensive position with your elbows protecting your ribs. The only difference from the typical survival stance is your rear hand now holds an impact weapon.

Remember Chapter 11 on generating power and the discussion of the Rodney King event? If the subject is aggressively resistant, you are legally justified in using an impact weapon. You are better off striking him once and causing an injury that prevents the aggressive resister from continuing to resist, than you are hitting him multiple times with weak, ineffective strikes. If you are justified using a particular level of force, then use it. And use it to the best of your ability.

One officer who attended our DT instructor course several years back told me of an incident in which he used his ASP baton against an aggressive, violent resister. During the fight (which was truly a fight for survival for the officer), the officer had managed to break the resister's arm. The break was a compound fracture, broken at a 90° angle. At one point, the subject was knocked to the ground and used the "stump" of his broken arm to get back onto his feet—apparently feeling no pain. The officer described it as a terrifying event, realizing how committed this bad guy was to hurt him. The officer was fortunate to be able to use his baton effectively and eventually control the subject.

How do you generate maximum power with an impact weapon? Let's consider a sport in which you use one hand to swing a tool similar to a baton with the intention of hitting with power. That sport would be tennis. I hope I don't lose the nontennis fans on this explanation, but bear with me.

Professional tennis players strike the ball with incredible power. The best are capable of making that little yellow ball travel faster than 140 mph. My guess is they would be able to do significant damage swinging a police baton. So how similar is a tennis stroke to a baton strike? If done correctly, the baton strike should be almost identical in terms of the body mechanics deployed.

ASP is one of the most popular expandable batons in use today, and many officers are familiar with the ASP terminology, so I will reference it here. ASP refers to strikes originating from the strong side of the body as a weapon strike, and the opposite side as a reaction strike. ASP used to also teach a straight strike, which was a straight jab with the tip of the baton to the subject. Almost everyone I know who attempted this strike with an expandable baton had the baton collapse at least once as they did the strike. The result is a major "ouch," as the baton shafts collapse, pinching the skin of the hands and the fingers. It's a good strike with a solid baton, particularly from a riot formation, but I wouldn't recommend it for any expandable baton.

To continue the tennis analogy and for simplicity, instead of *weapon strike* and *reaction strike*, I'll refer to them as a *forehand* and a *backhand* strike. We'll look at the forehand strike first. As typically taught, the officer has the weapon/strong side back (right foot for right-handed officers) and the baton held back in a raised position. You may think the weapon-side strike is accomplished by pivoting the hips just as you would do for a rear hand strike, but there are two problems with this. First, you are not striking with your rear hand; you're striking with a club. The body mechanics are different, just as the body mechanics are different for delivering a right cross and swinging a baseball bat. Second, a primary advantage of using a baton is the extra reach it provides. The farther away from your adversary, the safer you are. Try this at home. Assume the survival stance. Now pivot your hips and see how far you can reach with your rear hand. Now do the same thing with a baton in your rear hand. Swing the baton in an arc to determine how much extra reach you have gained when you have your strong foot back in your stance. The answer is very little. Now step forward with your strong-side foot and extend the baton. How much reach have you gained now? It's a substantial difference.

To take full advantage of this reach, I'm advocating that you either step forward with your strong foot as you strike a forehand blow or you step back with your weak foot. Which you do depends upon if you are either moving away from an attack or moving toward the aggressive resister at an angle to strike. Either way, your strong foot will be forward as the strike lands, and you will extend your reach considerably. It's also more tactically sound as you are moving rather than remaining a stationary target (Figures 14.1 and 14.2).

One reason for striking with your strong foot forward is it increases your safety, as you are able to reach out and strike the bad guy from a greater distance. But there is another important reason. You can generate considerably

Figure 14.1 The limited additional reach when you strike with the baton initially positioned to the rear.

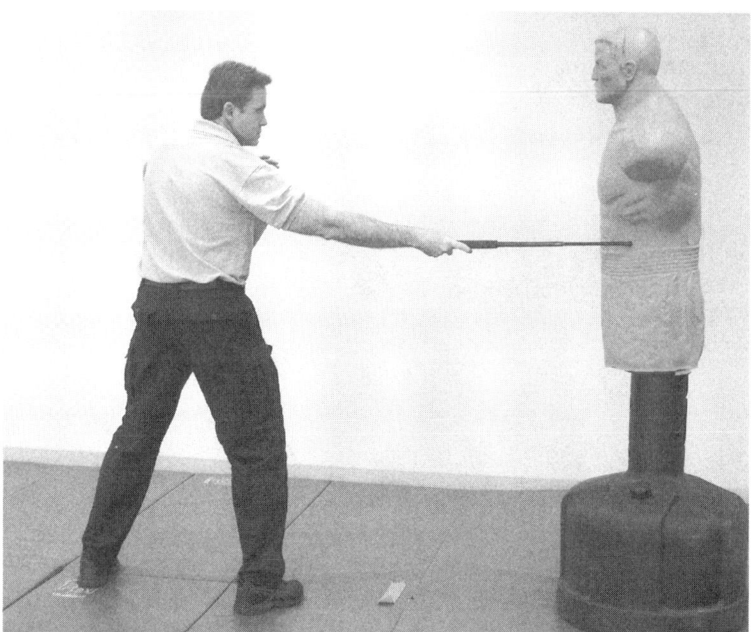

Figure 14.2 The additional distance obtained when the strong foot is forward during the forehand strike.

more power using this technique. I've experimented with both methods and determined that using the strong foot forward forehand strike is approximately 16% more powerful than the conventional method. In a study using a LAJUST Sports power indicator, I had a test group of officers strike a bag using the traditional stance with the baton to the rear and the modern Survival Sciences stance with the baton forward. Not only were the forehand strikes 16% stronger, but the backhand strikes were approximately 17% stronger. Most of the test group were DT instructors and quite adept at using proper body mechanics to obtain maximum force.

I also discovered the improvement in striking power is even more noticeable in individuals who are not instructors and not particularly athletic. Most officers, recognizing the awkwardness and weakness of the reaction strike, abandon it. Instead, they use a weapon strike and then recock the baton to the beginning or "loaded" position. By using the Survival Sciences method, this group was able to strike effectively with the backhand motion.

Common sense also supports this. Looking again at professional tennis players, the forehand stroke has changed over the last few decades. In the mid-1900s, tennis players would hit a forehand with their weak shoulder facing the net, their racket back, and then swing across their body (Figure 14.3). Modern tennis players discovered a more ballistic-style swing in which they

Figure 14.3 The old-fashioned tennis forehand swing.

Figure 14.4 The modern tennis forehand swing, which permits better use of the hips and body weight.

actually hit the ball off their strong foot with an open body position, allowing them to rotate their hips more fully into a more explosive stroke (Figure 14.4). The same is true for a baton strike (Figure 14.5). The conventional method restricts a free flow of the hips. The tennis forehand method allows you to fully deploy the hips and your body weight into the strike.

Going back to the traditional baton strikes, what was commonly taught was for the reaction strike to follow immediately after a weapon-side strike to return the baton to the original loaded position. This is a good concept, but the traditional stance and body mechanics weren't conducive to generating power. If your weak side is forward and you attempt to bring the baton back around, there is just no more room to pivot your hips to generate power. It becomes a very weak, arm-only strike. After watching videos of officers using baton strikes, I quickly learned officers almost never deploy this particular strike. The reason is they recognize there is no power in it, so instead they strike with a weapon-side strike and then recock the baton for a second weapon-side strike. This is not necessarily bad; it just takes more time and is predictable. The lag time allows an aggressive resister the opportunity to charge the officer.

Figure 14.5 The same swing motion with a baton.

A better option is to again use a tennis analogy. If your strong foot is forward and you have completed a forehand strike, you are now in perfect position to deliver a backhand strike. Rather than having your hips working against you, your hips are now coiled to deliver an incredibly powerful blow. Rather than having a weak strike to return the baton to your initial position, you now have a strike as strong as, or stronger than, your original forehand strike.

Again using the LAJUST Sports power indicator, I was able to determine officers using the Survival Sciences method were actually able to generate *more* power with their backhand strike than they were with the forehand strike. This is logical, as the hips are in a more coiled, explosive position (Figures 14.6 and 14.7).

The path of a baton strike is an arc. Consider at what point in the arc of the swing the greatest power is delivered. If you stand in a neutral stance and just swing a baton in an arc from side to side, you'll easily be able to tell the strike would be strongest when the baton tip is near your strong-side foot. When the baton is swinging near your weak-side foot, it is either too late in the stroke for a forehand to have much power, or it is too early in the stroke for a backhand.

To increase power, not only should you use the Survival Sciences stance as outlined above, but you also strike near the tip of the baton. Physics explains

Figure 14.6 The proper position at the beginning of the backhand strike.

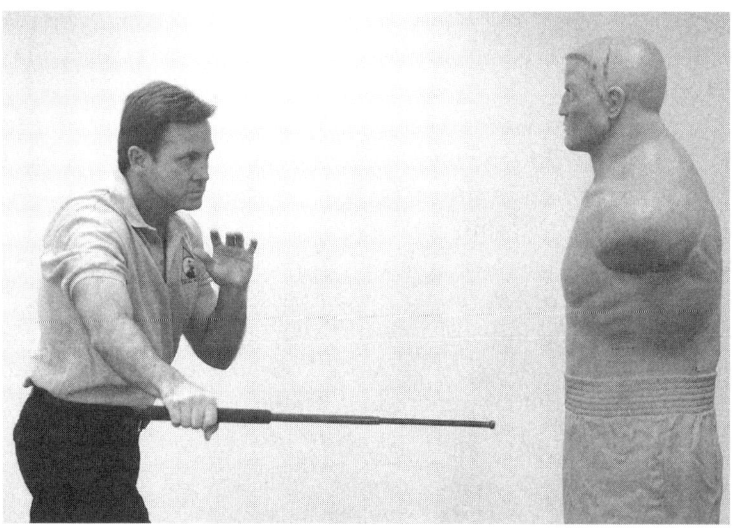

Figure 14.7 The completion of the backhand strike. The officer has swung through his target, and now his hips are coiled and in a position to deliver another forehand strike if necessary.

why this is true. Any object traveling in an arc is creating centrifugal force. If you swing a rock at the end of the string, the rock is moving faster than the string near your hand. This is because even though they both are making one revolution, the rock is traveling a greater distance. The same is true for a baton. The tip is moving faster than near the grip, so the greatest power is being generated in the tip of the baton.

Following is a drill to increase the power of your baton strikes: Stand at the appropriate distance from a heavy bag in a good Survival Sciences stance (strong side forward). At first, use only the wrist to hit the bag. After a few strikes, allow your arm to pivot at the elbow. You should notice an increase in power as you are now increasing the weight behind the strike (your arm as opposed to just your wrist and hand) and the speed of the strike (since the arc of the strike is much greater using the arm from the elbow down as opposed to just the flexion of the wrist joint). Next, continue to strike the bag using the entire arm, from the shoulder joint down. Next, strike the bag rotating the shoulders. Now, strike the bag using all of the above body parts, but also sharply pivoting the hips into the strike. Finally, assume the survival stance with your strong foot to the rear and your baton in the loaded ready position. While stepping forward with your strong-side foot, drive with your legs, rotate your hips sharply, turn your shoulders, and let your elbow and wrist pop into the strike. You should notice a significant increase in power at each stage. You are also training to use correct body mechanics to develop maximum power. As was mentioned in Chapter 11 on generating power, a tight muscle slows you down and weakens the strike. The same applies here. You must pay particular attention to your grip so that you don't have the baton in a death-vise. A relaxed but firm grip will suffice in providing maximum "whip" to the strike.

Now that we know when to use an impact weapon (against an aggressive resister) and we know how to generate more power (using the correct stance and rotating the hips), let's discuss more of the tactical application. If the aggressive resister is charging you, the first thing you want to do is get out of the way. As covered in Chapter 6, first avoid the attack by side stepping. As you do so, you can simultaneously strike the attacker as he passes by.

If you are moving forward to strike the aggressive resister, recall that you never want to step straight in on the resister. Instead, step at an angle to place you outside of his strength and defensive position and strike to an available target. If the subject has an outstretched arm, it is a great target that

> Please see Video 14.1 at www.SurivalSciences.com for a demonstration of the increasing power drill. Use the user name and access code listed in the introduction to gain access to the video.

See Video 14.2 at www.SurvivalSciences.com for an example of side stepping and striking your attacker.

you can strike effectively at great range. The legs are always good target areas, as most people have difficulty avoiding strikes to their legs. Once you strike, continue to move and continue to strike until you obtain control and are able to handcuff the subject. Once you've struck someone with a baton, don't allow him to leave the area. This is a violent encounter; he must be arrested and you shouldn't just let him say, "Okay, you win" and walk away. Or worse, "Okay, you won that one, but now I'm going to my car to get a gun and then I'll show you!"

If you are caught off-guard and an attacker has invaded your safety zone, don't forget close-in strikes. An expandable baton can be used effectively in the closed position, just as the butt of a standard baton can be used if necessary. An expandable baton in its closed position is exactly the same as a yawara or kubotan (small handheld stick used in martial arts). You can strike with the end of the closed baton as you hold it in your fist to add power and impact to your close-range strikes. The strikes are similar in the closed mode as they are in the open mode. You can strike in a forehand or backhand fashion, as well as "hammer fist" style strikes at a downward 45° angle. Your mindset is to use these close-range techniques to give you a chance to create distance, deploy the baton to full length, or transition to another weapon.

As mentioned in Chapter 1, the baton has the highest rate of injury, and that's not a big surprise. However, what I like about the baton is I never have to worry about a baton losing it's charge, dropping it in water, confusing it with my handgun, breaking it, having a canister explode in the heat, running out of the contents, or having it expire. It's a low-tech, reliable piece of equipment, and sometimes you have to appreciate that.

Drills

1. As was mentioned in the beginning of the chapter, determine the extent of your reach with a baton in the strong-side back stance. Then determine the extended reach of the baton by assuming a strong-side forward stance.
2. Shadowbox moving and striking with a baton. Visualize sidestepping away from an attack as you simultaneously strike with a baton, and then visualize stepping in at an angle to an aggressive resister as you strike with the baton.

3. Practice the power increasing drill demonstrated in Video 14.1.
4. Practice striking a heavy bag using proper footwork and striking with forehand and backhand strikes. Give clear, loud commands as you strike.

15 Pepper Spray

In this chapter we'll discuss the history, purpose, characteristics, effects, first aid, and tactical use of pepper spray, or oleoresin capsicum (OC).

Even though pepper spray use is fairly recent in law enforcement (since about 1973), its use in battle has been documented as early as 2300 B.C. The Chinese created "stink pots" by burning pepper in hot oil to produce an irritating, suffocating smoke. At the time, warfare typically involved massive frontal assaults. If the wind direction and velocity were favorable, the Chinese armies would use the stink pots to affect opposing forces prior to an attack. Samurai and Ninja were known to hide finely ground pepper wrapped in paper in their clothing. At an opportune time, they would fling the pepper into the eyes of an adversary as a distraction.

OC is a good tool for law enforcement, as it is safe in any concentration. Chloracetophenone (CN) and orthochlorobenzalmalonitrile (CS) have specific toxicity formulas that must be calculated by a grenadier prior to deployment in an enclosed structure. There is no toxicity for these chemical agents outside as they disperse quickly. A grenadier is responsible for determining the incapacitation level and toxicity level for CS or CN prior to deployment. It is important to know when a subject will be affected and at what time the exposure to CN or CS would become lethal. This mathematical calculation is avoided entirely when using OC. OC is made of cayenne or chili pepper, which is a naturally occurring, organic compound. No level of exposure is considered toxic, and the effects are almost instantaneous. Other advantages of OC are that it is relatively inexpensive, effective, and simple to use.

OC is classified as an inflammatory agent (its primary effect). OC usually appears as a dark red liquid and is commonly in an isopropyl solution (rubbing alcohol). Its effects may include lacrimation (causing the eyes to tear), blepharospasm (involuntary closing of the eyes), swelling in the lining of the throat reducing the airway passage, temporary paralysis of the larynx, burning and swelling of mucous membranes causing heavy secretion, inflammation of the skin, and temporary loss of muscle coordination (primarily because the eyes are forced closed). It's not unusual for someone sprayed with OC to drop to his knees and attempt to rub the OC out of his eyes.

I've been exposed to OC over ten times. Each time has been a different experience. Since I have fair skin, it would be expected that I would be particularly susceptible to the effects of the skin inflammation, or that I would feel as if I had a bad sunburn. However, this has never been an even minor effect for me. On the other hand, my wife is dark skinned, so it would be expected any discomfort from skin inflammation for her would be minor. She told me the skin irritation was a major element in her discomfort (and yes, I was smart enough to ensure someone else gave her the OC exposure). My perception of the effectiveness of the OC has ranged from instantly debilitating to very little effect. This could be explained by environmental differences or just my pain tolerance was greater on some days than others. All of the exposures were by the same product of OC, same percentage, and same manner of exposure (directly into open eyes at two to three feet). All this is to say there is no guarantee how each individual will respond to OC.

OC can be very effective on animals, particularly dogs. However, dogs, like people, can be trained to fight through the effects and still operate. I've had great success using OC against dogs with only one exception. Even on that one occurrence when the dog didn't flee, he at least didn't attack, but instead just held his ground as he rubbed his eyes against the grass. I will say that OC seems to have no effect on mice (don't ask me how I know this).

OC has proven effective on people under the influence and on people who had previous exposure to OC or other chemical agents. One advantage of OC over CS or CN is the effects of OC are both psychological and physiological, while the effects of CN and CS are primarily psychological. In a worst-case scenario, the subject exposed to OC should at least have difficulty seeing you, as it is painful to keep the eyes open. Please be aware that no chemical agent is 100% effective against all people.

Another benefit of OC is that decontamination is simple. Decontamination for CN and CS is almost impossible. On SWAT we were told if we fired CS into a house, we just bought that house as the owners would never be able to get the CS out of the carpet, drapes, and vents. For OC all that is needed are fresh air and perhaps soap and water. Clothing can be washed normally to decontaminate.

First aid is simple. The best results are obtained by exposure to fresh air. After several OC exposures, I finally discovered I recovered the quickest by turning my vehicle's air conditioning on the highest fan setting, prying my eyes open with my fingers, and placing my eyes directly in front of the vents. Free-flowing cool water, such as from a garden hose, also works wonders. I've seen some departments use buckets for the officers to dunk their heads into after being exposed. This works great for the first officer, but every subsequent officer is using OC-tainted water. Baby shampoo can also be used to wash out the eyes, face, and hair. Once you overcome the effects, I can tell you what will happen. Everything is wonderful until you take a shower that night. Forgetting you still have remnants of OC particles in your hair, you'll duck your head under the water. The stream of water will then carry those OC particles down your face and back into your eyes. Reexposure! To avoid this, just remember to back into the shower so the water runs off the back of your head rather than into your face.

Things you should *not* do include using oil-based creams or soap. It will trap the OC particles onto the skin. If you spray a subject, at no time should he be left unattended. You also have a responsibility to provide first aid as listed above as soon as it is safe to do so. Be careful of the position you place a handcuffed prisoner after exposure to OC. Since the subject's breathing is expected to be restricted, be sure the subject is not in a position that further restricts breathing. If the subject seems to be experiencing difficulty breathing, get medical help immediately.

People can die when in custody regardless of whether they have been exposed to OC, hit with a TASER, or if the officer just gave the bad guy a loving hug. Normally when subjects die, it is because of excited delirium. As one doctor explained it, there are some people who can drop dead at any second due to drug use and their physical condition. It is not surprising that these individuals would die after an intense struggle due to resisting arrest, causing sky high blood pressure, body heat, and dopamine levels.[1] Contributing factors that would put a resister at higher risk are if they are male, obese, exhibited bizarre behavior, have acute heart or pulmonary disease, or if the officers had difficulty in subduing the subject, which caused the subject to be exhausted.

The individual protective devices (IPDs) containing OC vary. Dispersal can be by mist, spray, or foam. Each has benefits and drawbacks. I would recommend mist for most law enforcement officers. A mist has a wide range of coverage so you don't have to be as precise in aiming. Also, the OC remains airborne longer, increasing the possibility of affecting the subject. The mist dispersal method has both visual and respiratory effects and is effective even if the subject is wearing glasses.

A stream IPD has a longer range than a mist IPD. It also has a greater concentration at longer distances, but it is target specific. The primary effect of the stream is visual. Foam is an even more target-specific dispersal method. Its use has typically been restricted to hospitals and courtrooms, where the residual effects are more likely to be more serious or less acceptable.

Now let's talk about the tactical use of OC. Most importantly, when can an officer use OC? In which of the four subject categories of the Dynamic Resistance-Response Model (DRM) is it appropriate to use OC? A famous court case occurred in Humbolt County, Oregon, in which nine environmental protesters brought a lawsuit against Humbolt County, the Humbolt County Sheriff's Department, Eureka City, the Eureka Police Department, and individual officers.[2] The plaintiffs claimed the use of pepper spray on nonviolent protesters was excessive force and violated their Fourth Amendment rights. Using the DRM, the protesters would be classified as passively resistant.

As background of the event that led to the lawsuit, the plaintiffs were protesting the logging of redwood trees in the Headwaters Forest. For several years, the protesters had used a strategy in which they would link themselves together using a device known as a black bear, which was a self-releasing locking mechanism. The black bear devices immobilized the protesters' arms and prevented them from being separated. Typically, law enforcement in Humbolt County would respond by cutting the cylinders with a handheld electric grinder to allow them to remove the protesters. Beginning in 1997, officers began using OC (pepper spray) on the protesters to persuade them to release themselves from the black bear devices. At the first event addressed by the court, seven protesters linked themselves together in the headquarters of the Pacific Lumber Company and refused to disperse when ordered to do so by law enforcement. Humbolt County sheriff's deputies warned the protesters they would use pepper spray if the protesters did not release themselves from the black bear devices. When the protesters refused, the deputies applied OC using Q-tips. The protesters who continued to refuse to release themselves from the devices were eventually carried out of the building and an electric grinder was used to cut them free of the locking devices.

In a second event, protesters again used the black bear devices while outdoors on Pacific Lumber property. After the protesters refused to leave, officers initially used Q-tips to apply the OC and later sprayed OC into the face of the protesters. As before, after some protesters continued to refuse to release themselves, officers cut the devices using an electric grinder.

In the third incident, four protesters linked themselves together in the office of a congressman. The events were similar to before in terms of the application of pepper spray and the eventual use of an electric grinder.

The court determined the acts of the officers in these three events were excessive force, as it violated the "objectively reasonable" standard of *Graham v. Connor*.[3] The court stated the force used must be balanced against the need for the force. In this case, pepper spray was clearly not used to subdue or arrest the protesters, since that was done later by using an electric grinder in much less time than was used with the pepper spray. The court also noted the use of the electric grinder to remove the black bear devices caused no pain to the protesters.

The court cited the policy of the Eureka Police Department, which stated pepper spray could be used against "active resistance," but then went on to define active resistance as when the subject attempts to inflict pain or physical injury on the officer. This was obviously not the case in these events. The Ninth Circuit Court of Appeals advised that a reasonable officer should undoubtedly recognize it is excessive force to use pepper spray against a nonviolent protester under the circumstances described above. Continuing to use the reasonable officer standard and citing *Lalonde v. County of Riverside*,[4] the court stated it was also excessive to repeatedly use pepper spray once the subject is under control, and it is unreasonable to fail to alleviate the effects of the pepper spray once the subject is subdued. Finally, the court stated most departments recognize using pepper spray against nonviolent protesters is excessive.

In this situation the protesters had been given prior warning, they were in clear violation of the law, they were illegally affecting commerce, and the officers had been professional and calm in the application of the pepper spray. However, the Ninth Circuit Court primarily focused on the lack of an immediate threat presented by the protesters. Various courts have continued to determine it is not appropriate to use pepper spray (or batons or TASER or personal weapons) on passive resisters. The DRM was patterned specifically on these decisions.

As an officer, think of it this way: Would you feel comfortable punching the person in the nose for his offense? Would you think it is reasonable? I'm certain no officer would think it is okay to walk up to the chanting, seated protesters described above and punch them in the nose. Therefore, it is also not reasonable to use a baton, TASER, or pepper spray. It is evident the courts do not favor using pepper spray against a passive resister, or one in which the officer cannot articulate a threat. Therefore, using the DRM as the guide, an officer may only use pepper spray against an aggressive resister. Now that we know when we can use OC, how do we use it?

FBI policy mandates that OC must be drawn and deployed with the weak (nonweapon) hand. Other departments have a different policy, but I agree with the FBI on this one. Drawing the OC with the nonweapon hand is required for several reasons. First, by drawing and holding the OC IPD in the weak hand, your strong hand is still free to draw your handgun if necessary. Second, drawing the IPD with the weak hand reduces the possibility of you mistakenly drawing and firing a handgun when your intent was to use OC spray. Next, when the weak hand is extended toward the subject, the weapon side is situated farther from the subject, theoretically making a weapon disarming attempt by the subject more difficult.

If you are working with other officers, they would probably greatly appreciate it if you give them some warning prior to spraying a subject so they know to stay back. "I'm going to use OC" or "Stay back, I'm using pepper spray" will usually suffice. If you have two officers, designate one as the OC sprayer and the other as a cover officer ready with deadly force if necessary.

As you draw and point the IPD, there should be a minimum of 2 to 3 feet between the IPD and the resister's face. Any closer than that endangers you (as you are closer than you need to be), and the spray of the OC will not be at optimal dispersal. Maintaining this distance also ensures the aggressive resister's eyes will not be unintentionally damaged from the pressure of the OC as it is being dispersed. If you can do so safely, give commands prior to spraying and while handcuffing. Aim for the face while maintaining a good survival/response stance. A key tactical point, as stressed throughout this book, is you must move and continue to move. You should spray a one- to two-second burst and then immediately move to a different position. Even if the aggressive resister is greatly affected by the OC, he may still swing about wildly in an attempt to strike you. Knowing this, you must continuously move. As you continue to move, you also continue to disperse the OC in short bursts until you are able to safely control and secure the subject. As the courts repeatedly have told us, stop spraying once you achieved compliance or control. Then handcuff the subject as soon as possible and conduct a thorough search. Once the subject is handcuffed, you may need to move him a few feet out of the general area to conduct your search and get away from the OC. Never let the subject out of your sight once he has been sprayed. Then provide proper aftercare as outlined above.

You should expect to receive some residual effect from the spray. This may lead to some coughing, constriction of the throat, and possibly some tearing. Make sure you know which way the wind is blowing before using your IPD. As Jim Croce once sang, "You don't spit into the wind." Well, you don't spray OC into the wind either. It may incapacitate you more than the bad guy.

Knowing you will probably have some exposure during an actual deployment of OC gives credence to exposing officers during training. If you had a prior exposure, you realize it won't kill you; it will just be a little unpleasant for a while. Prior training exposure also increases your confidence in OC and allows you to experience firsthand the effects and limitations. If you have been debilitated by OC, you can also easily articulate why it may be necessary to use deadly force against a subject armed with a chemical agent. A word of caution: When exposing officers to OC, ensure you remove all weapons. On at least two occasions I've seen officers react very badly to OC exposure—screaming, cursing, and swinging about wildly. And these are officers who wanted to be chemical agent instructors. I would have sworn some would have shot someone else or themselves if given the opportunity.

I have a few final precautions. Do not store the OC canister by clipping it onto your automobile's visor. Depending on where you live and the time of year, it can get incredibly hot and burst. You don't want to be driving down the road and hear a "pop" as your car fills with pepper spray. Also, be cautious of how and where you wear the pepper spray. During a SWAT call, as we were driving down the road in a convoy, I happened to look in my rearview mirror and see the two operators in the car behind me. Both were hanging their heads out of the car like dogs out for a joy ride and enjoying the fresh air whipping by. But these two SWAT operators weren't having much fun. One had sat on his OC canister's trigger, releasing pepper spray throughout the car. We never let them live it down.

Please see Video 15.1 at www.SurvivalSciences.com for a demonstration of the tactical use of OC spray. Use the user name and access code listed in the introduction to gain access to the video.

Endnotes

1. Pearson, A., "Can 'Excited Delirium' Get Cops Off the Hook?" 2009, http://www.newscientist.com/article/mg20327204.500-can-excited-get-cops-off-the-hook.html (accessed August 27, 2009).
2. *Headwaters Forest Defense v. County of Humboldt*, 240 F.3d (9th Cir. 2000).
3. *Graham v. Connor*, 490 U.S. 386 (1989).
4. *LaLonde v. County of Riverside*, 204 F. 3d 947 (9th Cir. 2000).

Electronic Control Device 16

I'm an unabashed fan of the TASER. It's more accurate to use the term electronic control device (ECD),[1] but since I'm familiar with the TASER, and since most officers call all ECDs a TASER (much like we tend to refer to facial tissues as Kleenex), I'll refer to an ECD as a TASER in this chapter. I like the TASER because I'm for anything that allows officers to safely control an aggressive resister while maintaining distance. Although I also like batons and pepper spray, I think the TASER has some distinct advantages. First, it can be deployed from a greater distance. Second, it's more effective in that it is more likely to stop all resistive action immediately. Third, it doesn't require a high degree of skill to use effectively. Fourth, the subject suffers no after effects. What have been the results of the increasingly widespread use of TASER? The results have been reduced officer injuries and reduced subject injuries. This also means there are fewer workers' compensation claims and reduced liability for the department.

As was mentioned in Chapter 1, the TASER has an excellent safety record for use against an aggressive resister. Personally, if I had my choice of you beating me with a baton, pepper spraying me, punching me in the nose, or using the TASER, I'd pick the TASER. A baton strike can result in permanent injuries. If the person swinging the baton knows what he or she is doing, I may have a broken bone or two. The effects of pepper spray wear off in no more than forty-five minutes, but sometimes it's an agonizing forty-five minutes trying to pry your eyes open. Getting punched in the nose could break my nose and cause other problems. Not that getting "energized" by a TASER is any fun (it's not), but once it's over, it's over. Once the power is turned off, you're as good as new. Ask yourself this: If you had a loved one who was suffering from a mental illness and was a threat to others (including family members) and himself, how would you want the police to respond? You'd want the police to respond quickly before the loved one killed another family member or himself, correct? If it were me, I'd want the police to use a TASER, as I believe the TASER is the best option. Many officers I've talked to spoke about numerous occasions when the TASER was used successfully to prevent the suicide of a distraught person. Any attempt by civil rights groups to ban the use of a TASER is misguided at best.

While I was attending a TASER instructor course, Officer Hans Warren of La Mesa PD told me about one arrest in which he received the effects of both pepper spray and TASER. This was the first time I had heard of an officer having been the victim of both methods in a single occurrence, and it struck me as funny. I'm not sure if Hans found it as humorous as I did. The subject was fighting with Hans and repeatedly grabbing for Hans' duty belt as they struggled. Another officer on scene initially fired a burst of pepper spray and Hans was also exposed. As they continued to struggle, the other officer then fired a TASER. Unfortunately, one of the probes got caught in Hans' belt. As he continued to try to subdue the subject, Hans tried to pry open one of his eyes to see, and he would receive a jolt every time he came into contact with the TASER wires. Of the two, Hans described the pepper spray as more painful, but the TASER as more effective.

As with any use of force tool, we must first know when we can use it. I already gave the answer away in the first paragraph. The TASER, as is true for the baton, pepper spray, and personal weapons, can only be used against an aggressive resister. You can use the TASER when you can articulate why you or someone else is physically threatened. Unlike some department's policy, the courts have decided you can't use a TASER just because someone didn't do what you told them to do. ("Please show me your license." "No." "Show me your license now." "No." ZAP!) As mentioned in the previous chapter on pepper spray, an easy way to determine if you can use a TASER is to ask yourself if you are justified in striking the subject. If you aren't, then you shouldn't use the TASER. If you are, then it is much safer for both you and the subject if you use the TASER rather than trying to go hands on. If given the option, I would only choose to use personal weapons because I was taken by surprise or close quarters prevented me from initially using one of the other weapons available (i.e., TASER, pepper spray, or impact weapon). But as soon as I created sufficient distance, I would immediately transition to one of the nonlethal weapons.

In a December 28, 2009, Ninth Circuit Court decision,[2] the court advised "the objective facts must indicate that the suspect poses an immediate threat to the officer or a member of the public" prior to using an ECD. Officers must articulate some immediate threat to justify the use of a TASER. On the surface, this is a reasonable ruling and appears to be based on earlier decisions such as *Headwaters Forest Defense v. County of Humboldt*[3] in the pepper spraying of protesters. It is also consistent with civil court decisions in which settlements have been paid to passively resistant people who had a TASER deployed on them. The courts have clearly and repeatedly indicated they don't like officers using an ECD, pepper spray, impact weapon, or personal weapon on someone who is passively resistant.

The only problem I have with the decision is, from reading the facts of the case, I think the officer could have articulated a very real threat existed. Based on *Graham v. Connor*,[4] the courts first look at the nature of the incident that brought the subject and the officer together. In this case, the subject was stopped for a seatbelt violation. This is obviously a minor traffic offense; however, don't forget that even a jay walking ticket could escalate to a deadly encounter.

Continuing to follow the guidance of *Graham v. Connor,* the court will also determine if the subject was fleeing or otherwise attempting to evade arrest. In this case, both the officer and the subject agreed he was not. Finally, the court will seek to determine if an immediate threat existed. If there is no immediate threat, then tools such as a TASER, pepper spray, or personal weapon cannot be used. In this case, it could be argued two bad things happened quickly. The subject stepped out of his car after the officer directed him to remain in his car. This is a bad sign. Anyone who doesn't obey your commands should cause your threat antennae to go up. Already you have someone who is not compliant and there are going to be a few problems, at a minimum. The next thing that happened is the driver was only dressed in shoes and boxer shorts. What's the first thing you think of when you see someone step out of a car not fully dressed? You probably think this guy is probably under the influence. You may also think that based on your training and experience, he may be on PCP. Methamphetamines or PCP users can have incredibly high body heat. Therefore, because of overheating, they strip off their clothes.

The officer then observed the driver beating his thighs with his fists and shouting gibberish. This was described as a "bizarre tantrum." What do you think of when you hear the word *tantrum*? I think of a child throwing a fit. A child behaving in a spoiled manner is not a threat. I wouldn't describe this as a tantrum. I think it's more accurate to describe this behavior as aggressive and indicative of someone under the influence of a dangerous narcotic and mentally unstable. I also know that people under the influence of PCP appear to be impervious to pain and require many officers to successfully subdue them. I don't know about you, but I'd feel uneasy and threatened about now. I would also be calling for backup and assistance from medical personnel.

The distance between the officer and the subject was reported to be about 20 to 25 feet. The court seemed to think this was a reasonable distance for safety. We know it's not. The average adult can cover this distance in 1.5 seconds. A young, athletic person can run it in less. It doesn't give you much time to respond. I would include all of this in my report because it is now clear a "reasonable" officer would feel physically threatened by this behavior. Based on the above, it would indicate an immediate threat did exist. But the Ninth Circuit ruled otherwise. Why did this happen?

Sometimes, courts reach decisions such as this because the use of force report failed to clarify the immediate threat. When you are involved in a use of force incident, particularly one in which injuries were sustained, expect to get sued. Recognize your report will be carefully reviewed by a judge (or judges) and possibly jurors. Take special care to educate them as to the nature and immediacy of the threat. As the Ninth Circuit Court wrote in its decision, "A simple statement by an officer that he fears for his safety or the safety of others is not enough; there must be objective factors to justify such a concern."

The court cited two factors, among others, for its decision. First, backup was called, yet the officer chose to use the TASER instead of waiting for the backup to arrive. I'm certain there are very good reasons why the officer chose to use the TASER at that time. However, nowhere in the court's statement does it reference those reasons. Second, the officer used the TASER without warning. We are not required to give a warning if it compromises our safety, but again, the court doesn't cite anything in the officer's report that would explain why a warning could not have been given without compromising safety. As in using pepper spray, an impact weapon, etc., the courts prefer you to give a warning if you can do so safely. It's not likely that upon hearing your warning an aggressive resister will say, "Oh wow! I didn't realize you were serious. I'll do what you want now." But the courts still consider it appropriate if you can do so without endangering yourself or another person. As I'll mention again in Chapter 18, it's not enough to be reasonable in the application of force. You also must thoroughly document why the force used was reasonable.

The courts allow using the TASER against someone who presents an immediate threat and against someone who is fleeing if you would be justified in tackling that person. I would argue it would be better to have an officer deploy a TASER on me rather than tackle me. If I get hit by a TASER, I lock up and fall down. If you tackle me, not only am I falling, but I now have your body weight on top of me, increasing the likelihood of injury. There are several reasons not to tackle someone. Among them are you are likely to be injured, you are now in a fight on the ground, and the weapons you carry are now accessible to the subject. Using a TASER avoids these problems.

We know we can use a TASER against an aggressive resister. There are several models manufactured by TASER International that are quality products. These are the X26, X3 (which can shoot three sets of probes in a manual or semiautomatic mode), and XREP (eXtended Range Electronic Projectile), which is fired from the X12 shotgun launching platform or a smooth-barrel shotgun. If your department still has the M26 in service, I'd recommend an upgrade. Not that the M26 is a bad product; it's just the X26 is that much better. Officers I've talked to liked the M26, but said it was sometimes difficult to keep it charged properly. If you do a spark check as instructed, you don't have to worry about the X26. Also, there is a shelf life to about anything, and the M26 has been around since 1999. It's time to buy the new product.

The effective zone for a TASER is the entire body. The recommended zone is all of the back of the body below the neck and the front of the body below the chest. There was a huge uproar when TASER International changed the preferred target area of the front of the body to below the chest. Many officers accused TASER International of succumbing to pressure from some groups with their own agenda, claiming the TASER may cause damage to the heart if one of the probes hit the chest area. No credible medical research supports such a claim. Research has indicated that the likelihood of a TASER deployment causing heart problems is almost zero. However, TASER International had already recommended that officers not target the chest area for females because removal of the probes could cause scarring of the breast tissue. The preferred target area is now the same for males and females. Also, it's a *preferred* target area—not a mandatory prohibition against aiming at the chest area. It makes sense to avoid the chest area for two additional reasons. One, the TASER is more effective when there is a greater spread of the probes. It has also been determined that the TASER is more effective when the probes impact the lower torso, or split the belt line, with one probe impacting above and one below the waist. The recommended target area increases the chances of this spread. A second reason is bad guys have been successful in suing if a probe should hit them in the face or eye. Similarly to the head being a prohibited target area to strike with a baton on an aggressively resistant subject, the head is also a prohibited target area for a TASER probe deployment. It doesn't hurt to create a cushion or a margin for error. If a probe should strike the chest area, you are not in violation of the law or the policy as recommended by TASER International. It's just that it would be more effective if the spread of the probes was above and below the waistline. As stated in an October 15, 2009, memo by TASER International's vice president of training, Rick Guilbault, the preferred target area was changed to improve the effectiveness of the TASER and improve risk management. It sounds like a logical argument to me.

Common sense dictates when use of the TASER may result in elevated risks. These include the presence of flammables or explosives. It's never a good idea to introduce a spark in that environment. In one notorious case many years back, officers saturated a violently resisting offender with an alcohol-based pepper spray. When that failed to work, they then used an old version of an ECD. Not too surprisingly, they set the subject on fire.

Other scenarios that increase the risk include when the aggressive resister is elevated (e.g., standing on a chair, on the edge of a bridge, etc.), driving a vehicle, riding a bike, in a body of water, or running. The issue of using a TASER on someone in water may not be for the reason you think. There is not a danger of electrocution. In fact, there is a video of one of the founders of TASER International being hit with a TASER while standing in a pool of water. The concern is if you use a TASER on someone in a body of water, you may not be able to get to him before he drowns.

Courts also haven't looked favorably on using an ECD on the elderly, small children, sickly, frail people, and pregnant women. However, as long as you can articulate a viable, immediate threat, you should be able to use the

TASER, even on a sickly ninety-year-old pregnant woman (but I would like to see that report).

Like any law enforcement tool, you should be consistent in how you carry the TASER and how you deploy it. It's a bad idea to wear your handgun on your strong-side hip one day, in a cross-draw holster the next, then in an ankle holster, and then in a shoulder holster. Train as you are going to play. The same is true for the TASER. Your department probably has (or at least should have) a policy as to how the TASER will be worn. Stick with it and be consistent.

In a tragic event, a Bay Area Rapid Transit (BART) officer shot and killed a person suspected of fighting on a train on New Year's Day 2009. The officer was charged with murder. To many, including me, it looked as if the officer had confused his TASER with his handgun. Supporting this belief were several witness accounts of hearing the officer announce his intention to "tase" the subject, the officer's apparent difficulty in getting his handgun out of the holster, and the officer's reaction immediately after firing a shot in which he appeared stunned, brought his hands to his head, and said "Oh my God!" repeatedly.[5]

There have been other cases in which officers have confused handguns with a TASER. These are almost always a result of the TASER and the handgun both being positioned on the strong-side hip. In the BART case, it was reported that there were not enough TASERs or holsters for each shift. It was also reported that three different holsters were used: strong-side carry, cross-draw, and weak-side carry. Officers would grab whichever holster was available at the beginning of the shift. If this is true, it violates the need for consistency in how we carry our weapons. If it is true, it was a recipe for disaster.

Following TASER International's lead, I would suggest you do some risk management of your own. Carry the TASER in such a manner that is clearly different and requires different motor functions to draw and deploy than your handgun. As is evidenced every day, bad things can happen under stress. You want to be certain that your muscle memory for firing a handgun is distinctly different than that of deploying the TASER. I recommend carrying the TASER in a weak-side, cross-draw holster. I've talked to too many departments that have told me stories of close calls when they position the handgun and TASER on the same side. The only argument I've seen made for having the TASER and the handgun on the same side is it simplifies weapon retention. I don't think this is a strong argument. If someone tries to get my TASER, but my handgun is still accessible, I'm grabbing my handgun as the bad guy is making a grab for my TASER.

TASER International recommends a 4-inch spread of the probes to increase effectiveness. To get this spread, you can't be too close to your adversary. It's best to deploy the TASER into the back of the aggressive resister since there are larger muscle groups and the clothing typically fits tighter in the back lessening the chance that one of the probes will get caught in loose clothing. It's always better to be behind the subject in any tactical encounter ("behind is better"), but I recognize most of the time it's just not an option.

Hopefully you've been successful in maintaining the appropriate distance from the subject, as outlined in Chapter 5 on the fundamentals. It is recommended you deploy the X26 or X3 at a distance of 7 to 15 feet. You may need to step back to create this much distance. Move and continue to move as you deploy the TASER. If that safety zone has been breached (i.e., the subject is closer to you than the length of his rear leg), continue to move and create enough distance to deploy the TASER successfully. Failing that, use the TASER in the "drive stun" mode to get the attacker off of you. As when using any weapon, use any physical barrier and cover available, and use the cover officer concept if you're working with a partner. The cover officer should be ready with deadly force if necessary. Have a custody plan in place before deploying the TASER. Heck, you should have a custody plan in place before you even arrive on scene. As suggested by several court decisions, give a warning prior to deploying the TASER if you can do so without jeopardizing your safety.

Also have a plan if the TASER doesn't work. There are several reasons it may not work. Any electronic device can fail. The subject may be wearing clothing too thick for the probes to penetrate. Or, you may have just missed with one or both of the probes when you fire the TASER. If you hear a loud crackling noise, then you don't have a good connection. If you know one probe hit its mark, you can follow up with a drive stun to another part of the subject's body to complete the circuit and obtain control.

What if you missed with both probes or don't know what happened? If you are using the X3, you still have two more cartridges you can fire. If you have the X26, you have three options: close and use the TASER in a drive stun mode, load a fresh cartridge and fire it, or maintain distance and go to another tool. In Chapter 6, I already outlined the reasons it is typically better to disengage rather than engage. I also don't like the idea of rushing in when I have had a tool not work. This is particularly true if you don't know why the ECD didn't work. Rather than sitting there trying to figure it out, go immediately to plan B. And you always have a plan B—a backup plan for when things don't go as originally desired.

For the vast majority of officers, it is better to stay at a safe distance and reassess the situation. When we rush, we have a tendency to make mistakes that can get us killed. However, if you can safely load a fresh cartridge and deploy the probes, do so. If you are not able to maintain a safe distance that allows you to reload, then you may consider the drive stun. Only go to the drive stun option if you are certain you have the tactical advantage and surprise is on your side. Remember, the drive stun is not as effective as the deployment of the probes. The probes cause neuromuscular incapacitation (NMI), which affects both the sensory and motor nerves, so the person "locks up." A drive stun is dependent solely upon pain compliance to be effective. TASER International discourages the use of the drive stun as a first response because it doesn't cause NMI. A drive stun may be useful, however, if you are trying to get a subject's body part to move, for example, if the subject has his legs dangling out of the squad car and refuses to pull them in so you can shut the door. It can also be used to get the subject to release his grasp on an object. Recognize the natural reaction is for the person to pull away from the drive stun and the source of the pain.

One reason officers may miss with the TASER is they fail to orient the TASER in the same plane as the subject. If the subject is standing, the TASER must be fired in a straight up and down position and not "gangster style," in which the TASER is held parallel to the ground. A tip by Senior TASER Instructor Bernie Gaona is to extend the pinky finger of your shooting hand as you aim the TASER. On the X26, the laser and mechanical sites will show you the path of the top probe. Your little pinky will show you the trajectory of the bottom probe.

It's always safer to work in teams. The more officers, the safer it is for the good guys and gals. Once the TASER has been successfully deployed, a second officer can control and handcuff the subject while "under power" (i.e., the TASER is still cycling). Once you have control, don't waste time. Move in, handcuff, secure, and search. The cycle for the X26 is five seconds, so you have five seconds to move in and secure the subject. If you are working alone, think about what you are going to do with the TASER as you move in to handcuff. Don't just throw it aside. You may need to hit the trigger again to reenergize. Similar to a one-handed, wounded officer reload, one option is to place the TASER behind your knee as you kneel down to handcuff the subject. Using this technique, the TASER is easily accessible and you can quickly grab it as you move to a standing position and away from the subject as you apply another cycle as needed.

I have repeatedly stressed the need to move when facing an aggressive resister and the need to continue to move. Even once the TASER has been deployed, you must continue to move. Move to keep slack in the wires (so the probes don't come out rendering the TASER ineffective), move to avoid additional attacks, and move to be in the most advantageous position to control and handcuff. As is true after any physical confrontation, we are required to observe the subject for any medical distress or injuries and request medical assistance if necessary.

In January 2010, I had a conversation with Julian Coleman, a Houston PD SWAT officer. He had nothing but praise for the TASER. Julian said Houston PD had close to a 100% success rate using the TASER. The TASER has been used by Houston PD SWAT for about eighteen years, originally using the M26 and now using the X26, X3, and Shockwave. Julian estimated they have used TASER products approximately twenty-five to thirty times during that

Please see Video 16.1 at www.SurvivalSciences.com for a demonstration of the effectiveness of the TASER.

time period, and he has personally used the TASER X26 twice. On both occasions he was impressed with the product.

One occasion occurred during his off-duty job when he noticed several males in a car casing a parking lot in an apparent attempt to steal a car. Julian saw the car drop off one male, who then appeared to be looking for a car to break into and steal. Julian moved in and confronted the would-be car thief, temporarily losing sight of the moving subject vehicle. The subject began looking around as if to find an avenue of escape. Julian warned the man he would be tased if he tried to run. Sure enough, the bad guy started to run, Julian deployed the TASER, the bad guy went down, and an arrest was made without incident. Not only did Julian say he was happy that he didn't have to wrestle with the large subject, he also liked the fact that he remained in a standing, upright position, which allowed him to continuously scan for the vehicle containing the subject's friends as well as any other threats.

I find it interesting, and a little more than disturbing, that some courts and activists groups seem more interested in the safety of criminals than the safety of officers trying to uphold the law. The TASER is a great tool that allows us to safely make an arrest of an aggressive resister. Please don't cause us to lose a valuable tool by misusing it or maintaining bad policy.

Endnotes

1. Special thanks to Rick Guilbault, Vice President of Training, TASER International, and Bernabe "Bernie" Gaona, Senior TASER Instructor, for the information they provided for this chapter.
2. *Bryan v. City of Coronado,* December 28, 2009 (9th Cir. 2009).
3. *Headwaters Forest Defense v. County of Humboldt*, 240 F 3d 1185 (9th Cir. 2000).
4. *Graham v. Connor,* 490 U.S. 386, 394 (1989).
5. Shields, B., "Former BART Officer Johannes Mehserle Will Be Tried for Murder," *Kron 4 News*, June 4, 2009, www.kron.com/News/ArticleView/tabid/298/smid/1126/ArticleID/1703 (accessed January 16, 2010).

Weapon Retention and Disarming

17

Handgun Retention

Looking at the FBI statistics of officers killed in the line of duty,[1] it is apparent that every year, approximately 10% of the law enforcement officers killed in the line of duty are killed with their own handguns. Not surprisingly, officers are killed when they approach subjects. Over half of the officers killed each year are less than 5 feet away from their assailant when the attack occurred.[2]

While teaching a course to certify defensive tactics (DT) instructors from other agencies, I was told by one officer that there was an individual named Raymond who was infamous and well known within their jurisdiction. It seems as if Raymond was somewhat of a nut. For his own amusement, he would regularly call a police dispatcher and report a suspicious person, providing a detailed description of himself. He would do this just to interact with the police. Although this was a waste of the department's time and resources, it soon became a more serious game. After receiving one such call, two school police officers responded to Raymond's call as he was on a campus. When the two officers approached Raymond, he promptly and deftly removed both officers' weapons, threw them on a roof of a nearby building, laughed, and walked away before later being arrested. It seems as if Raymond was quite adept at weapon disarming and enjoyed proving his prowess. This happened more than once and escalated until Raymond eventually shot two officers. The bottom line is there are people out there who are very good at taking weapons away from you. There are prison videos showing prisoners practicing various disarming techniques.

If you should be so unfortunate as to see someone taking your handgun out of your holster, statistically speaking, there is over a 90% chance you are going to die. What does this tell you if someone makes a grab toward your gun? It tells you that you are now in a fight for your life. The bad guy doesn't want to look at your weapon to admire its craftsmanship and then hand it back to you. He wants to kill you with it. There is at least one weapon in every confrontation we have as law enforcement officers—and we brought it. The important thing is to keep it.

A well-made, secure holster can greatly assist in preventing your weapon from being taken, but it's not the complete answer. As is discussed throughout this book, the answer is to maintain proper distance, remain alert, expect to be attacked, and be prepared to move out of the way. The first line of defense in preventing your gun from being taken is being cognizant that you are carrying a gun. Do you remember the first day you were issued a handgun? It was a heady experience, wasn't it? Every few seconds, you'd lay your arm against the weapon to make sure it was still there. Somewhere along the way, we get so used to carrying a weapon, we take it for granted. We become less aware that it's just sitting there begging to be snatched by a bad guy.

There are several videos that, unfortunately, show officers being killed by their own weapon. One of the more notorious is of Constable Darrell Lunsford of Texas. Constable Lunsford was a very large man. He also had a talent for identifying vehicles carrying illegal drugs. One night his instincts were again correct. He pulled over a vehicle with three males. At Constable Lunsford's request, one of the men opened the trunk and a large quantity of marijuana was clearly visible. Constable Lunsford bent over the trunk to view inside, exposing his weapon to two males that had since exited the vehicle. Constable Lunsford then turned to one of the males and asked him, "What is this?" indicating the marijuana in the trunk. The male spoke in Spanish to one of his accomplices. They then tackled Constable Lunsford to the ground, removed his service weapon, and shot and killed him. The purpose of this story is not to speak badly of the dead. The purpose is to learn from other's mistakes so we don't keep repeating them. Sometimes in law enforcement we have a bad habit of glorifying a dead officer (as we should), but ignoring the events that led to his or her death (as we shouldn't). The only good thing that can come from such a tragedy is we learn from it, teach it, and prevent other officers from being murdered.

Another example of a lack of awareness to the vulnerability of your service weapon was shown on an early episode of *Cops* when the show focused on a department in Florida. A deputy had stopped a suspect in what appeared to be a mini-market parking lot. After being told by the suspect that there were no drugs or weapons in the car, the deputy asked permission to search the car. After being given consent, the deputy crouched over to look under the front seat, completely exposing his weapon to the suspect. The deputy quickly discovered a revolver under the car seat. He placed the revolver in the palm of his hand, extended the revolver toward the suspect, and asked, "What is this?" The suspect could have taken his revolver at that moment and he could have disarmed the deputy as he was bent over looking under the seats. Fortunately for the deputy, the suspect chose not to.

Always be aware you are carrying a weapon. If you are in uniform, the weapon is exposed for the world to see, making weapon retention even more challenging. Even if your weapon is covered, it is still easily accessible to someone with even marginal skills. Don't make it easier for the bad guy. Maintain distance and stay alert. If someone does make a grab for your gun, remember Chapter 6 on movement. Get out of the way, get off the tracks, and draw your weapon to prevent an additional attack.

Now let's say something went horribly wrong. For whatever reason you failed to maintain proper distance, you weren't alert (not enough sleep, exhausted, distracted with home issues), and the bad guy actually grabbed your gun. What now? First, recognize you are in a fight for your life. Your primary goal is to keep that gun in your holster. At the first sign of danger, I hope your instinctive reaction was to lower your center of gravity in a low, wide, stable position. Your weapon hand should sweep up and grab the gun from underneath as your opposite hand covers the top of your weapon. *Do not* attempt to pull away from the attacker. This is a natural reaction and exactly what the attacker expects you to do. By stepping away, you are assisting the bad guy in removing the gun from the holster. Instead, step *into* your attacker while simultaneously striking his elbow with your forearm. You accomplish several things by stepping into the attacker. First, it's a surprise move. Second, you take the attacker's balance if you lower your center of gravity and "stand where he stands." Third, you attack the elbow joint weakening the attacker's grip on your weapon (Figure 17.1).

Using proper body mechanics (i.e., using your entire body weight and momentum), you violently step and rotate into the attacker's elbow, hyperextending it. Once the bad guy's grip has been broken, immediately step away, make distance, and draw your weapon. If the first strike fails to break the attacker's grasp, continue to strike and continue to move. Also, don't forget the finger jab to the attacker's eyes. If you jab your fingers into the attacker's eyes and push, he may pull back and away from your weapon to avoid damage to his eyes.

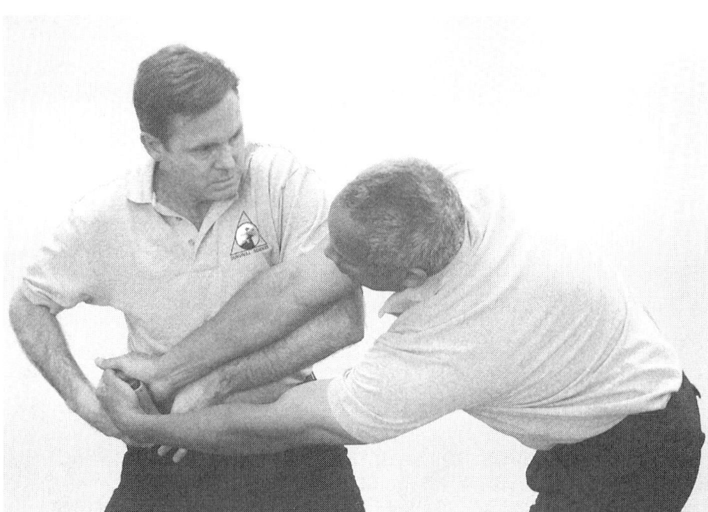

Figure 17.1 The proper position for attacking the subject's elbow.

Video 17.1 at www.SurvivalSciences.com demonstrates the weapon retention technique when your handgun is grabbed while it is still in your holster. Use the user name and access code listed in the introduction to gain access to the video.

In summary, the steps to retain your handgun when the handgun is in your holster are (assuming you failed to abide by the tactics mentioned earlier of effectively moving out of the way) retain the weapon in your holster, step into the attacker, attacking his elbow, and once contact has been broken, create distance and draw your weapon. You should practice this technique simulating attacks from the front, rear, and side.

Next, what happens when you have your handgun in your hand (rather than the holster) and someone tries to grab your gun and take it away from you? This is an even scarier situation because now the barrel of the gun may be waving to and fro as you and the bad guy struggle for your gun. First, maintain proper body mechanics. Don't let the gun and your hand extend away from your body. Keep everything in as close as possible. Now for the technique—look at the palm of your hand. Yes, that's right. With the gun in your hand, rotate your hand so the palm area faces you. Simultaneously drop your body weight as you bring the gun-side elbow to your belt level (Figure 17.2). This accomplishes a couple of things. First, if your attacker has

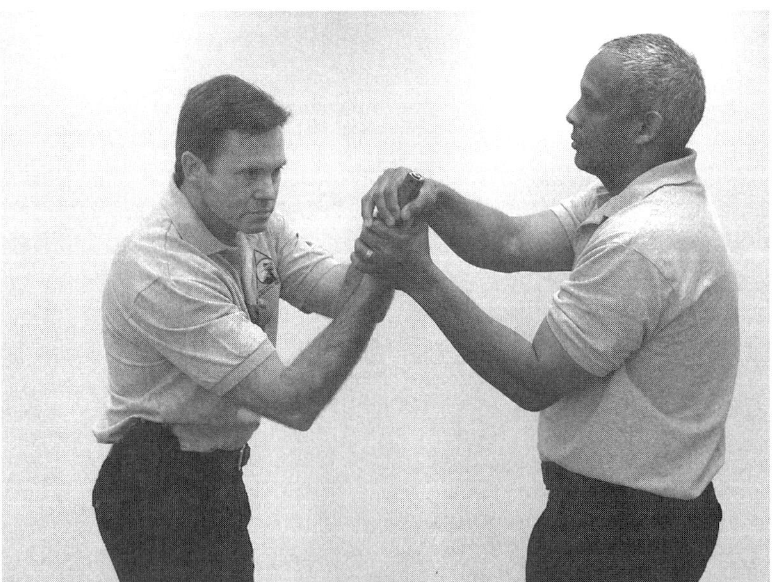

Figure 17.2 The position of looking at the palm of your hand while dropping your body weight.

Video 17.2 at www.SurvivalSciences.com demonstrates the complete retention technique if someone grabs your handgun when it is in your hand.

maintained a grip on your gun, it has twisted his wrist in an unnatural position. If you continue this motion, the bad guy must either release your gun or have his wrist sprained. Second, you take the bad guy's balance by combining the wrist twist with the drop and shift in your body weight.

Handgun Retention with Multiple Subjects

Prison videos show inmates practicing weapon disarming techniques against officers. Sometimes, the inmates would practice working as a team to disarm and murder an officer. Working in tandem, one bad guy would distract an officer from the front, while a second bad guy attempted to take the officer's weapon from behind. Sometimes, one bad guy would grab and immobilize the officer's gun hand while an accomplice would take the officer's handgun from the holster. As bad as this may initially sound, if you follow the technique described above, you should still be okay. If there are one or more assailants, you still react in the same manner.

As before, you should first be aware of your surroundings and those who are infringing on your zone of safety. The first defense is being aware of the threat and not letting them get that close to you. Failing that, all is not lost. Let's take the worst-case scenario in which one attacker has grabbed your hand as his accomplice tries to take your handgun. Just as before, you will move. As your hand is grabbed, instinctively you should drop into the low, centered, balanced response/survival stance as your hands come up for protection. As you quickly bring your hand that has been grabbed upwards, be sure you rotate it so your palm faces you (exactly as was described in Chapter 10 on counters to common attacks). Remember to look at your palm. By doing this you are twisting the attacker's wrist in a position that will cause him to release his grip or sprain his wrist. Simultaneously as your hands come up, your elbows are brought in tight to your sides in the proper survival stance position. Your elbow in this position will cause it to cover your handgun in your holster, making it more difficult to grab. Finally, as always, you continue to move using your entire body weight in a balanced fashion. All three aspects are done simultaneously—bring up your hands as you look at your palms, drop your elbows to protect your weapon, and move using your body weight.

Video 17.3 at www.SurvivalSciences.com demonstrates the handgun retention technique against multiple attackers working together as a team.

Handgun Disarming

The next topic under this chapter is weapon disarming. I originally thought the primary value of practicing a weapon disarming technique was to reinforce how easy it is for someone to take your weapon if you allow him to get too close or are careless in weapon handling. Early in my martial arts training and later in my law enforcement training, we had great fun practicing with rubber-tipped dart guns and later with paint guns and Airsoft guns. What we all learned was that with a minimum of practice, it was quite easy to disarm an opponent if we were allowed within arm's reach. Beyond that distance, it was almost impossible to succeed without getting shot. This practice, which I later duplicated with FBI agents and other law enforcement officers, emphasized the need to stay out of range of a subject's hands and feet, and the more critical need to stay alert and expect to be attacked. Those lessons alone are well worth the time practicing disarming techniques with a partner.

I thought the possibility of any of us ever having to do an actual weapon disarming technique was remote at best. I was wrong. I've since done two in my lifetime—once against a pistol and once against a revolver. For me at least, it was practice well spent.

The first rule of disarming an opponent is to be fairly certain the bad guy is going to kill you. I realize that sounds somewhat facetious, but there is a reason for it. You may be a master at weapon disarming. You may be able to successfully take a weapon from someone 999 times out of a 1,000. The problem is what if this is the one time in a thousand you fail? Bad times. The first step is the mental preparation that should have taken place long before the actual incident when you are staring down the barrel of the gun. Can you do it? Will you do it? Are you committed? Are you ready to change the equation and take control from your attacker? Totally make up your mind prior to acting. Hesitation and second thoughts will get you killed.

There are a few key elements of a successful disarming technique, but there are hundreds of techniques for disarming an opponent. Which one is best? It may not be the technically best technique, since the technically best technique may require constant training, or size, or strength, or speed to be successful. I know of complex moves that are highly effective when done correctly, but I also know few people can perform these moves reliably in a high-stress encounter. I also have seen highly touted techniques that involve grabbing the barrel of the gun and lifting it upwards. Think about that. If a gun is pointing at your chest and you start raising it skyward, where is the muzzle going? It's tracking up your body, to your head, and eventually (if you're lucky) over your head. This technique violates my number one rule in a disarming attempt. Here is the most important rule: **do not get shot!** If you obey that one rule, every thing else is gravy. Having a bad guy's gun track up my body is not the best method of abiding by rule 1. Unless you are wider than you are tall (and if you are, perhaps you shouldn't be in law enforcement), the quickest way to get a muzzle from pointing at your body is for it to move horizontally, not vertically. And, going once again to our fundamentals, you will simultaneously move. Move out of the way as you deflect and control the barrel of the gun.

So what is the best technique? The best technique is the one that works for you all of the time. To be successful, you need to be within arm's reach of the weapon, the technique must get your body out of the line of fire as quickly as possible, the technique must be simple but effective, and you must be aware of the location of the weapon.

So you are in this really bad situation looking down the barrel of the gun and you're pretty well convinced the bad guy is going to drop the hammer on you. You are mentally prepared and are ready. What do you do? The same things the bad guys do. When you tell bad folks to raise their hands, do they ever get it right? No! They typically half-heartedly raise their hands to about head level with arms bent at a 90° angle. They don't lock out their elbows and extend their hands fully as you'd like them to do. You do the same. Keep your hands at about the level of the gun with your elbows bent. Stay in a balanced stance so you can move quickly. Now for an important side note—I know you're Billy or Bobbie badass, but this is not the time to be Godzilla. Being Godzilla when someone is pointing a gun at your face is a good way to get killed. This is a great time to be Bambi. "Anything you want." "Please take my wallet." I know it's hard, but be Bambi. You get to be Godzilla soon, I promise. Distractions are also useful as every microsecond counts. If you can get the bad guy to talk, it is the perfect time to move. People respond more slowly to a stimulus when they're talking. Next, don't stare at the gun. If you had a bad guy at gunpoint and he kept staring at your gun, it would make you nervous (as it should). If a bad guy stares at the gun, it may mean he's thinking of trying to take it from you. It makes you nervous, and it will make the bad guy nervous too if he is the one holding the weapon. Remember, this is Bambi time, for now.

Finally, when you move, **move!** Explode into action. It's interesting to me to see officers practice disarming techniques by slowly inching forward toward the gun. That will get you killed. Make the decision and commit!

Some instructors of weapon disarming techniques use the acronym GUN for grab, undo, and neutralize. I think it's missing the most important element. **Get out of the way! Do not get shot! Move!** After you accomplish that very important goal, you can then deal with the niceties of removing the weapon and neutralizing. So I created the acronym MISS for **move, immobilize, strip,** and **secure**. I don't want to get shot, so my primary objective is to move out of the way as I immobilize, or control, the weapon. I then strip the weapon from my attacker and secure the situation by controlling the attacker.

There is literature that tells you what to look for prior to attempting a gun take-away. For example, is it a revolver or a pistol? Is the revolver a double action? Is the hammer back? Theoretically, if it's a double-action revolver and the hammer is down, you can grab the cylinder to keep it from firing. Theoretically, if the hammer is back, you want to grab the revolver in such a manner as the web of your hand or a finger will prevent the firing pin from coming forward and striking the primer of the cartridge. I say "theoretically" because it's all BS. Having been in that situation, I wasn't too concerned about those intricacies. Here's what we know: in times of stress, when our system is flooded with adrenalin, our large muscle groups work really well so we can run faster, jump farther, and lift heavy objects. In times of stress, our fine motor skills pretty much go in the toilet. How fast can you run 100 yards? How fast can you run 100 yards with a 500-pound grizzly bear chasing you? How much trouble do you think you'd have putting the correct key into the lock of the front door of your house with the grizzly getting ready to pounce on you? So, don't worry about the type of gun or if the hammer is down or not. Just worry about getting out of the way. Use your large muscle groups to blade your body (getting those vital organs out of the line of fire) as you simultaneously sidestep and push the barrel away from your body.

Weapon Disarming from the Front

Which direction should you move? Do you push the gun to your attacker's inside (toward his midline) or do you push it to the outside? Theoretically, you'd want to step to the outside as you push the weapon toward the attackers' midline. There are several reasons for this. Going back to the chapter on fundamentals (Chapter 5), we never want to be directly in front of the attacker. The position of survival is one that is at least to the side or behind an attacker's outstretched arm (Figure 17.3). Additionally, people are stronger resisting a push of their arms to the outside than they are to the inside. Finally, pushing the gun to the inside begins to bend the wrist toward the attacker. This means if the gun should go bang, guess who takes the bullet? The bad guy gets it and not some innocent person.

Recall I said "theoretically" again? That should be a clue by now. The way you move is whichever direction you can move the fastest and with the highest degree of success. If that's not the theoretically "best" direction, then so

Figure 17.3 The proper position after the initial deflection of the handgun.

be it. If the direction you feel most comfortable moving is the theoretically best direction, then great. The bottom line is just don't get shot.

Okay, so you've succeeded so far. You have the muzzle off of your body, sidestepped, and you've bladed your body. Now what? Grab the barrel or the entire gun in a baseball grip. I think all of us have swung a baseball bat at some time in our lives, so it shouldn't be too difficult to think of grabbing a bat and swinging for the bleachers. To greatly simply the technique, that's exactly what you will do. Grab the barrel and handgun in a baseball grip and swing; but use a good baseball swing that is likely to result in a homerun (Figure 17.4). Keep you hands near your center (belt buckle), elbows in, and swing with your hips using your body weight. The muzzle of the gun should immediately be directed toward your subject's body.

One concern once the weapon has been taken away from the subject is the subject will instinctively "convulse" back on the gun and the struggle for control continues. You add one more step to the above technique to prevent this. As throughout this book, it involves stepping out and down at a 45° angle to take the subject's balance. Once the muzzle has been directed back into the subject, step at a 45° angle to the subject's rear and down simultaneously. This is the exact same technique as discussed in Chapter 8 on subject control to take a subject's balance. The result should be you successfully stripped the gun from the subject, the subject is now lying on the ground, and you have continued to move a safe distance away as you draw your weapon and obtain control.

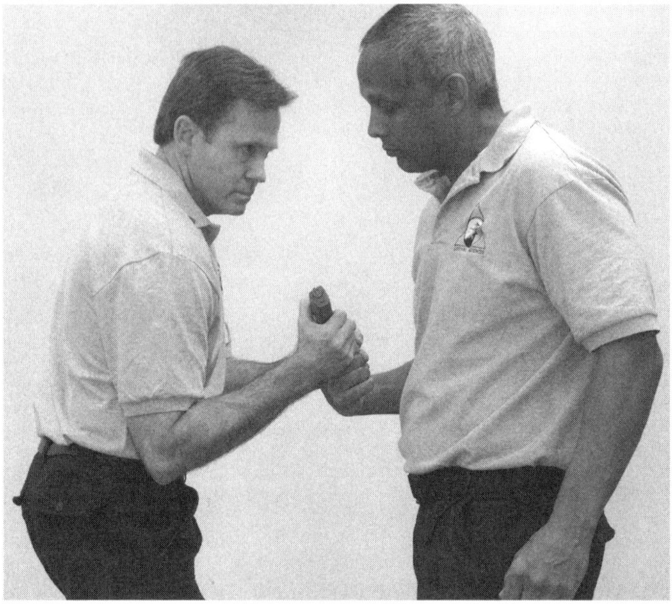

Figure 17.4 The position of the baseball swing disarming technique.

A very similar technique is called a run-through, in which the officer, upon securing the weapon, uses body weight to run past the subject at a 45° angle. The run-through can also be used as a weapon retention technique.

Video 17.4a at www.SurvivalSciences.com demonstrates the basic weapon disarming technique. Video 17.4b at www.SurvivalSciences.com demonstrates a variation of the weapon disarming technique in which you take the attacker to the ground to prevent him from "convulsing" on the weapon. Video 17.5 at www.SurvivalSciences.com demonstrates a slight variation to the disarming technique by using the run-through approach.

Weapon Disarming from the Rear

The technique to disarm an attacker standing behind you is almost identical to a disarming technique when the attacker is in front of you. The only difference is your initial move to deflect the gun off your body and not get shot. If the attacker is behind you, you must first look to see where the weapon is situated. You can't just spin around and then hope to deflect the weapon blindly. If you try this, you are likely to violate my primary rule and get shot.

Figure 17.5 First looking over your shoulder to locate the weapon.

Video 17.6 at www.SurvivalSciences.com demonstrates the disarming techniques when the weapon is behind you.

Your first move is to casually and in a nonthreatening manner look over your shoulder to locate the weapon (Figure 17.5). It helps to talk as you look. "Hey, no problem, whatever you want." Once you see the weapon, spin toward the attacker and sidestep as you deflect the weapon away from your body (Figures 17.6 and 17.7).

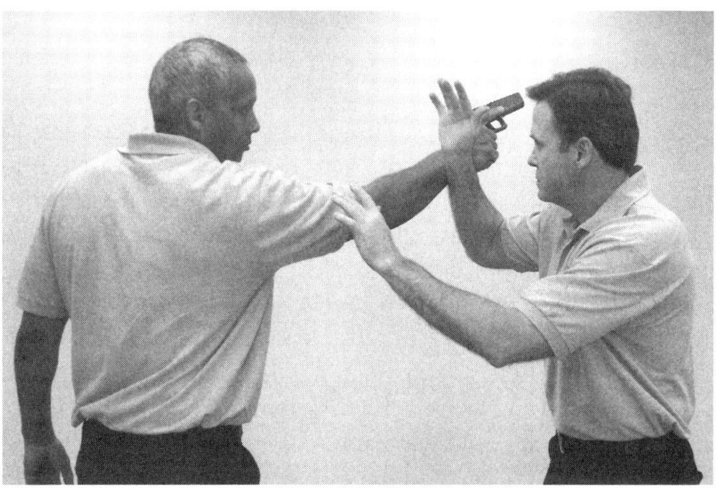

Figure 17.6 Spinning and sidestepping as you deflect a weapon held in a high position.

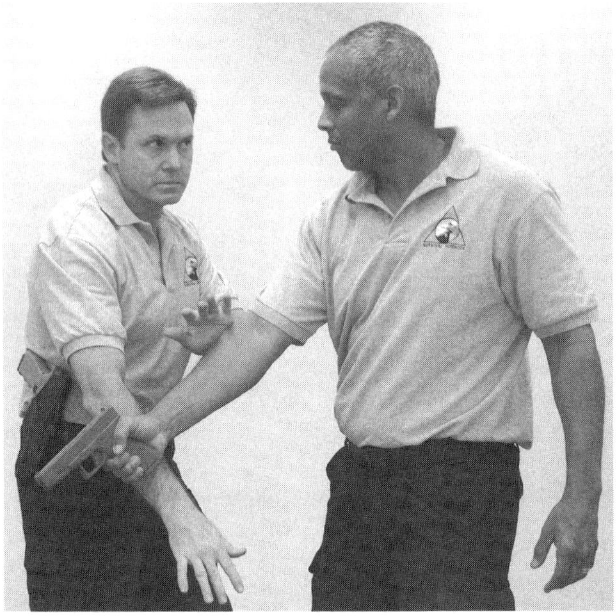

Figure 17.7 Spinning and sidestepping as you deflect a weapon held in a low position.

Once you have reached the position of deflecting the handgun and blading your body, the technique is identical to that described above for a weapon disarming to your front.

Long Gun Retention

Departments typically will have some instruction on handgun retention, but I've seen very few departments that even mention long gun retention. This may be okay if your officers never carry a long gun, but I'll make a wild guess that some of your officers, at least some of the time, carry a long gun. Particularly in close quarters such as clearing a house or other structure, officers with long guns are likely to be in close proximity to bad guys. As with handguns, the first rule to long gun retention is never let the weapon get close enough to a bad guy where he can reach it. For whatever reason, let's assume things turned bad and you are now holding onto a shotgun (for this example) and a bad guy is latched onto the barrel.

The first option is the easiest retention technique known. Before we discuss this surefire technique, there are some questions I need to ask. First, having read the above information, do you believe that once any bad guy grabs your weapon, you are now in a life-or-death struggle? Yes? Good for you. Next question, is the muzzle of your weapon pointing toward the bad guy? Yes? Excellent! Okay, here's the technique: wait for it, wait for it … **press the #*!#* trigger!** That's it. Probably the safest and easiest retention technique is to shoot the assailant. Don't forget that one.

Now let's assume you violated the first rule and allowed the bad guy to grab your long gun. And the bad guy isn't quite dumb enough to stand there with the muzzle covering his body, so the press the trigger technique is kaput. We will stay with the fundamentals and theme throughout this book. Don't fight, don't resist. If the bad guy tries to force the barrel of your gun upwards, let him. If he tries to force the barrel of the gun downwards, let him. As he does so, you will do the one thing we discussed continuously, and that is move. As the barrel of the gun is moving up or down, you will maintain your grip on the weapon and step to the side of the subject. As you do so, an incredible thing will happen. The subject's arms will become crossed, making his grip weaker. Also, by stepping next to the bad guy as the movement of the muzzle is going either up or down, you have also begun to take his balance. Now it's a simple matter of continuing to step out at a 45° angle as you rotate the weapon away from his crossed arms. As always, continue to move and address the threat (Figure 17.8).

The key to success is to remember not to try to use strength against strength, but simply allow the muzzle to go in the direction the attacker is taking it. By stepping to the side of the attacker and supplementing his movement, you cause the attacker's arms to cross and take his balance. Continue to move as you regain control of the weapon.

(A)

Figure 17.8 (A) The position of both the officer and the attacker when the long gun has first been grabbed. (Continued)

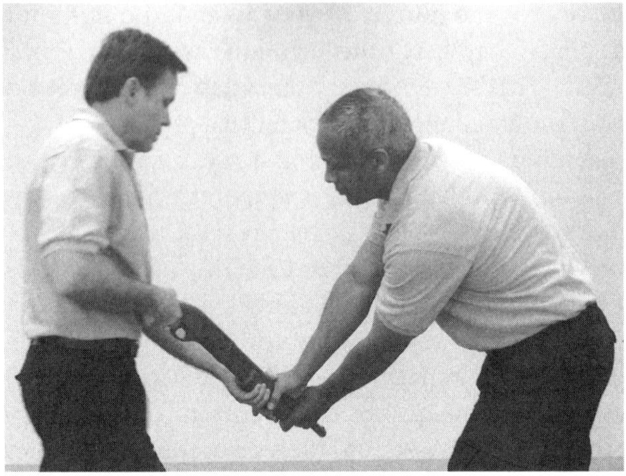

(B)

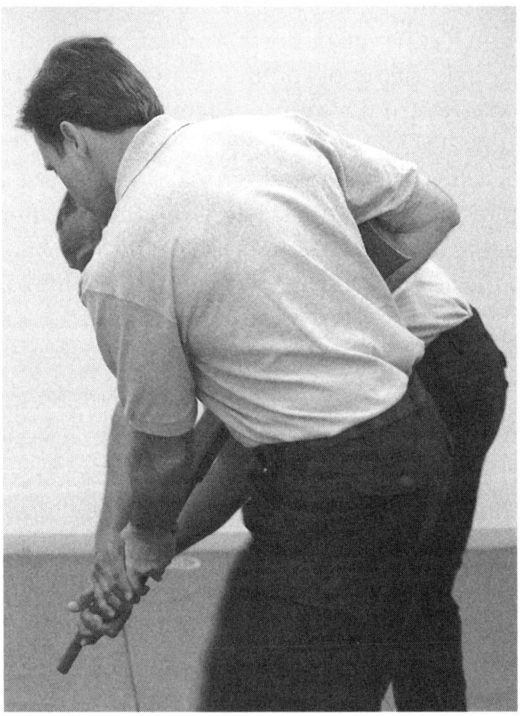

(C)

Figure 17.8 (Continued) (B) The attacker trying to wrestle the gun away from the officer in a downwards direction. (C) The officer continues the motion of the attacker. Notice the officer supplements the direction (redirection of force rather than force against force) and steps to the side of the attacker.

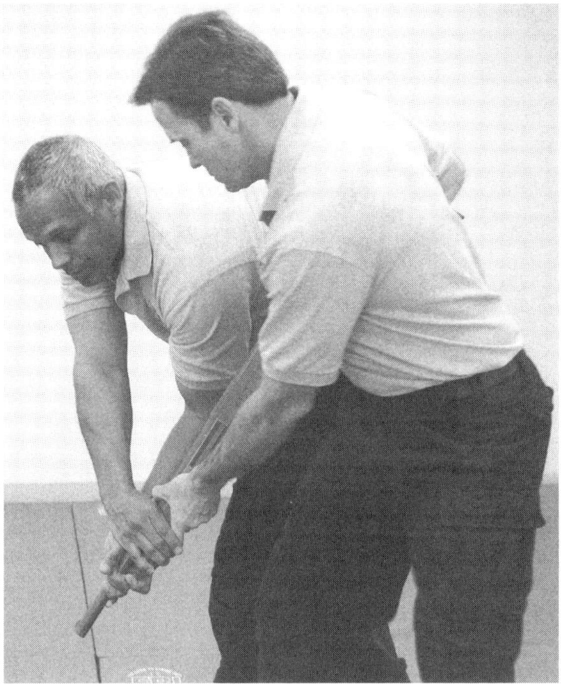

(D)

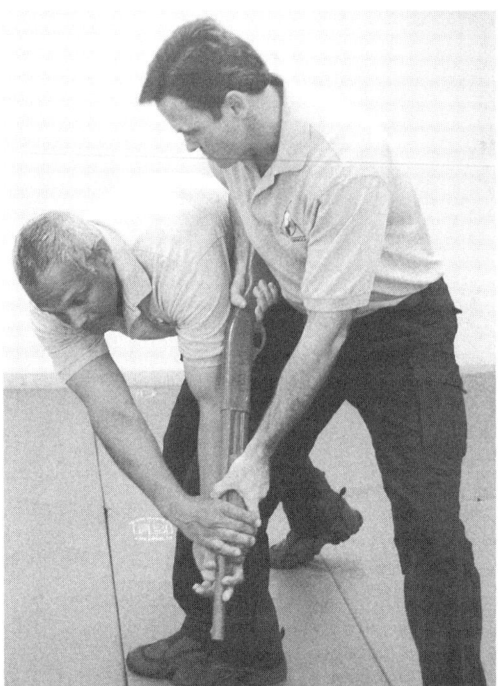

(E)

Figure 17.8 (Continued) (D) The officer continues the attacker's original motion and stepping to the side, causing the attacker's arms to begin to cross. (E) The attacker's arms cross as he loses his balance and begins to fall forward.

Video 17.7a at www.SurvivalSciences.com depicts the entire sequence of a long gun retention technique as the attacker attempts to force the weapon up. Video 17.7b at www.SurvivalSciences.com depicts the entire sequence of a long gun retention technique as the attacker attempts to force the weapon down.

Long Gun Disarming

As with the handgun, one benefit of practicing long gun disarming techniques is to recognize how easy it is to take a weapon away from someone if you allow him to get too close. What was the number one rule mentioned above when attempting a weapon disarming technique? Don't get shot! It still applies. To avoid getting shot, you must be within arm's reach of the muzzle and you must immediately get your body out of the line of fire. Once you do that, you have to make sure the bad guy isn't able to bring the muzzle back to you and shoot you. You must get to the side of the muzzle with your body weight preventing the muzzle from sweeping back on target.

If your body is positioned correctly, as demonstrated in Figure 17.9, the bad guy will have to move your entire body weight to move the muzzle in

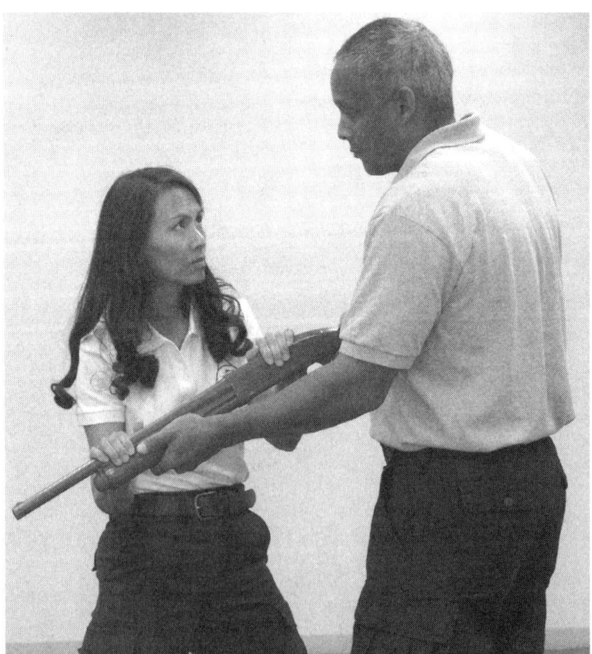

Figure 17.9 The proper position once you have redirected the muzzle off of your body. Notice the bent arm as well as the position of the body.

Video 17.8 at www.SurvivalSciences.com shows the result of being in the proper position, even with a much larger and stronger opponent.

your direction. Here is the really great thing about this position: even if your attacker is so strong he is capable of moving you, all that will happen is he will continue to move the muzzle, and you, in the same direction. As long as you keep your bent arm in the same position, the best the bad guy can do is continue to move you.

Once you are in position and avoided getting shot, you will always be in constant movement. In this case, the movement is to step into the bad guy and with your near, free hand, grab the butt of the long gun. Recognize you now control the weapon from its pivot points and you have the best leverage. By rotating the weapon, you force the attacker to cross his hands and release the weapon. The key to this technique is not using your strength. The key is to use your body weight properly. As you begin to rotate the weapon, you step in with your full body weight and then drop back and down at a 45° angle (Figure 17.10).

Video 17.9 at www.SurvivalSciences.com demonstrates the entire long gun disarming technique.

(A)

Figure 17.10 (A) The proper position as the officer first gets out of the way of the muzzle (don't get shot!) and begins stepping in to grab the butt of the weapon.

(Continued)

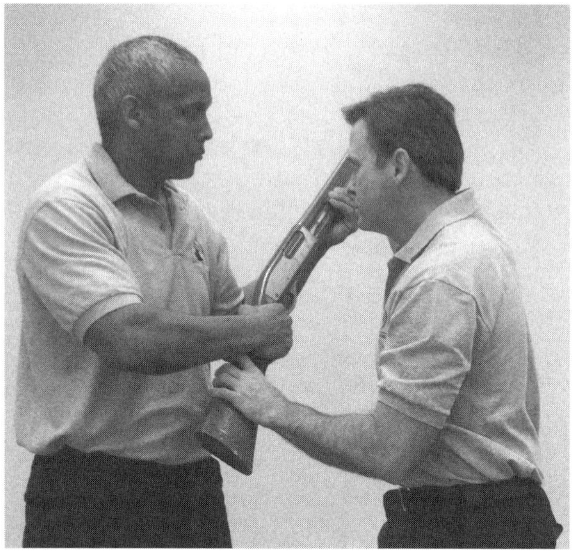

(B)

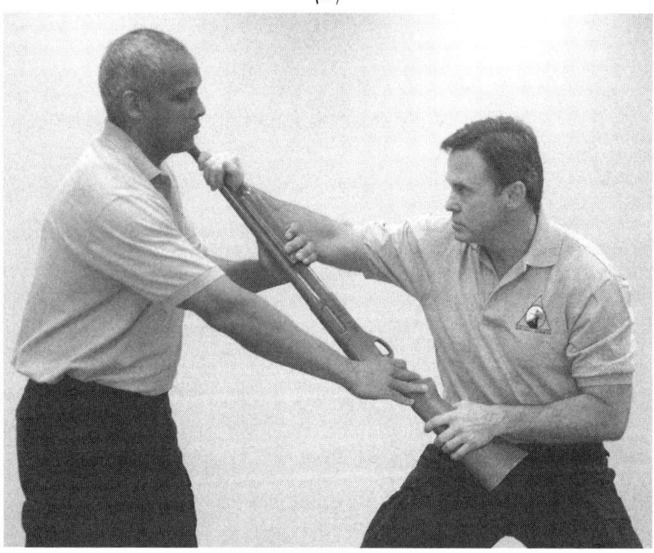

(C)

Figure 17.10 (Continued) (B) The officer has grabbed the butt of the weapon and begins to rotate the weapon as he steps out. (C) The officer is stepping back using his bodyweight while continuing to lever the long gun out of the hands of the attacker.

In summary, the best defense against a bad guy attempting to disarm you is to maintain proper distance, stay alert, and be prepared to move. Failing that, don't panic. Move properly using your body weight as described above and don't give up!

Drills

1. With a rubber (or other nonfunctioning) training gun, practice weapon retention with a partner. Allow your partner to grab the butt of your handgun and then *gently* attack the elbow to break your partner's grip as depicted in Video 17.1. Practice with the attack originating from a variety of angles.
2. With the training gun in your hand, again allow your partner to grasp the weapon. Immediately assume a survival stance and "look at your palm" as you step out and down at a 45° angle. As before, practice with the attack originating from a variety of angles, as demonstrated in Video 17.2.
3. With multiple partners or by visualizing other attackers, practice handgun retention against multiple attackers working as a team to disarm you, as shown in Video 17.3.
4. As shown in Videos 17.4a and b, 17.5, and 17.6, practice disarming techniques from various angles.
5. Practice long retention as demonstrated in Video 17.7a and b.
6. Practice long gun disarming as shown in Video 17.9.

Endnotes

1. FBI Uniform Crime Reporting Program, "Law Enforcement Officers Killed and Assaulted 2005," Table 14, www.fbi.gov/ucr/killed/2005/index.htm (accessed February 9, 2010).
2. Ibid., Table 35.

18 Just for Law Enforcement Executives and Use of Force Instructors

Okay, some of you peeked and you are neither an executive with your department or an instructor, are you? That's okay. There are no secrets here, and it is useful for all officers to be aware of the following issues. They are just more pertinent to those who make policy and those who prepare lesson plans and conduct the training.

The purpose of this chapter is to discuss preventing and defeating excessive force/police misconduct claims. We'll look at what can go wrong, how plaintiff's attorneys will attack you, and how to defend yourself against these attacks.

First the good news: According to a study conducted by the National Institute of Justice (NIJ), police use force infrequently. The report indicated about 1% of people who had contacts with police reported the officers used or threatened force. The International Association of Chiefs of Police (IACP) also collected data indicating less than a half percent of calls dispatched for service resulted in a use of force incident beyond presence and verbal commands.

Now the bad news: 27% of police officers reported having been sued.[1] As mentioned in the first chapter, research has consistently indicated an officer's use of force is most likely to occur when dealing with someone who is either under the influence or mentally ill. Once an officer uses force, the officer and the department are likely to be scrutinized, criticized, and possibly sued. Take a look at your own department. How many times has your department been sued in the last decade, and how much have you paid out—not just in settlements, but also in attorney's fees, lost time from work, etc.? If the answers are zero and zero, then congratulations. But even if that's the case, please take a look at the statistics and do a cost-benefit analysis to determine when your turn is up. Typically, regardless of the size of the department or the location, it's simply a matter of time before you will have to deal with the court process. One court decision can lead to an exorbitant settlement. A May 25, 2001, article in the *Los Angeles Times* stated that the Los Angeles PD paid out over $161 million in civil suits in one year alone.

If you have been successful in avoiding these claims, you need to ask yourself if it is because you have instituted the necessary precautions (as will be outlined below) or if you have just been lucky. You have a moral and fiduciary responsibility to your community, to your municipality, to your department, and to your officers to provide legally sound, life-saving training. Exceptional training leads to safer, more professional officers. And that leads to reduced liability. Everyone wins.

Let's look at how bad it can get. Having worked on SWAT during the LA riots and the subsequent gang sweeps afterwards, the situation that leaps to my mind is the Rodney King incident. Rodney King was a reported alcoholic and convicted felon for armed robbery (later described simply as a "motorist") at the time of his encounter with the LAPD and the California Highway Patrol (CHP). On March 3, 1991, Mr. King led officers on a chase that exceeded 100 miles per hour. During the subsequent traffic stop, Mr. King violently resisted arrest, behaved erratically, and was hit with an electronic control device (ECD) twice and struck with a baton over fifty times. Mr. King suffered a fractured facial bone, a broken leg, and lacerations.

As a side note, what many forgot, or never knew, is that Mr. King wasn't alone in his car. He had two passengers with him. What happened to them? Nothing. Why? They didn't resist arrest.

What was the aftermath of the Rodney King incident? There were riots in Los Angeles as well as other cities in the United States. These resulted in 53 deaths, 2,383 injuries, 7,000 fires, almost $1 billion in financial losses, and a $3.8 settlement paid to Mr. King. Later, four officers were charged with felonies and two officers were eventually convicted and sentenced to thirty months. It was not a good time for Mr. King (other than the settlement), the police, or the taxpayers. The media and public perception was clearly that the police have all of the power and control the amount of force used. Using the flawed ladder/continuum model, the public viewed the incident as fifteen officers with batons and an ECD pitted against one unarmed man. They didn't seem to consider the incredible danger created by driving at such a high rate of speed through residential areas. They didn't consider one strong, large man effortlessly threw off multiple officers who attempted to "swarm" him. They didn't consider the ECD seemed to have no effect on him. (As a side note, the ECD deployed in 1991 was far inferior to the ECDs in use today.) They also didn't consider that he continued to disobey lawful commands even after repeated blows from a baton. It was an ugly incident and almost all of Los Angeles paid a price for it. I'm certain no mayor, city manager, police chief, or sheriff wants to see a Rodney King incident occur in his or her jurisdiction.

Why did this occur (other than an illegal act and resisting arrest)? Several bad things led to this event. First, according to LAPD Chief Daryl Gates and LAPD Sergeant Stacey Koon (who was one of the convicted officers), the prohibition against the carotid restraint contributed to the excessive force claim. Both men argued that if the carotid restraint had been available to officers who were on scene, it would have been applied early in the confrontation and the subsequent baton and personal weapon strikes would have been unnecessary. **This is a training and policy issue.** In Sgt. Koon's book, *Presumed Guilty: The Tragedy of the Rodney King Affair,* he commented that Officer Laurence Powell was counseled for weak and ineffective baton strikes. It is clear that the baton strikes were feeble, as significant baton strikes should do enough damage to discourage continued resistance. **This is a training issue.** The swarm technique commonly used by LAPD at that time also proved ineffective. **This is a training issue.** At several times in the event, Mr. King no longer appeared to be a threat, as he was on his hands and knees and either immobile or crawling slowly. Officers commanded Mr. King to lie down and not move. Mr. King ignored those commands. The officers continued to issue commands and occasionally strike Mr. King, but no one moved forward to handcuff and secure him. **This is a training issue and possibly a policy issue.** Finally, once Mr. King was handcuffed, he was seen unattended for several minutes. **This is a training and policy issue.** Finally, LAPD used the continuum use of force model, which failed to accurately depict the use of force encounter. In almost every successful suit against a department, you find problems with policy, training, or both.

As was mentioned in Chapter 1, excessive force claims are most likely to occur just about any time an officer physically controls a subject. Any time a subject resists an officer, injuries may occur to both the resister and the officer. And when there are injuries, a lawsuit will likely follow. Recognizing this phenomenon, previous chapters specifically addressed use of force options. Officers will be safer if they clearly understand their force options (via the DRM) and are proficient in deploying these options (i.e., control holds, personal weapons, pepper spray, TASER, and impact weapons). This use of force knowledge and competency will result in greatly reduced liability for the officer and the department. It is critical officers know how to use all of their possible defensive devices effectively and to comprehend with absolute confidence when each tool can and cannot be legally used.

It is also imperative that officers know what to do after they have used force. Plaintiff's attorneys will look closely at all reports related to a use of force event, so those reports must be accurate and thorough. Officers should expect to use force a number of times during their careers.[2] Officers and their management should expect to be closely scrutinized and possibly sued after a use of force occurrence, particularly if there was an injury.

To successfully combat a use of force lawsuit, an officer must do two things. First, and most importantly, the officer needs to be right in the use of force. Being right has been defined in *Connor v. Graham* as the use of force must be "reasonable."[3] If the force used was not reasonable, then open the department's wallet now and pay for this error. Second, the officer must carefully and clearly document why the use of force was reasonable. Any inaccuracy or omission in the report will be used to attack the officer's integrity and professionalism.

When describing the appropriate response, it is imperative officers painstakingly document their perception of the threat and their fears. Without feeling threatened, the officer has no legal right to use higher levels of force. If the officer doesn't feel his or her safety, or the safety of another, is threatened, then only passive techniques may be used. As was mentioned in Chapter 16 on ECDs, the Ninth Circuit Court wrote in its *Bryan v. City of Coronado* decision, "A simple statement by an officer that he fears for his safety or the safety of others is not enough; there must be objective factors to justify such a concern." A use of force decision is based upon the officer's perception of the level of threat, so that perception must be thoroughly documented.

Officers must recognize the gravity of the situation after a use of force incident and take adequate time to prepare a proper report. Supervisors and reviewers of the report have the responsibility to their officer and to their department to ensure the report is "court ready." The report must document the subject's resistance, the officer's response to the resistance in an attempt to gain control and compliance, and how the officer's response was reasonable, proper, and lawful.

An additional strategy, which I support, is some departments file reports for every arrest or encounter. Although this increases the volume of paperwork, it documents how rarely officers use force. It also establishes a pattern for every officer in the department of how often he or she does *not* use force. This information can be invaluable later if a plaintiff's attorney attempts to portray an officer as a rogue, civil rights-violating rebel. The department can then pull documents that would indicate that this same officer had been involved in hundreds of contacts with the public in which no force was used. This would then lead a reasonable person to logically ask, "What did this one subject do differently than the other hundred people the officer had contact with? What did this subject do to cause the officer to respond with force since this officer has a pattern of not using force?"

I had the privilege of attending a number of seminars presented by and for plaintiff's attorneys who specialize in suing police departments. Some of you may question spending my hard-earned cash and giving it to a group of attorneys who sue us, but it was a great investment. It was like being invited into the enemy's camp, sitting around the campfire, and the enemy explaining their attack strategy. In subsequent seminars, I also listened to a number of defense attorneys who lectured on the tactics they use to embarrass and discredit officers on the stand. It's all incredible knowledge to have, and I admire those attorneys who are willing to speak to law enforcement groups to provide such information.

In the first plaintiff's attorney seminar I attended, some attorneys present seemed uncomfortable and suspicious to have an FBI agent in their midst. Since I paid my fee, I don't think they could have kicked me out. I did have a rather lengthy discussion with one presenter prior to class, however. He asked why I was there and what I expected to get out of the conference. I explained my primary responsibility in the FBI was providing firearms, defensive tactics, and tactical training to FBI agents and other law enforcement officers. Therefore, it was beneficial for me to know how we (law enforcement) were being sued so I could modify training and correct these issues. My goal was to provide the best training possible, so agents and officers could provide the best service possible (to protect and to serve). This seemed to satisfy them. A theme I heard throughout this and subsequent seminars was the plaintiff's attorneys were seeking systemic change and improvement in law enforcement training. They freely admitted to going after deep pockets. They expressed no interest in going after an individual officer, but preferred to target departments and municipalities for perceived misconduct and then have the courts force the department to receive training to correct these deficiencies (in addition, of course, to large settlements). Many of the attorneys stated they always ask for additional, mandatory training to be imposed by the court as part of the settlement. They saw this as their way of contributing to the safety of the public and increased professionalism of law enforcement. I know some of you are gnashing your teeth at this, but think about it. What do we want? We want the best training we can get, so we can do the best job possible in protecting and serving our communities.

So what did I learn? What is their attack strategy? When plaintiff's attorneys consider filing a lawsuit, they look at the facts surrounding the incident. They want to find a way to attack the department to establish agency liability. The best way to get their hands into deep pockets is to find a policy, custom, or lack of supervision, discipline, or training that leads to a foreseeable violation of a federally protected right.

The plaintiff's attorney must prove some violation by the officer, but the attorney will ultimately put the department on trial. A court may find an underlying constitutional violation but then grant qualified immunity to the officer. If, following this grant of qualified immunity, a court finds that the violation was the result of some policy or training issue, then the agency is still liable.[4] So, to protect itself, an agency must strengthen policy, training, and supervision.

First, let's look at policy. If your policy is outdated or, worse, in conflict with recent court decisions, you will have problems. For example, many departments still have a policy that states officers will use the "minimum amount of force necessary." First, this is in conflict with *Graham v. Connor*,[5] which clearly states the force used only has to be "reasonable" and not necessarily the lowest possible level. In *Plakas v. Drinski*,[6] the court also specifically stated officers are not required to use less intrusive alternatives; the only test is whether the officer's actions were reasonable. A good plaintiff's attorney can easily argue that lesser force could have been used in any situation in which force was used. Now that the attorney has demonstrated that policy has been violated, the next step is to indicate how this violation of policy is actually due to negligence.

As an example, let's assume Officer Doright is a competitive mixed martial arts (MMA) fighter, 6 feet tall, and 210 pounds. The subject is unknown to the officer, about 5 feet 10 inches, 175 pounds, and aggressively resistant. Could the officer possibly subdue the subject using a control hold or takedown? Possibly, but it wouldn't be the safest option for the officer. Not knowing the subject's background or if he may have a concealed weapon, Officer Doright instead chooses to first use pepper spray, a baton, or a TASER on the aggressive resister. Is this reasonable use of force? Absolutely. Is it the minimum amount of force necessary to overcome resistance? No. If any physical force is used by an officer, the plaintiff's attorney could always argue that if the officer had just talked to the bad guy for another five minutes and asked nicely, the subject would have complied. Beware of policy such as this, as it puts officers in a bad position and compromises their safety (as well as subject safety).

In addition to policy inconsistent with court decisions, plaintiff's attorneys also look for policy that is largely ignored by officers. Policy is meaningless if it is not adhered to and enforced. The department's culture and customs may be in conflict with its policies. Rules and regulations don't matter nearly as much as actual customs and practices. If this is the case, then even good policy becomes useless. If the culture and customs of a department are in conflict with policy and the law, this is a failure of leadership.

Plaintiff's attorneys will also closely scrutinize your training. Was there a lack of training, inadequate training, or poorly documented training? Going back to Officer Doright, the plaintiff's attorney will want to know the last time Officer Doright had pepper spray, baton, or TASER training. Is this training documented? Was there a test or some method of ensuring Officer Doright actually comprehended the training? If a department failed to adequately train its officers, and the department should have known this lack of training could have reasonably resulted in violations of the public's constitutionally guaranteed rights, then your department will most likely be successfully sued.

Failure to train can be established two ways. The first is a lack of training in an area where there is an obvious need for training. For law enforcement officers, the courts have determined use of force training is an obvious need. Officers must be trained in the types of force available to them and the circumstances when that force may be legally used. The second method of establishing a failure to train by an agency is to establish a pattern of conduct by officers that would put the final policy maker on notice that officer behavior was inconsistent with the law, and yet the policy maker failed to respond with appropriate training.

When I was still in graduate school, I worked for the City of Pensacola in Florida with a city manager noted for his witticisms. One of my favorites was, "An unwritten agreement isn't worth the paper it isn't written on." I also had a supervisor in the FBI who repeatedly would say during agent file reviews, "If you didn't document it on paper, you didn't do it." It's the same for training. You may have the best use of force training in the world, but if it's not properly documented, it didn't happen.

We know bad policy, bad training, failing to document, and failing to properly supervise officers lead to successful lawsuits. "Bad facts" make great cases for plaintiff's attorneys. Now we'll discuss how not to give them any bad facts.

G. Patrick Gallagher is a respected police practices expert. Mr. Gallagher developed a six-layered liability protection system to provide guidance to law enforcement agencies. Generally, Mr. Gallagher said the cornerstone of a liability protection system is good (i.e., lawful) policy must be in place. Once good policy is established, the officers who are expected to abide by those policies must be trained so they understand and act in a manner consistent with the policy. Not only should the policy frequently be discussed, but training should be structured that requires officers to demonstrate their comprehension of the policy and of the law. Training must include use of force situations that officers are likely to experience. Training should entail an evaluation of officers' responses to a full range of possible force options.

Mr. Gallagher advised that departments must make a concerted effort to hire the best possible personnel, to regularly evaluate their performance, and to commit to training and excellence of each officer. If you hire good people and give them the necessary training and feedback, there should be little need for discipline. However, if an employee has the necessary tools and knowledge to perform effectively, but fails to do so, then supervisors must discipline immediately and fairly once a policy violation is discovered.

A department must constantly review internal as well as external information to ensure quality performance and liability avoidance (risk management). Policy makers must stay abreast of changes in the law relating to policing.

Municipality attorneys must also remain current on the laws affecting law enforcement. In addition, they then must be aware of what is being taught to officers and ensure it complies with the law. The best way to do this is to review lesson plans and actually witness some use of force training. This may make some use of force instructors unhappy, as they may see it as an "outsider" meddling in their territory. But it is imperative your attorney, the person who will defend your officer and your department against a claim of excessive force, is familiar with what is being taught to officers in use of force training. There must be a continuing dialogue between your organization's attorneys and the use of force training staff. It's important that the attorneys and instructors recognize and respect each other's areas of expertise. Use of force instructors must understand the law, and your attorney must understand your use of force training. A defensive tactics (DT) instructor shouldn't try to argue the value of a particular law, and an attorney shouldn't try to interject on the training of a technique. However, your attorney must ensure the information provided to officers is legally correct. The attorneys must ensure the use of force options being taught comply with recent court decisions for that department's region of responsibility.

Scenario training is made even more effective by having a DT instructor critique an officer's performance and then having your attorney question the officer as to the officer's use of force decision-making process. For example, an officer may be placed in a scenario in which the officer has to respond with a baton strike to subdue a role player. Once the DT instructor has critiqued the application and tactics of the strike, the legal advisor will then question the officer as to the objective factors that permit the officer to articulate an immediate threat and deploy a baton. The better an officer understands use of force policy and the law, the less hesitation the officer will have in deploying lawful force.

I can name at least a few agencies that are currently teaching officers to use personal weapon strikes against a passively resistant subject. This will not be looked upon favorably by the courts. Once a law is clearly established by a court decision or legislative enactment, the departments within that jurisdiction will be expected to abide by that law. How many agencies still have policy permitting the use of a TASER on a passively resistant, nonthreatening subject? Civil courts throughout the country have repeatedly sided with the plaintiffs in these cases. In December 2009, the Ninth Circuit Court of Appeals specifically stated a TASER could not be used unless there was an "immediate threat."

Jack Ryan, a retired police captain and highly regarded instructor for the Public Agency Training Council (PATC), summarized the spirit of Gallagher's six principles during a June 2006 use of force conference succinctly: "One of the most effective methods of avoiding liability is through proper, thorough, and documented training."

Please take a minute and visualize you are now in court and one of your officers has been accused of excessive force. You have been called to testify as an executive in the department or as an instructor. You are on the witness stand and are being grilled by the plaintiff's attorney. He fixes an accusatory, steely gaze upon you and fires at you the following questions:

"When was the last time this officer had training on pepper spray (or baton, personal weapons, etc.)?"

"At the academy! You do realize, don't you, that it has been ten years since this officer attended the academy?"

"Surely you think some periodical refresher training is necessary and reasonable, don't you?"

"Do you know everything all your DT instructors are teaching?"

"What is in the lesson plans?"

"What! There are no lesson plans?" or "How do you know your instructors are sticking to the lesson plans?"
"How do you ensure consistency in what is being taught?"
"Do you know if what is being taught complies with all legal requirements?"
"Do you even have a roster to show who attended?"
"How do you know if your officers actually comprehend the training?"
"Do your officers know the law as it applies to the use of force?"
"Most importantly, where is all of this documented? Show it to me."

Visualizing the above scenario, how did you do? Would you be comfortable and confident on the stand answering these questions? Or would you be dancing a little? Or a lot?

As a chief, sheriff, city manager, or other concerned executive, you realize there are things you can do now to minimize your liability. Taking a proactive approach, you can implement sound, legally based policy. You can ensure modern, legally defensible use of force training is implemented and maintained for all officers. The instruction should include regular refresher training and documentation of officers' competency in required use of force topics. When a use of force incident occurs, you can require a supervisor from your department to respond to the scene. You can ensure officers write thorough, accurate reports that clearly articulate the objective factors of the immediate threat. Finally, you can see to it that well-trained, competent officers who willingly violate policy are properly disciplined.

Do an assessment of your department right now (later may be too late). Have these vital issues been adequately addressed? Are you confident of your policy, training, and documentation regarding use of force concerns? Or are there areas that have you a little worried? Or worse, do you know these critical areas need improvement?

You know the answer to increasing officer safety and minimizing your department's liability, but you also recognize it's not quite that simple. Particularly during a tough economy, budgets are tight, resources are scarce, and training time is limited. We are all trying to do more with less. What is your current DT training lacking? What is the cost for what you are doing now? When you look at your current use of force training expenses, are you considering not just your overall training budget, but the salaries of all personnel involved in the application of the program (both sworn and nonsworn)? Are you considering the time spent away from the streets as officers participate in training? Have you factored in the administrative costs of recording attendance and scores, as well as space requirements? After establishing the actual cost, determine if your use of force training is accomplishing what you want. Is it allowing you to sleep soundly at night knowing you are fully prepared to answer the plaintiff's questions mentioned above?

How do you provide modern, proper, thoroughly documented use of force training at a cost less than you're paying now? What is the solution?

The answer is the Law Enforcement Training and Tracking System (LETTS). LETTS is a proactive system that incorporates supervisor oversight, mandatory training, competency testing, and documentation of necessary use of force topics. LETTS is web-based training featuring a realistic, optimal DT program that automatically provides training, tests officer comprehension, records results, and stores data in a court-ready format.

My company, Survival Sciences, LLC, in collaboration with Decision Sciences, Incorporated (DSI), created LETTS. I embarked on this project with DSI due to DSI's recognized expertise in program development. DSI was founded in 1986 and is an information technology company specializing in the development of high-quality, cost-effective computer applications using advanced, web-based technology for the work place. DSI's primary clients include every branch of the U.S. armed forces, and DSI products are currently supporting the global war on terror.

LETTS is the answer to law enforcement executives' legal requirements to train officers in use of force, schedule training, record the training, and retrieve use of force documents. LETTS increases officer professionalism and safety, reduces liability, and is offered at a cost likely to be less than the current administrative expense of maintaining a paper system.

LETTS is a web-based use of force training program based upon the Survival Sciences Defensive Tactics (SSDT) program contained in this book. Topics are presented in short (ten- to fifteen-minute) video segments that can be viewed at any computer with Internet access, including squad cars' MDTs. After viewing a use of force training video, officers can take a brief computerized exam demonstrating their competency in that topic. The test scores are automatically saved in a database maintained in LETTS.

LETTS tracks use of force training to ensure all officers are current in required training. This prevents a department from being found negligent in providing suggested training due to an administrative oversight. LETTS provides notification to an officer and the officer's supervisor prior to the due date of training. LETTS will automatically begin notifying the appropriate chain of command if an officer becomes delinquent in training, so that corrective action can be taken.

LETTS is an invaluable management tool in that it has drill-down capability and supervisors have access to an easy-to-read, color-coded web page that clearly shows the training status of officers in their command. All officers are provided a personalized web page so they can track their personal training progress. LETTS is a "smart system" in that no proactive work is required of management.

Of course, you don't have to implement LETTS to comply with legal requirements. But you do have to provide proper, current, thorough, and well-documented training. The two areas most likely to be attacked by plaintiff's attorneys are failure to train and failure to document the training and competency of officers. You must ensure your department institutes and maintains a valid training curriculum, officers are receiving the required training, and the training is properly documented. It's up to you to determine how to best accomplish this. LETTS will increase training in minimal time, increase officer safety, increase officer professionalism, reduce liability, and reduce administrative costs. LETTS is cutting-edge technology to serve you.

Endnotes

1. Hall, D. E., Ventura, L. A., Lee, Y. H., and Lambert, E., "Suing Cops and Correction Officers: Officer Attitudes and Experiences about Civil Liability," *Policing: An International Journal of Police Strategies and Management,* 26, 529–47, 2003.
2. Joyner, C., "A Proper Use of Force Report; Reducing Liability," May 20, 2009, www.PoliceOne.com (accessed May 21, 2009).
3. *Graham v. Connor,* 490 U.S. 386, 394 (1989).
4. *Kuha v. City of Minnetonka*, no. 02-1081 (8th Cir. 2003).
5. *Graham v. Connor,* 490 U.S. 386, 394 (1989).
6. *Plakas v. Drinski*, 19 F 3d 114 (1994).

Conclusion

I'm confident *Advanced Concepts in Defensive Tactics: A Survival Guide for Law Enforcement* is a complete foundation in defensive tactics (DT) and beneficial to any department. However, not everything can be portrayed in the written format, nor should it be. I would prefer to limit the book's readership to those in law enforcement and the military. But because I have no control over those matters, I have purposely eliminated some practical, yet potentially dangerous techniques. I also purposely excluded counters to techniques commonly applied by law enforcement officers (e.g., arm bar, wrist twists, bar hammerlock, etc.). If you have any questions, please contact me through my website, www.SurvivalSciences.com. I'm always happy to talk about DT with anyone in law enforcement. I hope you have found the material worthwhile, that you practice the recommended drills at the end of the chapters, and you maintain your warrior spirit.

In closing, I'd like to relay a personal experience that occurred soon after 9/11. Like all FBI agents and law enforcement officers during that traumatic time period, I was working long hours, every day, with little rest. I was mentally, physically, and spiritually exhausted as I reported to work each day. As I was walking to my car parked in front of my house to report for another shift, I noticed an elderly neighbor walking toward me. We had never spoken before other than to say good morning or hello. With a stern look on her face, she hurried up to me as I was walking around my car. "I have a question for you!" she said. I really didn't want to hear it. I had been bombarded with images of horror, heard endless allegations against the FBI and the CIA, and I was exhausted. I just didn't want to listen to anything else that was negative. For some reason, I knew she just wanted to give me a hard time or insult the FBI. But because she was my neighbor and because of her age, I felt I owed her the courtesy to stop and listen. "You work for the FBI, don't you?" she asked. I thought I detected an accusatory tone to her question. I've always been proud to work for the FBI, and I hoped my pride was evident as I answered, "Yes ma'am, I do." As I prepared myself for the allegations or conspiracy theory I was sure would follow, she unexpectedly reached out, touched my arm, and said, "Thank you. And God bless you." I was shocked. I was ashamed. And I went to work rejuvenated with a much better attitude and appreciation for the opportunity to be contributing in even a small way.

I know all of you at times are discouraged, depressed, and wonder if the sacrifices you make are worthwhile. They are. What you do as a sheepdog is an incredible gift to those you serve. The other sheepdogs know this. And even though we sometimes forget, the vast majority of the sheep recognize it to.

To quote my neighbor, "Thank you, and God bless you."

Index

L

M

N

O

P

R

S